AN
UNCOMMON
ROAD

AN

HOW CANADIAN SIKHS

UNCOMMON

STRUGGLED OUT OF THE FRINGES

ROAD

AND INTO THE MAINSTREAM

GIAN SINGH SANDHU

EDITORIAL DIRECTOR John Burns
ART DIRECTOR Cathy Smith
DESIGNER Mauve Page
PHOTO EDITOR Adam Stenhouse
COPY EDITOR Marial Shea
PROOFREADER Renate Preuss

All images courtesy of Gian Singh Sandhu unless otherwise noted.

Library and Archives Canada Cataloguing in Publication

Sandhu, Gian Singh, author
        An uncommon road : how Canadian Sikhs struggled out
of the fringes and into the mainstream / Gian Singh Sandhu.

ISBN 978-1-987900-16-3 (hardcover)

        1. Sikh Canadians. 2. Sikhs—Canada. 3. Sikh Canadians—
Social conditions. 4. Sikhs—Canada—Social conditions. 5. Sikh
Canadians—History. 6. Sikhs—Canada—History. 7. World Sikh
Organization of Canada. 8. Sikh Diaspora. I. Title.

FC106.S55S26 2018   971.0088'2946   C2017-906406-1

Printed in Canada.

I dedicate this book to my parents, particularly my dear mother, Chanan Kaur (Kartari), who brought me into this world and nurtured a shy little toddler into the person I have become. And to my soulmate and my life partner, Surinder Kaur, who has walked beside me through all the peaks and valleys of my life and kept me grounded in our faith.

CONTENTS

FOREWORD

The ultimate measure of a man is not where he stands
in moments of comfort and convenience, but where
he stands at times of challenge and controversy.

—*Martin Luther King, Jr.*

SINCE GIAN SINGH Sandhu arrived in Canada in 1970, he has found his share of challenges and controversies. These are detailed between the covers of this book, and through them we come to see the measure of not just one man but the broader community he has served for much of his life.

The welcome waiting for him was nothing like the warm embrace that refugees from Syria and other conflict-torn nations find today. Canada, especially before it embraced its policy of multiculturalism, was cautious by nature. Practising Sikhs, with their distinctive turbans and facial hair, have long been an especially noticeable other — in this country and many others. The easiest route to assimilation, quickly adopted by newcomer Sikhs around the world, is to jettison what in their appearance distinguishes them. Gian Singh was no exception: like so many, he shaved his beard and unwound his turban before reclaiming his faith, embracing the very "difference" that defines him.

Other challenges have been much broader. Too many citizens believe that governments are powerful, monolithic entities impervious to persuasion. Yet the author has marshalled credible evidence of external state actors not only engaging in subversive activities in our communities but, to a considerable extent, hijacking Canada's systems of democratic governance, law enforcement, justice, and media.

Some of these interferences will be well known to readers familiar with developments across the Indian subcontinent during the Gandhi family's decades-long dynastic rule. Less well known are the historical and political factors that led to the Indian military's 1984 attacks in Punjab on the holiest of Sikh worship places — and the ensuing massacres of thousands of innocent members of India's Sikh community. The author relates the historical context of the Sikh genocide, and also brings it back to his adopted homeland to examine what happened to Sikhs in Canada when the New Delhi government dangled the pretty carrot of potential exports in front of a hungry Ottawa.

The most notable matter studied here is the crash of Air India Flight 182 in 1985. In that tragedy, 329 innocents were lost, mostly Canadians. Have we adequately addressed the weaknesses in our system to take effective and timely steps to find the real culprits? Have we implemented sufficient changes to prevent similar disasters in future? Judge for yourself after examining the revelations contained herein.

This book puts us on notice. To how effortlessly outsiders can plant propaganda in our naive media to make themselves look good or to justify oppressive practices back home. To how easily our political leaders can be compromised, tempted, and persuaded to muzzle community leaders. And to how quickly they will turn a blind eye to nefarious and destructive activities by foreign intelligence agencies.

Yet it offers hope as well. It alerts the leaders of some vulnerable minority communities to the potential dangers they may face, but also shows a proven path that can empower them and help get them on track to regain lost ground, move forward, and emerge stronger and more unified than ever. The author's message, and the message of the World Sikh Organization more broadly, is this: the Sikhs have done it. We all can.

DAVID KILGOUR
July 2017

David Kilgour PC is a human rights activist and author, and former lawyer, cabinet minister, and deputy speaker. With David Matas he was nominated in 2010 for the Nobel Peace Prize for their work opposing human organ trafficking in China.

CHRONOLOGY OF EVENTS

*A timeline of some of the major events from the
book. For details, visit the pages listed.*

1469   Guru Nanak, founder of the Sikh faith, is born in Punjab (in an area now in
Pakistan). *Page 29*

1577   Guru Ram Das, the fourth guru, begins construction of the town Ramdaspur,
later named Amritsar. *Page 61*

1601   Guru Arjan Dev, the fifth guru, completes construction of Darbar Sahib, often
referred to as the Golden Temple. *Page 15*

1606   Guru Hargobind, the sixth guru, builds the Akal Takht within the Darbar
Sahib complex. *Page 61*

1675   Guru Tegh Bahadur, the ninth guru, is beheaded in Delhi for defending the
right of Hindus to freely practise their faith. *Page 196*

1699   Guru Gobind Singh, the tenth guru, formally creates the order of the Khalsa
on Vaisakhi day. *Page 68*

1710   Banda Singh Bahadur establishes the first Sikh Kingdom. *Page 67*

1799   Maharaja Ranjit Singh establishes the Sikh Empire in northern India. *Page 67*

1849   Punjab becomes the last kingdom on the Indian subcontinent to be annexed
by the British. *Page 68*

1897   Capt. Kesur Singh becomes the first Sikh settler in Canada. *Page 44*

1906   Canadian Sikhs establish the Khalsa Diwan Society. (In 1908, they build the
first gurdwara.) *Page 170*

1914   The Japanese steamship *Komagata Maru*, packed with Sikh émigrés who
are all British subjects, is not allowed to dock in Vancouver and is eventually
escorted out of Canadian waters. Nineteen Sikhs are shot when they
disembark at Budge Budge, near Calcutta. *Page 46*

1919   The Jallianwala Bagh massacre, led by British Brig.-Gen. Reginald Edward Harry Dyer, kills close to 1,000 people, mostly Sikhs. The official death toll is 379. *Page 28*

1942   The Sikh All Party Committee submits a proposal for azad ("independent") Punjab to the British Raj. The proposal is denied. *Page 32*

1946   Jawaharlal Nehru (India's first prime minister) assures Sikhs that they will have a region where their religion is respected and where they can call their own political shots. *Page 34*

1947   India gains independence from Britain. Punjab is divided between India and Pakistan. *Page 35*

1966   The Indian government accedes to the demands of the Akali Dal to create a Punjabi-speaking state, but also unilaterally establishes the states of Haryana and Himachal Pradesh. *Page 38*

1973   Shiromani Akali Dal adopts the Anandpur Sahib Resolution, addressing a host of grievances, calls for minority and religious rights, and recommended changes to the Indian Constitution to allow political autonomy for the various regions. *Page 39*

1978   A clash between a number of devout Sikhs and a larger group of Nirankaris, an offshoot sect, takes place near Amritsar. Thirteen are killed, including 10 devout Sikhs belonging to Akhand Kirtani Jatha. *Page 42*

1982   Sikhs launch the Dharam Yudh Morcha civil disobedience movement to force the Indian government to concede to demands laid out in the Anandpur Sahib Resolution. *Page 43*

1984   In early June Indian Armed Forces, under the direction of Prime Minister Indira Gandhi, storm the Darbar Sahib and 38 other gurdwaras, destroying the highest Sikh seat of spiritual and temporal authority, Akal Takht. *Page 60*

1984   In late July delegates to the international Sikh convention at New York's Madison Square Garden decide to establish the World Sikh Organization (WSO). *Page 76*

1984   The Sikh genocide in Delhi in the first days of November follows Indira Gandhi's assassination by her two Sikh bodyguards. *Page 79*

2015   In *Loyola High School v. Quebec (Attorney General)*, WSO intervenes to support the right of the Catholic high school to teach the Christian portion of the mandated "Ethics and Religious Culture" curriculum in accordance with its faith. *Page 200*

2016   Prime Minister Justin Trudeau apologizes in the House of Commons for the 1914 *Komagata Maru* incident. *Page 225*

2017   *Trinity Western University v. Law Society of Upper Canada* and *Law Society of British Columbia v. Trinity Western University* revolve around the accreditation of graduates of the Christian university's law school, which requires students to conform their morals to a controversial "community covenant." WSO is granted leave to intervene. *Page 202*

MY HEART IS OPEN

My eyes are closed.
My heart is open.
I am at peace.
At long last, I am home.

HERE, ON THE top floor of the centuries-old site of Sikhism commonly known as Darbar Sahib, or the Golden Temple, you can lose yourself in solitude, even when surrounded. This parapet is crowded with visitors today, each craning for the least obstructed view. Next to me is my eldest child, my daughter Kamaljit. We stand side by side, appreciating the vista. Overcome by the profound beauty of this sacred spot, we do not speak.

Completed in 1601 by Guru Arjan Dev, fifth of the 10 Sikh gurus, or spiritual masters, this place became the centre of spiritual life to those of the Sikh faith. Accessed by a walkway that juts into the Pool of Nectar, a stunning rectangular water feature around which the complex is built, the Golden Temple comes by its nickname honestly: its dome, splendid and awe-inspiring, is gilded with nearly a ton of gold.

The sun in Punjab, merciless in summer, beats down on us. I draw a deep breath, exhale slowly, repeat. From this vantage point, I take in some of the most important creations in our history. To my right is the Sikh Reference Library, repository of so much of our people's heritage. To my left is the Central Sikh Museum; the light glints off its roof, a blindingly beautiful sight. Just beyond the walled complex are the hostels where I stayed when I was a young man preparing for the exams that paved the way for my enrolment in the Indian Air Force.

In the foreground is Amritsar, the main city in India's Punjab province, conceived in 1577 by Guru Ram Das, the fourth guru. Amritsar exists in a constant state of flux; today's version is just one more iteration in a transformative process that seems perpetual. In Amritsar today, the air is full of dust, a by-product of the development rapidly redrawing this place I once knew so well. But the breath I draw here at Darbar Sahib is not heavy with dust. It is heavy with memory.

From where I stand I can barely see the present for the past. The last time I was here was in 1978, as a pilgrim but also a tourist, not so different from the people around me now. Back then my hair was black and I was clean shaven. I am older now, of course, and more than a little rounder than I was in the prime of middle age. My hair is long and grey and uncut, tucked neatly into my dastar, or turban — one of the Five Ks, the articles of my Sikh faith that I embraced later in life. But the biggest change is invisible to the casual observer. I am here today as a man transformed. By my faith, certainly. But also by events that took place on this spot over three decades ago. In a sense, I was born here — politically, at least.

To the northwest is the Akal Takht, the seat of Sikh temporal and spiritual authority and the place where the political and social affairs of the community have historically been resolved. Since 1984, the Akal Takht has been rebuilt twice. First, by the government of India. And then, after tearing this version down, by the Sikhs of Punjab, who rebuilt it again themselves. Their reason for doing so isn't hard to fathom. In June 1984, the Akal Takht was bombed into a pile of rubble, part of a four-day assault by the Indian Armed Forces, acting on orders from Prime Minister Indira Gandhi. In the carnage that ensued, thousands of men, women, and children, most of them pilgrims who had come to commemorate the martyrdom of Guru Arjan Dev, were murdered in the Darbar Sahib complex, collateral damage to Mrs. Gandhi's aim (apparently at any cost) of eradicating a group of "militants" who were also allegedly holed up there. For Sikhs to allow the Indian government's rebuilt Akal Takht to remain standing would have been to allow the whitewashing of the slaughter to stand, too. After the tragedy, the only testament to the cut-short lives of those pilgrims who fatefully entered the complex that day were the horrifying photos of their corpses and the mountains of shoes they would never reclaim.

The volleys of gunfire targeting the Golden Temple echoed across the Sikh nation, here in Punjab and in the diaspora of which, by then, I was a part. The attack on our holiest shrine appalled us, shocked us, sickened us. In the next few months this violence would spread, claiming the lives of Indira Gandhi and, in the immediate aftermath of her killing, thousands of Sikhs in Delhi, who were slaughtered in revenge. It set in motion a widening spiral of violence in which thousands more perished in the ensuing months and years. Nor was this paroxysm confined to India: even those of us who had long ago left that nation to pursue a better life in Canada were not spared.

In 1985, a little more than a year after the attack on the Golden Temple, bombs were placed in the luggage compartments of two separate flights, both originating in Vancouver, British Columbia. In a matter of hours, 331 people, most of them Canadians of South Asian origin, were dead. The blame would be placed directly at the feet of the Sikh community in Canada. My community.

The Golden Temple invasion, the Delhi genocide, and what is commonly known as the Air India bombing heralded a dark new epoch for Sikhs, especially in the country I now called home. It would become our crucible.

REBORN

The Sikh community's roots extend deep into Canada's history — particularly in British Columbia, the closest port of call for ships making the journey from the Indian subcontinent to the New World. The first migration to the area, in the early 1900s, enticed Sikh men looking for employment abroad into manual service alongside other workers from Southeast Asia; Canada's western province was built largely on the backs of Sikh, Chinese, and Japanese labourers.

Their initial welcome was far from warm. As with the Chinese, who suffered the indignity of the infamous "head tax," Sikh men were barred from participating fully in Canadian society: to ensure that their stay in Canada was temporary, they were originally not even allowed to bring their wives. (The first Sikh community was literally a brotherhood.) Eventually, they broke through the tightest bonds of prejudice and began to jostle for a place within the emerging society. In B.C., many Sikhs ended up working in forestry or in the orchards of the Okanagan Valley. The community was small but significant.

A shift in immigration laws implemented in the late 1960s augured much change. No longer were newcomers from European lands granted preferential treatment; a points system that tied acceptance to a raft of qualities unrelated to national origin was put in place. By 1970, the year my family and I arrived to start our Canadian lives, thousands of Sikhs searching for a new and better life had begun to move here. At first we were viewed as curiosities, perhaps even benign "novelties" — especially in rural areas where turbans and beards, hallmarks of the observant male Sikh, were scarce. But by the 1970s and 1980s, as more and more people from India called Canada home, we were recast by some as a threat: to the social, cultural, racial, and, yes, even economic order. Denigrated as "Pakis" by those who couldn't accept the changes happening around them, South Asians were often singled out for abuse. And those who wore a turban? As you can imagine, their welcome was even less cordial.

Earlier, I told you that I was born, politically speaking, at the Golden Temple. That was not my only rebirth. In 1981, after a soul-searching decade, I made my own spiritual commitment and became a practising, or amritdhari, Sikh.

Although the decision was deeply personal, it was fueled by my deepening commitment to those around me. Shortly after arriving in Canada, I began to devote myself to helping out the small Sikh community of Williams Lake, British Columbia, where we had made our home, helping to establish the Central Cariboo Punjabi Canadian Association. (I was its founding president.) Over time, we channelled our energy into building a gurdwara, or Sikh place of worship. Involvement begat involvement — first within the Sikh community of Williams Lake, later across the province, and ultimately nationally and internationally. In the wake of the Golden Temple massacre my commitment only deepened: it was clear there was a need for a new organization, one that could press the Sikh case to the world. Later in 1984, a year that for us would be defined by pain and bloodshed, the World Sikh Organization International (WSO) was formed. In December, I was elected president of the Canadian chapter, incorporated in the same month, eventually becoming head of the international organization.[1]

There were repercussions. There is a reason it has taken me 38 years to return to Darbar Sahib. Shortly after becoming involved with the WSO in 1984, I, along with many others, was placed on a blacklist that prevented me from returning to India. It wasn't until 2016, when my name was published in an Indian newspaper as "No Longer Banned" that I learned that I might once more see the shimmering dome of this beautiful place of peace.

It is from this perspective — as someone who has been deeply immersed in Sikh affairs for the last half century, sometimes to the exclusion of all else in my life — that I will convey the story of how the Sikh community dealt with the extraordinary events of 1984–85 and their ongoing fallout. Those events would traumatize us, scar us, haunt us, and redefine us as a group and as individuals. They would make us angry, afraid, resentful, assertive, and defiant. Scapegoated by many, tarred as terrorists, our community nevertheless has extraordinary resilience. The maturity we have mustered sends a message of hope to others who, in this age of Islamophobia, anti-Semitism, and a broad fear of "the other," may find themselves in a similar position.

After the massacre at the Golden Temple, I, like the rest of the 20 million Sikhs worldwide, was outraged. I am not an inherently angry or emotional person; I prefer to think of myself as rational (perhaps to a fault). My default manner is to be calm, sometimes to the point of appearing detached. I am more likely to focus on solutions than to sit and brood over the problem. As an advocate for our community, a sort of innate level-headedness has served me well. As a storyteller, though, I may leave you wanting to look elsewhere for a more emotional narrator who wears his angst on his sleeve. I hope, though, that you will stay with me.

For the Sikhs, raising awareness of Indian abuses in Punjab, reclaiming our good name, and pushing forward together is a challenge that has spanned decades. Hard as it has been, I see a silver lining: this struggle has given me purpose and filled my days (and many nights!). As president of the World Sikh Organization of Canada, and then head of the international parent organization, and ultimately WSO Canada's senior policy advisor, I have had the chance to converse with every Canadian prime minister from Brian Mulroney on (with the exception of Stephen Harper). I have provided evidence in the legal judgment that put an end, once and for all, to the debate about turbans in the RCMP — an issue that seems almost quaint today but that was at one time the hottest of hot buttons. I have testified on behalf of Canadian Sikhs at the Air India Commission, headed by retired Supreme Court Justice John Major. I say this as a matter of fact — not to blow my own horn, but rather to let you know that my perspective is informed by years of work, often involving the highest levels of government, from the Canadian Parliament to the U.S. Congress and even the United Nations.

All this said, although I figure in it, this story is not about me. Rather, it is the tale of how a community, under great pressure and against overwhelming odds, clawed its way back from the brink, and in the process became not only a redeemed people but a political force. It is the story of making the leap from "despised other," a pariah among minorities, to a fully incorporated part of the Canadian multicultural quilt.

It is the story of the Sikhs of Canada. And I am proud and honoured to be the teller.

PART I

ANNUS HORRIBILIS

(JUNE 1984–JUNE 1985)

CHAPTER 1
THE STAGE
IS SET

I N EARLY SEPTEMBER 1948, a little over a year after India and
the newly created state of Pakistan officially went their separate
ways, I was about to turn six years old. Or, more accurately, I
had just turned five. A contradiction? Yes, clearly. But it is also true.

For many years the date of my birth was elusive even to myself,
the result of a white lie told by my grandfather, Kartar Singh, when
I was a child. Baba Ji, as we called him, was an imposing man with
piercing blue eyes. Earlier in his life he had traveled from Punjab
to England to make his fortune, eventually finding his niche selling
trendy high-end garments to British ladies. A bona fide success
story, he returned to our village of Rurka Kalan after two decades
abroad, arriving just before Partition — the divorce between the state
of India and what were once its Muslim majority territories to the
northeast and northwest, an area that included much of what was
then known as Punjab, the province where many of us Sikhs had
historically lived.

Rurka Kalan, a town of about 10,000, is surrounded by farmland.
Unlike the sprawling multi-section farms typical of Canada's Prairie
provinces, these were smaller family-owned plots where generation
after generation worked with animals to till the soil, hand-sowing

crops from bags of seed — traditions that, in many instances, continue to this day. While our family tended the fields of our 21-acre farm, planting and harvesting wheat, corn, sugar cane, rice, cotton, and vegetables, my grandfather, a stern figure who commanded respect among our neighbours, spent his days resolving land disputes, installing water pumps on public roads, and generally helping those in need. All this in addition to managing the household finances.

For years, my parents, sister Bhajno, and I lived with our extended family (two uncles, two aunts, and five cousins) in a house with no electricity, built from clay bricks and lit by kerosene lamps or mustard oil clay pots, the wicks throwing off a soft, warm glow. My mother, or "Beejee" — her birth name was Kartari, but since we already had one Kartar in the family, her name was changed to Chanan Kaur to avoid confusion — was the family's rock. She was always there for us, especially when times were tough: when Baba Ji punished my father, Bawa Singh, and one of my uncles, Sucha Singh, for their occasionally irresponsible ways with money by scaling back his support, my mother had to go to her father to ask for money for my school supplies.

In relative terms, though, our family was reasonably well off, and we were blessed with a good life. In part, this was due to Baba Ji's largesse. At one point, when I was still young, he divided his real estate holdings among his three sons. (Mehnga Singh, the third son, followed in Baba Ji's footsteps and went to England when I was in Grade 5, never to return.) My uncles got the nicer houses; we received the older ancestral home. About a block away was another, smaller brick guest house. This was where Baba Ji lived.

When one of my cousins, Charan, was seven years old, my grandfather took him to school to register for his first day. Two years younger than my cousin, I happily tagged along. Charan and I skipped down the dusty road, laughing and playing as we went. The six-room schoolhouse, for boys only, had no desks or even chairs — students sat on khuskhus mats (see Glossary on page 231 for Punjabi terms) or sometimes directly on the clay floor. After filling out the paperwork and registering Charan, my Baba Ji placed his hand on my shoulder. I looked up at him, confused.

"Do you have room for one more?" he asked the headmaster. I was a tiny kid compared to my cousin, and would remain small for my age until I was well into high school.

"This one?" the headmaster asked, looking me up and down. "You know he has to be six years old to go to school?"

"Oh, I assure you, he is," my grandfather replied.

"Really? When is his birthday?"

"As it happens, it is today."

And so my birthday — which much later I learned was actually July 23, 1943 — became September 10, 1942, the first day of the school year, magically aging me 10 months (and making a Virgo out of a Leo). My "rebirth" had occurred without fanfare or ceremony, entirely unlike that "other" birthday that had taken place almost exactly one year before, which was marked in ways that would alter the nation and scar Sikhs, Hindus, and Muslims alike.

A NATION DIVIDED

In the transfer of populations that occurred after the August 1947 Partition, millions of Muslims migrated from what was then India to the newly created state of Pakistan; going the other way, millions of Sikhs fled south. My family was lucky enough to live on the south side of the border — the Indian side. The sectarian violence that ensued was almost unimaginable, and second-hand stories of the horrific bloodshed witnessed by my family and neighbours haunted me throughout my childhood. I was very young, only four years old at the time, but I remember that when families from the nearby village of Nimahan were uprooted, two Muslim brothers, Atta and Fatha, brought their families to hide at our farm. For a few days they even hid in our home until the army arrived to give them safe passage to Pakistan. As Nisid Hajari writes in *Midnight's Furies: The Deadly Legacy of India's Partition*, a recently published account of this under-reported humanitarian disaster:

Gangs of killers set whole villages aflame, hacking to death men and children and the aged while carrying off young women to be raped. British soldiers and journalists who had witnessed the Nazi death camps claimed Partition's brutalities were worse: pregnant women had their breasts cut off and babies hacked out of their bellies; infants were found literally roasted on spits. Foot caravans of destitute refugees fleeing the violence stretched for 50 miles and more.

Between 1 and 2 million people died by the time the atrocities finally abated, which was roughly around the time I started school. After the dust had settled, so to speak, more than 15 million people had been displaced on both sides of a new border, forever altering the ethnic, linguistic, and religious makeup of the region.

Partition had been primarily about Muslims asserting their right to self-determination. But even before the horrors of 1947–48, the Sikhs of Punjab had worried about how we, as a distinct people and faith, might fare in a newly independent, Hindu-dominant India. In the run-up to the violence, Sikhs had been convinced by Jawaharlal Nehru's ruling Indian National Congress Party that in exchange for staying within the emergent Indian federation, we would be treated respectfully — and that a degree of autonomy would be granted to the Sikh nation in thanks. "The brave Sikhs of Punjab are entitled to special consideration," vowed Nehru, a year before India was granted independence and he became the nation's first prime minister. "I see nothing wrong in an area and a set-up in the North wherein the Sikhs can also experience the glow of freedom."[2] We took this assurance (and many others) to heart, throwing our lot in with India. For this, the Sikhs would pay an enormous price.

Nehru's promise, so blithely proffered, was never fulfilled. It would turn out to be one of several significant betrayals of the Sikhs by the newly created government of India. Over the years, there would be more deceit, more manipulation, more cunning games designed to derail any moves toward political autonomy, setting the stage for global conflicts. Nehru's unfulfilled promise would also play a foundational role in my own political evolution, manifesting in much of my life's work.

In the early 1980s, after a generation of broken promises and cynical attempts to mollify the Sikhs, the community reached a breaking point. The effects would be felt throughout Punjab and later within the worldwide Sikh diaspora, culminating in the terrible events of 1984–85, a time that would impact Sikhs, and others' perception of us, forever.

But those events, those terrible events, did not occur in a vacuum. Nor can their origins be pegged to any one moment, no matter how transformative or traumatizing. The factors that led to the boiling over of tensions had complex roots, fixed in the past. At school, I would study that past. In doing so, I was reminded daily of how what had come before informed so much of what followed.

THE MARTYR'S WELL

In Amritsar, about 100 metres from the Golden Temple, is a 6.4-acre field. Surrounded by stone walls, filled with lush gardens and water features, Jallianwala Bagh is an undeniably placid spot, a special place of manufactured serenity. Tourists wander the expansive grounds, armed with digital cameras and cell phones, capturing images that will animate their travel blogs, Instagram feeds, and Facebook posts. Some linger at the foot of a soaring sculptural monument that resembles a child's drawing of a rocket. Others peer into a 7-metre-wide hole in the earth, craning to penetrate the abyss — and, perhaps, the fog of time.

This is the Martyr's Well. Today, it is surrounded by a lattice of interlocking metal to prevent anyone from accidentally falling in. But on April 13, 1919, the well was at the centre of a dusty patch where over 15,000 people had gathered both to celebrate Vaisakhi, one of the holiest festivities of the Sikh calendar, and to protest against the Raj, or British rule. Around the well, there was no barrier.

On that day, Jallianwala Bagh became a killing field, the well itself a mausoleum filled with the bodies of men, women, and children who, harbouring the faintest hope or filled with the most profound desperation, had jumped into its depths to avoid the fusillade from British-led troops under the command of Brig.-Gen. Reginald Dyer. Dyer, who ordered his men to shoulder their .303 Lee-Enfield rifles and shoot indiscriminately into the crowd, hoped to inflict a teachable moment on those who had the audacity to challenge their colonial overlords. He succeeded, but not in the way he'd intended.

The massacre's official death toll was 379. Unofficial estimates put it closer to 1,000.[3] One hundred and twenty bodies were pulled from the well alone. Although Muslims and Hindus also died that day, by far most of the casualties were Sikh — a particularly galling fact, considering the enormity of the sacrifices Sikh soldiers had made fighting for the British mere months before, when the First World War still raged.

Although Dyer had his supporters in Great Britain, Secretary of State for War Sir Winston Churchill was outraged, and on July 8, 1920, clearly expressed his disgust in a speech to Parliament, calling it "a monstrous event, an event which stands in singular and sinister isolation." Although his umbrage was doubtlessly genuine, Churchill also likely viewed the massacre in strategic terms. He knew the carnage at Amritsar could ignite an opposition movement that might in turn threaten the primacy of British rule over South Asia. He was correct.

The Raj was a system of military, political, and social controls designed to bring order to the subcontinent, from Sri Lanka in the south and Burma in the east to the lands now known as Pakistan and Bangladesh. The British called this construct "India," but it was never a unified land in any relevant respect. Instead, it was made up of many separate and competing kingdoms with equally diverse systems of beliefs, including Buddhism, Jainism, Islam, Hinduism, and Sikhism. Adding to this patchwork of faiths and ethnicities was an almost unbelievable linguistic diversity: even today, according to India's census of 2011, there are more than 120 major languages spoken in India, in addition to another 1,600 lesser tongues. India is a "nation" to the same extent as Europe or the former USSR.

Respecting the subcontinent's longstanding ethnic, religious, and linguistic divisions was clearly not top of mind for the British in 1858, when troops loyal to Queen Victoria unified it under the Union Jack. But inflicting lasting order on India would prove much more difficult, due not only to the political events that would unfold in the coming decades but, in the case of my faith, the very tenets of our religion.

REVELATION AND REVOLUTION

Like most Sikh kids in Punjab, I'd been schooled in the origins of our religion from an early age. The youngest of the world's major religions, Sikhism can be traced back to 1469 and the birth of Guru Nanak, the first of 10 spiritual masters whose lives and lessons compose the great body of Sikh spiritual belief and ideology. At the time of Guru Nanak's birth, Punjab, a territory stretching from Delhi up to the Himalayas, was dominated by two competing religious visions: the Vedantic faiths, which comprised the various schools of Hindu philosophy, and Islam.

Sikhism includes concepts that would be familiar to both Hindus and Muslims, and culled its charter congregation from peoples of both faiths. But Sikhism was not just an incorporation of other, existing beliefs. Instead, it was born in Guru Nanak's realization of the unity of humanity under a common God, one who favoured no particular religion, language, gender, race, or caste. God exists within each and every human being (and indeed within every living creature), regardless of which faith one chooses to follow. Guru Nanak's philosophy stood in marked contrast to the status quo, which at the time included a key concept imported by the Aryan tribes who had much earlier invaded the area.[4]

The Aryans were a people whose beliefs were wrapped up in the natural world: they were, in a very direct sense, nature lovers.

The Aryans differed from the original inhabitants of northwest India not just philosophically but physically. The original inhabitants (Dravidians) were short in stature and dark-skinned. The Aryan invaders who made their way through the Khyber Pass from Europe into northwestern India (what is now Punjab), driving the Dravidians before them, were tall and light-skinned; many had blue or green eyes.

According to historian Khushwant Singh in *A History of the Sikhs*, in order to "maintain the purity of their race and reduce to servitude the dark-skinned inhabitants among whom they had come to live," the Aryans devised a social system built on five separate classes. At the top were the privileged Brahmins (priests), followed by Kshatriyas (warriors), Vaishyas (tradespeople), and Shudras (workers). A fifth group fell outside of these designations. Those whose bloodlines were dominantly aboriginal were relegated to this lowest class. They were considered so vile that even their shadow was polluting. In this new "caste" system, they became the Untouchables, the lowest of the low. (Women in all classes were placed even lower.)

In time, Aryan beliefs merged into Hinduism, as did the caste system and its entrenched inequalities. And this was anathema to Guru Nanak, an iconoclastic thinker whose emerging vision sought, among other things, to level the playing field for all people, regardless of belief or gender. Both progressive and revolutionary, the foundational principle of the Sikh faith is that meditation upon truth[5] is the cornerstone of wisdom, self-realization, and inner peace. But that wisdom and knowledge must be expressed fearlessly in conduct — in one's interactions with the wider world. Since God resides in each and every individual, for Guru Nanak it naturally followed that those who were guided by fearless action would actively oppose the caste system (and advocate for gender equality; Guru Nanak was the first among major religious figures to do so). Therefore, if one sees inequity or injustice, it is not just a choice but an obligation to stand up against it. In Sikhism, these values and principles would much later become codified in the articles of faith (often referred to in English as the Five Ks because each begins with the letter "k") worn by Sikhs; carrying the kirpan, a stylized representation of a sword, is a constant reminder that it is the duty of all Sikhs to protect those who need defending.[6]

By the time of Guru Hargobind, sixth of the ten gurus, there was much to defend against. After his father, Guru Arjan Dev, was taken into custody and subsequently tortured and executed by the ruling Mughals in the early 1600s, Guru Hargobind began nurturing a martial side to Sikhism, eventually taking up the mantle of armed resistance against Mughal injustice. In his time as guru, Hargobind gave rise to the idea of the Sant-Sipahi, or "saint-soldier," an individual who was grounded in meditation and compassion (sant) but who was bound to defend the rights of the defenceless (sipahi).[7] Taking up arms was to be a last resort, and only in defence.

A HISTORY OF NON-COOPERATION

The most tangible legacy of the Jallianwala Bagh massacre of 1919 was the boost it gave to the Non-Cooperation Movement. Spearheaded by Mohandas "Mahatma" Gandhi, a Hindu lawyer from Gujarat, the non-denominational protest movement called for a boycott of British goods and nonviolent opposition to British rule, with the end goal of compelling the Raj to loosen its grip on the subcontinent. (Even before the Non-Cooperation Movement began, Sikhs in Punjab had already been rallying against the British, holding peaceful protests in Punjab — for which many were imprisoned or hanged.)[8]

Although the movement, which ended in 1922, was ultimately unsuccessful, it did augur change — or, at least, it raised the possibility that change could be forced. Over the next two decades, Muslims, Hindus, and Sikhs actively pursued the course of independence, sometimes together but often at the expense of each other.

On the political front, Gandhi and his compatriot Jawaharlal Nehru transformed the existing Indian National Congress Party into a mass political movement. Founded in 1885 by English-educated, urban middle-class Indians (with the help of retired British officer

A.O. Hume), the Congress Party under Gandhi and Nehru included in its mandate pursuit of purna swaraj — complete independence. Originally it was an interfaith movement, but by 1942, onetime ally Mohammed Ali Jinnah had broken away and was pursuing a divergent path, one he hoped would lead to the establishment of a separate Muslim-majority state in the north. Purna swaraj shifted to embrace a Hindu-centric vision.

The Sikhs had not been idle, either: in the early 1920s they had to struggle to gain control of their own institutions from morally corrupt caretakers whose fealty lay with the British Raj rather than the Sikh community; the Akali Dal, a political party that would dominate Sikh politics for decades, formed to further their interests. Having fought bravely and suffered disproportionate losses in service of the British Empire during the First World War (83,005 turban-wearing Sikh soldiers died and 109,045 were wounded), the Sikhs were again called upon to make a sacrifice when the Second World War was at a critical juncture. Their leadership was willing, but this time, a price was attached — or floated, at any rate.

In March of 1942, a year that would see critical battles from Stalingrad to Midway, an all-party committee submitted a proposal for azad ("independent") Punjab. Their audience was parliamentarian Stafford Cripps, who had been sent by the British government to secure Hindu and Muslim cooperation in exchange for independence after the war. Being concerned mainly with keeping the peace between Muslims and Hindus, Cripps rejected azad Punjab, which called for the division of Punjab into Muslim and Sikh territories. He did agree on one thing: that joining the Indian federation should not in principle be obligatory — thereby opening the door to the possibility that other groups might be able to pursue their destiny outside of India. The talks, undertaken by the Akali Dal party and its leader, Master Tara Singh, failed, but the upshot for Sikhs was still significant: in admitting that there was no obligation for any province to join the emerging federation, Cripps had created room for Punjab as an autonomous state. (During the talks Tara Singh was, however, able to secure the Sikhs status as a distinct separate entity, which gave them standing in the Partition negotiations. Because of this, they were subsequently courted by both Congress and Jinnah's Muslim League, each party attempting to lure them to its side. Had the Sikhs not been granted this status, the entire Punjab region, which included the current states of Haryana and Himachal Pradesh, would have automatically been absorbed into Pakistan after Partition, since the majority population in Punjab was Muslim.)

By the end of the Second World War, after England had dominated India for more than a century, it was clear to all but the most myopic "defend the realm at any costs" Englishman that continuing to hold on to most of its far-flung colonies was impossible. Plus, the optics were terrible: how could any nation make the case for the continued suppression of another people, after what had just transpired in Europe and the Pacific theatre? The pro-colonial faction had next to no international sympathy or support. At home, too, there was no real appetite for maintaining the Raj.

So India would get its wish — there would be independence. But what would independence look like? The enmity between Jinnah's Muslims and the Congress Party would never be stilled. One thing was clear: "India," an artificial creation unified only through the use of British force, could not survive as a single entity. The territory would be divided. But rather than reverting back to the territorial boundaries of pre-British India, there would be Partition.

BLOODSHED UNLEASHED

The division of India involved Muslim-majority areas to the northeast, in the state of Bengal, and in Punjab to the northwest, another area dominated by Muslims but also home to the vast majority of India's Sikhs. With Partition inevitable, the Sikhs had to make a choice: either throw their lot in with the emerging Islamic Republic of Pakistan or stay within the newly independent India of Nehru and Gandhi.

The dance between the Sikh leadership and Nehru's Congress was long. As far back as 1929, the party had recognized the rights of the Sikhs as a separate entity entitled to special consideration. At a meeting in Lahore in December 1929, Congress passed a resolution assuring Sikhs that "no solution thereof in any future Constitution will be acceptable to the Congress that does not give [Sikhs] full satisfaction."[9] In March 1931, sharing a vision of a united, independent India, Gandhi himself had gilded the lily: "Sikh friends have no reason to fear that we will betray them. For, the moment it does so, the Congress would not only thereby seal its own doom but that of the country, too." Moreover, "the Sikhs are a great people. They know how to safeguard their rights by the exercise of arms if it should ever come to that."

Although composing a sizable minority, and certainly dominant in parts of Punjab — like in the city of Amritsar — Sikhs did not constitute a majority in any broad region. Even in Punjab, they numbered just 13 percent of the area's total population, making the emerging dream of an independent Sikh nation a bit of a fantasy — at least at the time. But for the Sikh leadership, ensuring that their religion would be allowed to flourish, as well as achieving a degree of autonomy after Partition, was critical. (The Sikhs had tasted this autonomy in Punjab from 1799 to 1849 under the rule of the Sikh king Maharaja Ranjit Singh and his successors, before the takeover by the British. They felt they had paid dues in defending India from Mughal forces and deserved to be recognized as an autonomous entity.) Nor was Congress their only suitor; Jinnah's Muslim League was also making a play for Sikh hearts and minds. For his part, Jinnah offered much: within the proposed territory of Pakistan, there would be a Sikh "homeland" with a separate parliament and armed forces. It was a tempting offer. For Sikhs to reject it — and remain within a Hindu-dominant India — they sought assurances.

In 1946 they received them from Jawaharlal Nehru: in exchange for signing on to the newly created Indian federation, the Sikhs would have a region where their religion was respected and where they could call their own political shots. Combined with other assurances from the Congress Party, some stretching back to 1920, the Sikhs of Punjab were convinced that, post-Partition, their religion and political aspirations would be better served by staying in India.

It was a fateful decision. Within months, the ethnic and religious enmity that had been bubbling beneath Partition discussions boiled over. Small skirmishes erupted. A flashpoint exploded in Calcutta in 1946 when the Muslim League's Chief Minister for Bengal, H.S. Suhrawardy, embarked on a series of speeches inciting his followers to turn on many of those whom he was supposedly representing. The massacres in Calcutta were replete with atrocities that mere months before would have been unimaginable. In all, 5,000 died.

With violence spreading, Britain officially announced the end of its rule in February 1947; the transfer to independent Indian control would occur "no later than June 1948." In fact, it happened sooner. In March 1947, Louis Mountbatten, the last of British India's viceroys, arrived in India. Finding the situation increasingly dangerous and untenable, he decided that, instead of overseeing what was beginning to look like civil war, he would cut and run: being unable to persuade Jinnah to remain within a united, independent India, Mountbatten announced that India and Pakistan would come into their own, and go their own ways, almost a year ahead of schedule, on August 15, 1947. The Raj was over, but violence would roil for another year.

In Rurka Kalan, we were fortunate: most of the atrocities took place a few hours north. That said, even my village had its scars. Memories of the time are vague — I was very young, whichever birthday you observe — but I remember a neighbour, Aas Kaur (we called her Taee, "Auntie"), picking myself and my cousin up one day from our farm. We left in a hurry, both dressed in just our underwear, as I recall, and followed this elderly lady down the main road away from our farm into town. As we tagged along with Taee Aus Kaur I can still picture army vehicles streaming by, on their way to the fighting in nearby Nimahan.

Years later, I would hear stories — horrible tales, circulated in whispers — about Sikhs caught on the Pakistan side of the border. My wife, Surinder, eventually told me the story of her own loss. Surinder was born in Chak 71, a village near Lyallpur in what would become the Pakistan part of Punjab. Three months before Partition, Surinder's mother, Dalip Kaur, was forced to flee with her family across the new border, leaving all their household belongings behind. While Surinder and her brothers were placed safely in the care of their paternal grandparents, Surinder's mother, with her infant daughter in tow, went to Lyallpur to withdraw funds from her bank. Surinder spent six months waiting for her mother and baby sister to join them on the Indian side of the new Punjab border. Finally, after a half-year journey that included four months spent in a refugee camp, Dalip Kaur arrived. But Surinder's baby sister, fragile and malnourished, died almost immediately.

By the time I entered second grade, the Partition violence had run its course. The area once known as Punjab had been split and ethnically cleansed, with almost 15 million Sikhs, Hindus, and Muslims fleeing both ways across the British-drawn border. It is the largest forced migration in history, a chapter no one would choose to revisit.

Yet for the Sikhs of Punjab, the trials were far from over.

EMPTY PROMISES

Almost immediately after Independence, the pledges made by the Congress Party to the Sikhs were shelved or altered. The first betrayal was a significant one.

In 1950, the newly formed Indian Parliament approved the Constitution. In it was a clause that caused much consternation within the Sikh community. On its surface, Article 25, titled "Right to Freedom of Religion," guarantees "freedom of conscience" and the "right freely to profess, practise and propagate religion." For Sikhs, it also includes a specific reference to our right to wear the kirpan. ("The wearing and carrying of kirpans shall be deemed to be included in the profession of the Sikh religion" is the rather stilted language used.) In addition, it ensures that the state can, if necessary, pass laws that throw "open Hindu religious institutions of a public character to all classes and sections of Hindus" — a necessary addition, one could argue, especially considering the long history of social castes.

Article 25 also contains an insulting phrase: "The reference to Hindus shall be construed as including a reference to persons professing the Sikh, Jain or Buddhist religion, and that the reference to Hindu religious institutions shall be construed accordingly."

By lumping Sikhs, Buddhists, and Jains together as "Hindus" in a document as important as the Constitution, the framers managed to disrespect three major religions and refuel longstanding Sikh fears of the subjugation of their faith and culture.[10] Hukam Singh and Bhupinder Singh Mann, the two Sikh members tasked with helping prepare the document, were enraged at what they saw as a betrayal of the spirit to which the Sikhs had agreed. Refusing to add their signatures to the most important document created by the Indian state, they walked out in protest.

More betrayals followed, from disputes over water rights in Sikh-majority areas — the importance of irrigation to the modern agricultural economy of Punjab cannot be overstated — to broken promises of more political autonomy. Over time, the grievances only grew. Disparities between "agricultural inputs" incurred by farmers (the cost of producing crops, including capital outlays) and the sales price set by the central government meant that profit margins shrivelled; since Punjab was the agricultural heartland of India, Sikhs were disproportionately affected. Few Sikhs were employed by government (even in Sikh majority areas). In 1955 the Golden Temple was invaded and hundreds of Sikhs beaten with long clubs, or lathis, a common form of crowd control. This invasion and desecration was both a reflection of Indian government arrogance and a portent of what was in store.

Of all the points of friction, one perhaps more than any other provided the spark for the discontent that would rage in the 1980s. Since the 1950s in India, territorial designations have been decided along mostly linguistic, rather than ethnic or religious, lines. This has proved pragmatic for a very good reason. People who share a language have something substantial in common; although they may be from diverse faith communities, this is the glue that binds them to a particular area.

After a decade of delay, in 1966 the Indian government finally acceded to demands put forward by Master Tara Singh, leader of the Akali Dal, that a separate region with limited autonomy be created in Punjab. It was to be based not on religion but, as with other states where these divisions had already taken place, on language. It would encompass the vast majority of the area's Sikhs, but also the many Hindus and other minorities whose mother tongue was Punjabi. To make this happen — to demarcate a region based on language spoken — those who lived in Punjab were asked to declare the language they spoke at home.

Many of the region's Hindus, wary of being part of a state where Sikhs would have significant control, simply lied: contrary to what was actually the case, they claimed Hindi as their mother tongue. The result: to reserve what was purported to be the linguistic contiguity of the region, the area in India that had historically been known as Punjab was split in three: Haryana, Himachal Pradesh, and, in a vastly reduced version of its commonly recognized borders, Punjab. (To be fair, disputes over the redrawing of borders were not confined to Punjab. Many other states within the Indian federation experienced similar clashes with the federal government. As leadership passed from Nehru upon his death to, eventually, his daughter, Indira Gandhi, the Congress Party became even more determined to impose tight, centralized control upon all areas of the country.)

Much would flow from this decision. Sikhs had been promised a region where we could "experience the glow of freedom." Instead, the government of India, with the Akali Dal's complicity, created a rump state. This further stoked fires of dissatisfaction within the Sikh community, and by the late 1970s, a consensus was emerging: the only way to move forward was to press the government for a series of concessions embodied in an almost forgotten list of demands, called the Anandpur Sahib Resolution.

Created in 1973 by the offshoot Shiromani Akali Dal party but overlooked until its resurrection in 1978, the Anandpur Sahib Resolution was a wide-ranging document. Its resolutions encompassed everything from past grievances and minority rights to the demand that a diaspora-focused radio station be allowed to operate on the grounds of the Golden Temple. Most importantly, it recommended that the Indian Constitution be reworked to allow political autonomy for the various regions. (In the 1960s, a regional autonomy movement had also emerged, but the Akali Dal and other parties from several Indian states[11] had failed to leverage it into lasting political change. In the protests that occurred during this period, my father was arrested and imprisoned for a month.)

The Anandpur Sahib Resolution was not a secessionist document — it did not call for an independent Sikh state — but it was cast as such by Indira Gandhi, who had already demonstrated her ruthlessness by jailing political opponents during a state of emergency imposed in the mid-1970s. As the decade came to a close, clampdowns on "subversive activities" escalated; in time, many young Sikh men, mainly from rural areas, disappeared or were killed in so-called false encounters — extrajudicial killings by police or government agents. Within the Sikh community, in both India and the diaspora, there was a growing feeling that we as a people had been taken for granted, and for a ride.

This was the state of the Sikhs in Punjab as the 1970s were ending. The promises of joining the Indian federation had rung hollow, unrest was spreading, and bloodshed was all too common. For those who felt the Sikhs were being shortchanged, it was a fertile birthing ground for a charismatic young preacher talking about broken promises. And revolution.

CHAPTER 2

OPERATION BLUE STAR

BORN IN 1947 in the small Punjab village of Rode, Jarnail Singh Brar was the seventh of eight children. Like many in the mostly agricultural region, his father was a farmer and the young religious leader's early life was likely similar to my own: surrounded by extended family, working in the fields, and playing with siblings or cousins as time allowed. By the time he was in his teens, though, he demonstrated a clear aptitude for religious studies and at the age of 18 began studying scripture at Damdami Taksal, the most prestigious Sikh religious school in India. He quickly became a star pupil.

Soon, he was living the life of a missionary, going from village to village exhorting young men to stay clear of the vices that had so many in their grip, from illicit drugs and alcohol to pornography; he called on them to devote their life to their faith instead. He was not simply a caricature spewing fire and brimstone: as anthropologist Cynthia Mahmood wrote in her acclaimed book *Fighting for Faith and Nation: Dialogues With Sikh Militants*, "Those who knew him personally uniformly report his general likability and ready humour as well as his dedication."

Some within Damdami Taksal's hierarchy took note of his gifts and his devotion to the faith. When his mentor, Giani Kartar

Singh, head of the religious school, was killed in a car accident in 1977, the mantle passed to his protégé. The young scholar who had come of age in Bhindran, the place where Damdami Taksal was headquartered, was designated "Sant Bhindranwale," or "great spiritual leader from Bhindran." Soon, legions of young men were choosing to follow him and his teachings, seeing in him a way of achieving a more meaningful life. Shortly after Bhindranwale became leader, an incident occurred that would shape his life and the course of Sikh history. On April 13, 1978, a clash between a number of devout Sikhs and a larger group of Nirankaris, an offshoot sect, took place near Amritsar. The Nirankaris, considered a cult by most mainstream Sikhs, had gathered in Amritsar for a convention during the annual Vaisakhi celebrations; to many Sikhs their very presence was blasphemy, and the fact that they decided to hold their convention during this particular holy holiday was seen as deliberately provocative.

How to deal with what was interpreted as an insolent gesture? Representatives from Akhand Kirtani Jatha (AKJ), a well-known religious group, sought advice from the charismatic young leader, Sant Bhindranwale. The AKJ members met with Bhindranwale at the Golden Temple. After conferring with him, they agreed that the slight should not go unanswered but that discussion, not violence, was the best way forward. With Bhindranwale's blessing the delegation left the gurdwara to confront the Nirankaris. But when the dust had settled, 13 people, 10 of them from the AKJ, were dead.

The larger Sikh community was outraged. Pouring salt into fresh wounds, the Nirankari leader, Gurbachan Singh — widely assumed to have been behind the violence — was allowed to leave the area, escorted by police to the safety of his home in Delhi. That the Nirankari leader had escaped justice for his role in the murders was met with broad disbelief. And suspicion that Indira Gandhi or one of her cohort (Zail Singh, the former chief minister of Punjab, is often mentioned) was behind the Nirankari provocation and Gurbachan Singh's timely rescue ratcheted the tension even higher.

The 1978 disaster on Vaisakhi Day (the same holiday that saw the massacre at the Martyr's Well in 1919) had longer-term implications, mainly by introducing Bhindranwale to a much wider audience. As time passed, thousands lined up behind the charismatic preacher. Many of his supporters were fervent, some zealously so.

Over the next few years, the spreading conflict was seen as increasingly intractable. In April 1980, Gurbachan Singh, the Nirankari leader, was assassinated. Although Bhindranwale was not formally named as a suspect, many of his associates were thought to be involved. (Three years later Ranjit Singh, who'd been present at the initial Vaisakhi Day incident, admitted responsibility and spent 13 years behind bars.) On September 9, 1981, Jagat Narain was murdered. He was the Hindu proprietor of Punjab-based newspaper *Punjab Kesari*, whose vitriolic editorials denigrated the Sikh gurus and incited right-wing Hindus against Sikhs. Bhindranwale was arrested this time, but later released without charges. (Although Bhindranwale had nothing to do with it, while he was in jail, five of his followers hijacked an Indian Airlines flight to leverage him out of custody.) His arrest and release only served to heighten his standing. Those in the Sikh diaspora couldn't help but notice.

Meanwhile, government-directed police clamped down on a spreading civil disobedience movement, the Dharam Yudh Morcha. Launched on August 4, 1982, by Harchand Singh Longowal, leader of the Shiromani Akali Dal, the morcha, which would last for several years, saw over 30,000 Sikhs arrested for exercising their right to peaceful protest. The Shiromani Akali Dal was not alone. After being invited to participate, in August Bhindranwale threw his support — and his growing base — behind Dharam Yudh, aligning himself with Longowal and other prominent Sikh leaders.

With Longowal planning and directing the morcha, Bhindranwale's stature grew, his defiance and message resonating strongly with the young men of Punjab. He was becoming a folk hero — something that Longowal likely noted. On December 15, 1983, members of the nascent Babbar Khalsa organization, with Longowal's consent, asked

Bhindranwale to join them in the Nanak Niwas residence adjoining the Golden Temple complex to more closely coordinate their actions. Bhindranwale agreed, and he and a few dozen armed followers, along with members of the AKJ, relocated to residences beside Sikhism's most sacred spot. They were joined by Maj.-Gen. (retired) Shabeg Singh, a highly decorated hero from the 1971 Bangladesh war. If violence erupted, he would coordinate the response.

Seen through the eyes of Indira Gandhi and her Congress Party, when Bhindranwale made the Golden Temple both his sanctuary and his operational base, he appeared to be symbolically aligning his cause with the Sikh faith. It's unlikely, however, that this was part of any strategy on Bhindranwale's part. That said, there was no doubt that an attack on him within the sacred grounds would be seen as an attack on Sikhs generally, and, indeed, on the Sikh religion. Bhindranwale's move did not go unchallenged. Tensions were growing by the day. As events unfolded in Amritsar, each development was carefully watched in Punjab, throughout the rest of India, and in the large diaspora communities in Britain, the United States, and Canada — the latter of which, by this time, I had become a part of.

BETWEEN WORLDS

My route to Canada was, as for many Sikh immigrants who arrived in the 1970s, paved by those who had come before. My family has roots that go deep into the non-aboriginal history of British Columbia, particularly through my wife, Surinder. We've been married since we were both 16, our engagement arranged by our grandparents when we were just 9. Surinder's grandfather Inder Singh was a true pioneer, arriving in B.C. in 1904, about seven years after Kesur Singh, a British Indian Army captain and the first Sikh to set foot in Canada in 1897. (Like many Sikhs whose Canadian welcome was less than warm, Surinder's grandfather stayed a year before moving on to California — and then back to Punjab almost three decades later.) These early Sikh immigrants, imported as a source of labour, were all bachelors: women were not allowed to accompany them.

This ensured that for the first wave of Canadian Sikhs there would be no real long-term future here, a strategy that was also used to manage other "undesirable" immigrant groups, notably from China and Japan.

Less subtle manipulation was also used to force these strange new people, with their beards and head coverings, to think twice about overstaying. In 1907, the Anti-Oriental Riots took place in Vancouver. Most people killed or injured were East Asian — Sikhs stayed inside, avoiding much of the melee — but the message to all was loud and clear. And for those who missed it, Sir Wilfrid Laurier, Canada's seventh prime minister, reiterated it in 1908 when he "invited" Sikhs to leave Canada. It was suggested that British Honduras (now Belize) had the kind of tropical climate that would make a more suitable choice.

Despite the cool welcome, in time a large and vibrant Sikh community formed. (In the 2011 census, the Sikh population of B.C. numbered around 200,000 out of a total of 468,700 nationally, making it the largest in Canada.) Most ended up in the Lower Mainland, a region that stretches north from the U.S. border to the cities of West and North Vancouver, abutting the Coast Mountains. Some immigrants were more intrepid and made their way to the orchards of the Okanagan or to the lumber towns of the Cariboo in the central part of the province.

As is the case with most transplants, at first the newcomers held fast to their language and customs; often networking within their own communities, they struggled to maintain their traditions within the context of a new and very different culture. But by the 1950s and '60s, the pull of the "old country" on B.C.'s Sikhs had begun to diminish.

For the second and third generations the ability to fit in became paramount; "assimilation" was the buzzword, long before it became a questionable one. In this evolving community the Five Ks, the visible proclamation of faith that had set Sikhs apart since the end of the 17th century, were being viewed as relics of a previous time and place. Turbans were folded away, and hair and beards trimmed. Many no longer wore kirpans or even the kara, the bracelet. Some changed their names to fit in; to avoid discrimination, many still do.

Sikhs in Canada were largely indistinguishable from any other Canadian of South Asian heritage. At the time, this was considered a significant accomplishment, especially in the context of what had come before, such as the series of early 20th-century race riots in Vancouver and the infamous 1914 *Komagata Maru* episode in which a Japanese steamship packed with Sikh émigrés, all British subjects, was not allowed to dock in Vancouver and was eventually escorted out of Canadian waters.[12]

In 1967, in what would become a pivotal development for me and my family, Surinder's mother, Dalip Kaur, and her brother Lehmber emigrated to Canada. Dalip Kaur was a remarkable woman. In her day, in rural areas of Punjab, girls were rarely permitted to go to school; as a result she was taught at home by her progressive husband. (Surinder, too, was home schooled.) A tenacious, fiercely independent woman, widowed in her forties, she decided to make a new life for herself and her youngest unmarried child in Canada. She couldn't speak a word of English, but upon being sponsored by Surinder's aunt,[13] she and Lehmber, then 22, settled in Williams Lake, about a six-hour drive northeast of Vancouver. There, Lehmber found work in a lumber mill.

That year, 1967, was the nation's centennial. A time of great change for Canada, it was celebrated throughout the land, but for us and many others, it was profound in another way as well. The next year, under the new leadership of Liberal Prime Minister Pierre Trudeau, Canada changed its immigration criteria, establishing a points system by which certain attributes — education level and facility with English or French, for example — were assessed a value that went toward determining suitability. The end result was that the nation, growing quickly and facing a dearth of skilled labour in a variety of areas, could now draw from a global talent pool. With strict quotas a thing of the past, the points system would bring a surge of non-European immigrants, forever altering the country's complexion.

We were part of that surge. In the winter of 1970, Surinder and I and our three children — our daughters Kamaljit and Palbinder, aged seven and four respectively, and our two-and-a-half-year-old son, Harjinder — joined a community of transplants that was growing quickly. We proudly became Canadians. I became something else, too. As a reasonably well-educated Indian émigré who had decided to start a new life in a country that was opening up in a dramatic fashion, I became one more symbol of the next wave of Sikh immigrants — still tightly tethered to the land we had left behind, the slights from India still viscerally felt.

FINDING MY PATH

Our new lives began with a flight from Delhi to Vancouver, with a stopover in Tokyo. After spending a week in Vancouver, we took a second, shorter flight to Williams Lake, arriving on December 19, 1970 (at the age of 27 by my real birthdate). Located about 550 kilometres northeast of Vancouver, with a population of around 2,500, our new hometown was little more than a hamlet. The day before we landed a storm had blown through the area, and the temperature was hovering around −30° C. The snow, something I had never seen before, was knee deep. I had always assumed that snow fell lightly, like flour spilling from a sifter. In Williams Lake it dropped in clumps — heavy, sodden, spectacular.

For me and my family, Williams Lake was like another planet. And talk about being visible! At the time, only 26 Sikh families lived in town — a fair number considering the overall size of the population. But for me, having lived my entire life in India, to be so plainly in the minority was a shock.

At first, we stayed with my wife's mother and her brother. Canadian Christmas festivities were something very new for us. Listening to carol singing was an experience to remember. After a few weeks of getting used to the place (and the weather), I set out to find work. I began my search at Lignum Limited, the lumber mill where my brother-in-law, Lehmber, worked. In India, I had been a member of the national air force in an administrative post, a fairly prestigious position. Here, I quickly realized that most likely I would be restricted to pulling lumber off the "green chain"— you spent your days outdoors in the freezing cold, snatching cut lumber off a mechanized line. It was hard work, but I needed the job. So I set out for the mill. As I would for any job application, I dressed respectably in a three-piece suit and tie, with briefcase in hand. My dastar was, of course, neatly tied.

I climbed the stairs to the foreman's office on the second floor. The door was closed and when I knocked, a commanding voice called to me to come in. Sawdust covered the floor. Papers were piled high on a desk. Two men, both smoking cigars, were crammed into what was little more than a cubbyhole.

"I'm Gian Singh," I said, offering my hand. They both shook it. Foreman Art Strand and quality control supervisor Norm Porter introduced themselves.

"Well, what can I do for you?" Art asked.

"I'd like to apply to work here," I said.

"Really?" he replied. His gaze narrowed. "And what kind of work would you like to do?"

"Anything you can offer. A spot on the green chain would be fine."

He looked me over again, eyes moving from my neatly knotted tie to my polished shoes, then he leaned back and blew a cloud of smoke into the stale air. A sly smile crept across his face. "Hey, Gee-yaaan — shake my hand again, would you?"

Confused, I complied. "Look," he said, shaking his head. "I don't know much. But I do know that those hands have never been near the green chain or done any hard manual labour."

The two men laughed. The five-kilometre walk back to my mother-in-law's was humiliating, and when I arrived back at the house, icicles were hanging from my beard and moustache. I had to pour warm water on my shoes to remove them. The laces had frozen.

Desperate to find work of any kind, I ended up at the Canada

Manpower Centre, the federally funded employment help agency. (You could refer to labour as "manpower" back then.) I'd met the manager, David Dieter, a few days before and he'd invited me to come by to discuss what opportunities might be available. In Williams Lake, most of the jobs revolved around the lumber industry and that meant physical labour. It's not that I was in any way unwilling or unable to do this kind of work, but I had heard so many stories of well-qualified professionals from India who, after immigrating to Canada, became menial labourers or landed in other jobs entirely unsuited to their training and education. I was determined to avoid that fate.

Instinctively, David understood. Like many in the small, tight-knit town, he would become a friend. He was impressed and wanted to hire me as a Canada Manpower counsellor, but the criterion of a year's residency in Canada disqualified me. After casting out a few options, he suggested I might have better luck in Vancouver; there, I could at least find enough work to put food on the table. After I met the required residency, I could then return to Williams Lake and he could hire me. But a year in Vancouver? With full rent to pay? Away from my family? (Or even with them. How could I uproot them again?) It was out of the question, I told him.

"I'm really sorry, Gian, but—" he stopped himself mid-sentence. "Gian, did you ever receive first aid training in the Indian Air Force?"

"Well, sure," I said. "We all did. It was standard."

David smiled. "You have options."

Because of the nature of the work, every lumber mill in the area had to have someone standing by who was qualified by the Workers' Compensation Board in industrial first aid. Surprisingly, there were many more jobs available than people who could fill them. With a bit of upgrading, in 10 weeks I'd be able to get my first aid ticket and be working — and pulling in much more than I could ever hope to make piling lumber.

In short order, I had companies lined up to hire me. This, in turn, led to other opportunities. I leveraged the administrative experience I had acquired during my stint in the Indian Air Force to move up

the ladder, and within five months I landed a supervisory position —
ironically, at Lignum, the mill where I first applied.

Through Lignum owner Jake Kerr's sponsorship, I eventually
enrolled in over a dozen professional development programs. In
time, I got my Certified Professional Purchaser (CPP) designation
and even went on to attend the University of Western Ontario to get
senior management education. The Canadian School of Management
became my vehicle for getting an MBA. I taught Industrial First Aid
and Purchasing and Production Management courses at Cariboo
College, the region's best-regarded institution of higher learning. It
was, to say the least, a delicate balancing act: juggling family, work,
education, and, in time, a lot of service work, too.

In March 1981, I decided to strike out in partnership with a
couple of my relatives[14] and jumped at the opportunity to buy a
small, six-employee lumber mill that, with a lot of effort, we turned
into a much larger operation, providing a good life for ourselves
and our families, as well as adding more than 70 jobs to the local
economy. We called the business "Khalsa Enterprises." (Roughly
translated, khalsa means "pure" in Punjabi.) My first real hire? Art
Strand, the foreman who had initially laughed me out of his office
that cold winter's day more than a decade before. Over the years, we
had become friends.

In time, the town of Williams Lake became our true home.
Our children were raised there, did well at school, learned how to
pronounce "Saskatchewan." Saturday nights were spent gathered
around the television for *Hockey Night in Canada*, cheering on
our favourite teams. We made great lifelong friends, both Sikh and
non-Sikh. I joined the Rotary Club and the Industrial Development
Committee for the City of Williams Lake, which were gratifying
volunteer experiences. We became part of the fabric of the community
— one that for the most part proved warm and welcoming.

I don't mean to imply that everything was rosy. The kids,
especially, faced their share of racism growing up in rural British
Columbia. I still vividly recall how upset I was when one day

Kamaljit, my eldest, came home with a broken tooth — one of the other students had pushed her face-first against a school locker. Years later, I would learn more about what my children endured, from bullying and name-calling to having rocks thrown at them as they walked home from school.

The business front, too, was not all cherries and cream. The lumber business is tightly tied to the broader economy, and when new home construction lags or softwood lumber quotas or punitive countervailing and anti-dumping duties are slapped on Canadian exports, so goes the mill business. As well, stiff competition from national and international corporations can be disastrous for a small company. We faced some lean times. I'm reminded of the English expression, "When the going gets tough, the tough get going." For my partners, "getting going" meant bailing on the business. For me, it meant reaffirming my resolve, even when I came close to losing everything, including my house — at one point, I had to borrow money from my good friend Khushbag Singh just to meet my mortgage. But with rock-solid support from my wife and a strong sense of faith, I was determined to provide a good and decent life for my family. I persevered.

In this regard, mine was the classic immigrant "success" story — no more, no less. As a testament to the kind of opportunity available in this land, it speaks volumes. But soon after arriving in Canada, I also embarked on a second path that would take me in a different direction from many who arrived in pursuit of a more solid and plentiful future. This path would give me purpose and define much of the rest of my life, and that of my growing family.

THE HOLLOW MAN

Not long after we arrived in Williams Lake, a family friend, Ajit Singh Hothi, invited me to a reception. The guest of honour was author and journalist-turned-politician Paul St. Pierre, then the Liberal member of Parliament for our riding. St. Pierre had just returned from a landmark trip to the People's Republic of China with Prime

Minister Pierre Trudeau, the first Western leader to visit that country since the 1949 revolution.

The reception was held at the home of Bob Leckie, a local radio station owner. Since I was new in town, I stood out. Plus, I was still wearing my dastar — my decision to remove it would come later — and that made me stand out even more. At the time, seeing a turban, especially in rural B.C., was almost like spotting a unicorn. People were curious and wanted to know about me, where I was from and what I was all about. (They were likely even more impressed by the fact that I was fluent in English — such were the times.) After being urged to do so, I spoke for about five minutes, touching on my time in the Indian Air Force and mentioning the wars that India had fought against China and Pakistan that coincided with my time in the armed forces.

This was enough to impress our host, who, for reasons I still don't entirely understand, invited me to come down to the station the following day ... to be interviewed along with Paul St. Pierre! Although I had no idea what to expect, I must have performed moderately well. The interview was a turning point, and certainly had the effect of getting my name out in Williams Lake, as well as establishing my reputation in the Sikh community.

When our family arrived in Williams Lake, the Sikh community hadn't exactly been flourishing. There was no gurdwara, or even a Sikh cultural centre. After discussing this with many in our town, we made a decision: we'd build one. Toward that end, we set up the Central Cariboo Punjabi Canadian Association and the membership selected me as the founding president. It was my first formal community role — but by no means my last. Until the congregation raised money for the construction of a gurdwara, we celebrated Sikh religious days like Vaisakhi in the gymnasium of Glendale Elementary where my kids attended school.

The community grew rapidly. In the 1970s and '80s, Williams Lake experienced the highest per capita increase in Sikhs in Canada, growing from 26 families to between 400 and 500 families who made their living primarily in the lumber industry. Due to this growth, we finally raised enough money to build the Guru Nanak Sikh Temple in 1974, a landmark accomplishment for us. By the early 1980s, after more than a bit of bickering and infighting among rival factions in the gurdwara — each had a different vision of what they wanted the gurdwara to be — I was once again requested to serve as president.

Because of my business commitments and gurdwara position, I often traveled to the Lower Mainland, where I'd network with the leaders of the much larger, longstanding, and very active Sikh community. Going back and forth on a regular basis, I had the chance to know the Sikh leaders throughout the province, and, because of the sheer number of Sikhs who were represented in B.C., well beyond our borders as well.

With Surinder's blessing, I devoted an increasing amount of time to the Sikh community. To do seva, to serve, was a great honour. It added a dimension to my life that career success couldn't provide, giving me a deep satisfaction and, in a way, tying me more tightly to my roots, to my religion. Yet despite all of this, for many years I held my faith at arm's length.

I was the holdout in my family. For Surinder and the kids, a 1978 family trip to India had been transformative. Punjab is rich in Sikh history, and throughout the region thousands of historical gurdwaras dot the landscape, marking places where historic events took place. With a car and driver, we visited dozens of such places, from the gurdwara marking where Guru Nanak lived with his sister to where the very young sons of Guru Gobind Singh were brutally executed by the Mughals.

We traveled outside of Punjab, too, from the outskirts of Bombay to the Taj Mahal. But the trip's pinnacle was visiting the centre of Sikh spiritual life, the Golden Temple in Amritsar. The splendour and richness of history were palpable and entrancing, even overwhelming, for anyone steeped in the Sikh tradition. Even our Canadian-raised kids, who really only had passing familiarity with the history and importance of the Golden Temple, could not help but be affected.

In fact, they made the decision then and there to become practising Sikhs, and on Vaisakhi in 1979, a few months after we returned to Canada, all three underwent a Sikh initiation ceremony.

My wife and children became amritdhari — which, very roughly translated, is the Sikh equivalent of being "baptized." In addition to dedicating oneself to one's faith, it also means adhering to the Five Ks, a tradition that goes back to the tenth guru, Gobind Singh: kesh (uncut hair), kangha (wooden comb), kara (iron or steel bracelet), kachhera (cotton undergarment), and kirpan (a stylized representation of a small sword worn sheathed and in a cloth belt next to the body, commonly misconstrued as a dagger and controversial to this day, as we shall see.) I made excuses for not joining them. Some of the Five Ks were simple to follow — wearing the kara, for example, was something I'd always done. Not a big deal. (And tellingly, not a choice that came with any real sacrifice.) But to wear the turban every day (and to not cut my hair or even trim my beard) would be a different level of commitment entirely. At the time, because of the extent of immigration from India, there was a swelling backlash against newcomers of South Asian descent, regardless of faith: Muslims, Hindus, and Sikhs were lumped under the generic "Paki" epithet. To stand out even more in my career than I already did? Like most, I just wanted to fit in.

That way of thinking was long ingrained. Shortly after arriving in Canada in 1970, worried about my ability to adequately provide for my family, I did what I thought I had to do. On May 7, 1971, while most of the Cariboo was focused on Queen Elizabeth's visit to Williams Lake, I walked into a barber shop on Second Avenue wearing my turban; 20 minutes later I emerged clean shaven, my head uncovered. Later that day on my way to work, I passed my daughter Kamaljit coming home from school. She did not recognize me until I spoke. I remember her looking stunned and confused, and I hugged her while trying hard to hold back my tears. Out of necessity, hesitantly, I had "assimilated." (Well, as well as any darker-skinned South Asian guy could.)

Almost a decade later, on Vaisakhi Day, 1981, all of this changed. To mark the occasion, I was asked to speak in our gurdwara about the significance of the celebration. During my speech I touched on many subjects, among them the five articles of faith. (Since I was speaking in the gurdwara, I had worn a turban.) Several of our non-Sikh friends were in attendance, so I decided to speak in English rather than Punjabi. As I spoke, I noticed John Bas, a manager at BC Hydro and a friend, listening attentively. After the speech, he approached me. "Gian," he said. "Can we talk?"

"Why don't we eat first?" I replied, gesturing for him to join me downstairs in the langar hall, where a traditional Punjabi vegetarian meal was being served.

"Sounds good, but first let's talk," he said.

"Sure. What's up?"

He paused for a moment, and took a deep breath. "I've never seen such a phony as you, Gian."

The look on my face must have registered somewhere between amused and irritated. "Excuse me?"

"I can see your bracelet, that's fine," he said. "I can see your turban. But under the turban, I know your hair is cut. I know you trim your beard. I know you don't carry a kirpan."

"I'm sorry — what are you trying to say, John?"

"You've just given a very eloquent speech talking about how important these things are to your faith," he continued, "and yet you don't even practise what you've just preached. If this was a church, my church, we would never have allowed you to speak."

There were reasons I could have given him, solid explanations that could have served as a rationale. I could have told him that, since I was still teaching part time at the Cariboo College, I was concerned about how I'd be perceived by my students; would they still be able to relate to me, and see past the trappings of my religion? I could also have said that in business, the turban and beard could hold me back — and in a worst case scenario impact my ability to provide for those I love. I could have said all of this. I did not. Because he was right. I was a hypocrite. And the realization stung.

For a long time, I'd known there was something missing in my life. Regardless of my successes, I'd felt unfulfilled, lacking — hollow. I was a practising Sikh, no question: every day, for my entire life, I'd done my daily prayers. At home we had placed the Guru Granth Sahib, or the Sikh scripture, in a dedicated room and we read from it daily. But I realized that by forgoing the Five Ks and distancing myself from the beauty behind this most visible declaration, I had never fully embraced my own faith. It caused me not only mental pain, but moral anguish as well. To this day I remind myself, "Practise what you preach, Gian."

In the Sikh faith, being born into a Sikh family and believing in the principles of Guru Nanak may be enough to call oneself a Sikh and be an active member of the community. (It was for me, for a time.) But at some point, making a formal commitment is essential. In a ceremony that involves drinking the initiation nectar amrit, a syrupy sugared water, and embracing the three basic tenets of the faith — to remember God, to live honestly, and to share with those who have less — I formally vowed to live according to the lessons of my faith.

When I was 38 years old, I became amritdhari — a little late, I suppose, but nevertheless. Since then, I have never cut my hair or trimmed my beard. According to the tenets of my faith, I present myself to others, and to God, in a natural state.

A DETOUR INTO THE LABYRINTHINE INTRIGUE OF INDIAN POLITICS

By 1982, news coming out of Punjab was dire. Seeing law and order deteriorating, and power slipping away from the Akali Dal, the Dharam Yudh Morcha was launched in August 1982, under the direction of Harchand Singh Longowal and with the support of Jarnail Singh Bhindranwale. It changed the game in Punjab: by the time the peaceful protests finally ran their course, more than 30,000 Sikhs had been jailed.

For the Indian government, the continuation of the morcha was the result of an opportunity lost. In 1978, Longowal's Shiromani Akali

Dal faction presented the Anandpur Sahib Resolution to a coalition government, but in April 1980 the coalition collapsed. Now the Akali Dal faced a belligerent Indira Gandhi.

Of the 40 demands the Resolution comprised, these 5 were critical:

- River water rights: only water in excess of Punjab's needs could be allotted to neighbouring jurisdictions, for which they would pay a royalty to Punjab
- Punjabi-speaking areas left out of the 1966 reorganization should be territorially reintegrated into Punjab
- Chandigarh, the capital designed by famed French modernist architect Le Corbusier to replace Punjab's former capital Lahore (now in Pakistan), would officially become part of Punjab
- The Indian Army quota system, imposed in the 1970s, should be dismantled. (The system had dramatically reduced the number of Sikhs eligible to serve. In 1947, Sikhs made up 30 percent of enlistees; by the early 1980s, that had been reduced to 2 percent.) With armed service one of the few stable and viable career paths available, and in light of our proud Sant-Sipahi traditions, this was not a trivial demand
- The pursuit of provincial autonomy, along the lines originally conceived of in the Federation of States' founding constitution, should be pursued for Punjab and all other states

The conditions were far from unreasonable. Meeting them would have required some political courage, but the payout (peace in Punjab and much improved Sikh–Hindu relations) would have been huge. Indira Gandhi, however, ever mindful that in opposing the Sikhs she could gain votes elsewhere, chose to dismiss the demands out of hand. Complicating things further, it was an election year. The Sikhs had provided Gandhi with a classic wedge issue, and in the coming months "Sikh terrorism" would become a prominent theme for the Congress Party.

Diaspora Sikhs in Britain, the United States, and Canada, appalled at rising unrest and Gandhi's history of unfulfilled promises and crass manoeuvres, offered aid and assistance to activists in Punjab. In September 1982, I joined a contingent of Sikh leaders from across the province who'd gathered in the small town of 100 Mile House in central British Columbia. After banging out the details over the course of a full day, we formed the Morcha Action Committee, whose mandate was to provide moral support to Punjab Sikhs for the protests that would soon become commonplace. To this end, we sent two jathas (groups mustered for a particular purpose), one formed from members of Vancouver's Ross Street gurdwara, the other from Guru Nanak gurdwara in Surrey. These two groups would travel to Punjab to represent the Sikhs of British Columbia in the protests, marching alongside other jathas from many countries, from Singapore and Hong Kong to the U.S. and Britain.

During the meeting, Jagjit Singh Sidhu, a prominent community member from Abbotsford, B.C., was chosen to act as Morcha Action Committee president. I was selected as vice-president and assigned the responsibility of maintaining a dialogue with the leadership of the Dharam Yudh Morcha in Punjab. It was through my time as VP of the Morcha Action Committee that I got to know Harchand Singh Longowal and Jarnail Singh Bhindranwale, both of whom would play critical roles in events that, by the spring of 1984, were getting well out of hand.

Although Longowal and Bhindranwale had agreed to work together to persuade the government of India to implement the Anandpur Sahib Resolution, over time it became clear that there was little love lost between them. (Initially some in the Akali Dal thought Bhindranwale was secretly aligned with the Congress Party — a misrepresentation fueled by Congress's early bungled attempts to use the then relatively unknown Bhindranwale as a counterweight to Longowal's support in the community.) By 1984, the competition between the two factions had grown violent; clashes between Longowal's supporters and followers of Bhindranwale became commonplace. A rumour that Longowal had put out a contract on his rival's life was being taken very seriously. Finally, on April 14, 1984, Bhindranwale's right-hand man, Surinder Singh Sodhi, was shot and killed. Suspicion immediately fell on those aligned with Harchand Singh Longowal.

The Sikh leadership in the diaspora was naturally concerned. Most of us were recent emigrants from Punjab, and our ties to the homeland, the place where our faith has its origins, were still very strong. For the past several years, as tensions grew in Punjab we had been networking, formulating strategies designed to challenge the Indian government to accept the Anandpur Sahib Resolution and restore peace in Punjab. Our goal was to put an end to the unrest. Now, we were forced to split our focus and mediate an internal dispute.

Although I was based in rural British Columbia, word of my seva had spread; through my work with the Morcha Action Committee, it became my job to talk with both Longowal and Bhindranwale, since I had established a working relationship with each of them over the past two years. After the killing of Sodhi, and the innuendo that swirled in its wake, the action committee wanted to penetrate the static. It fell to me to find out what was going on.

First, I called Sant Longowal, who, prior to becoming a politician, was a well-respected expositor of Sikh scripture. After a few pleasantries, he staked out his position in no uncertain terms. "Gian Singh Ji," he said respectfully, "these guys, these friends of Bhindranwale, are characterless goondas and deserve to die."

I was taken aback but pressed on, asking Longowal whether one of his men, Gurcharan Singh, was involved in Sodhi's murder, as was widely rumoured. From Longowal, there was much equivocating. "Bhai Sahib Ji (respected brother)," he finally said, "you do not know what goes on inside the precincts of the Golden Temple."

This, I assured him, was what we in the diaspora were trying to find out. After about 10 minutes, though, I realized he was not going to provide any truthful answers. Longowal had become a politician through and through.

We hung up, and I dialed the number I had for Jarnail Singh Bhindranwale in the Golden Temple compound. Bhindranwale's response was calm, careful — and without guile. He did, in fact, believe that Longowal's camp was behind the killing of his friend.

"Gian Singh Ji, I am told that Gurcharan Singh was directly or indirectly involved," he began. But he was willing to look past this, in the hopes of preserving a unified coalition that could continue to challenge the Indian government to accept the Anandpur Sahib Resolution. "Everything that happens is God's will. Tell the Sikhs in Canada to pray for peace." He wasn't finished; he had an olive branch to extend. "And please, do not blame Sant Longowal! He is the leader of our morcha, and he deserves our support."

It was such a contrast to the conversation I'd just had. It was clear to me who had the moral authority in this situation.

AN UGLY, DESPICABLE ACT

On June 1, 1984, my phone started ringing off the hook. At first, the accounts were vague. We had already heard that the Indian army, under the command of Maj.-Gen. K.S. Brar, had surrounded the Golden Temple with 6,000 soldiers, along with commandos. It was, most thought, more posturing than substance. The consensus: no matter how much Gandhi's government wanted to present a show of strength, there was no way they would launch a full-blown military assault against Jarnail Singh Bhindranwale when he was safely within the Golden Temple — it would be tantamount to, say, the Italian Army attacking the Vatican. (I mean this literally: imagine if the Vatican had been built by Jesus Christ, and that will give you an idea of the significance of the Golden Temple to the Sikhs.)

There was another reason most thought that the presence of the army was more show than anything: in preparation for the annual celebrations honouring the 17th-century martyrdom of the fifth guru, Guru Arjan Dev, thousands of pilgrims had been allowed inside the complex — a relaxation of the previous army-imposed curfew. Older women milled about; children leaned over the edge of the sarovar, or Pool of Nectar, the massive water feature that surrounds the Darbar Sahib and acts as a centrepiece. Assembled outside, the Indian Army would be laying siege to a holy shrine filled mainly with civilians, in addition to a few hundred of Bhindranwale's men. All this strongly argued against imminent military action.

Still, those of us who were monitoring the situation from abroad were concerned, although our worry was probably more out of habit than anything concrete. We knew that inside the complex, Sant Bhindranwale himself had taken refuge in the Akal Takht, the "throne of the timeless one," a gleaming gold-domed structure that functions as the primary seat of power in our faith and is the physical embodiment of miri and piri — the spiritual and the temporal. It was said to have been built on the very ground where the sixth guru, Guru Hargobind, played as a young child in the 17th century.

To launch an attack on a site imbued with this kind of meaning? Full of innocent worshippers? It simply couldn't happen. Yet at 4:00 a.m. on June 4, 1984, the sound of machine gun fire began ricocheting off the walls of Sikhism's most sacred place, echoing throughout Punjab and the Sikh diaspora.

As reports of the attack spread, urgent calls, mainly from relatives, came through. In turn they called others until the word got out. (Yes, life before the internet.) Accurate accounts of what was happening were difficult to come by. In a cynical yet strategically astute move, Indira Gandhi had imposed a media blackout prior to the attack, and although there were journalists in the vicinity — Mark Tully, the BBC's Delhi-based correspondent, had been in the compound until about four hours prior to the attack — almost all were quickly shuttled out of the area, witness only to the sounds of 105mm squash head shells exploding in the distance.

Desperate for actual on-the-ground accounts, I tried to call both Bhindranwale and Longowal. It was naive of me to think I could get through. Distressed and wanting to share their concern with others, people started simply dropping by our home. First to come was my friend Avtar Singh, from the nearby town of Quesnel, about a 90-minute drive from Williams Lake. He'd called earlier but grew restless waiting for any news at his home and decided that he needed company. Next, my friend Khushbag Singh dropped in, then Nagina Singh and others. Soon, our living room was full. Not everyone spoke, but from their faces you could read their emotional state. They were traumatized, unable to make sense of the news they were hearing. How could this have happened? I glanced at Surinder and the kids. They were stunned, silent, as anecdotal accounts of the Indian government's attack on such a peaceful, tranquil place went from bad to catastrophic.

We huddled around the radio, tuned to BBC International, but the vast bulk of our news came from the occasional phone call from Amritsar, shushing the gathering when anything approximating actual information was relayed — a rare occurrence, especially early on. On June 5, the third day of the attack, around 1 p.m. (1:30 the next morning in Amritsar) Avtar Singh got through to a telephone number that Bhindranwale had once used. The person picking up the phone identified himself as Bhindranwale's brother and told Avtar Singh that there was heavy shooting going on, not just small arms or machine gun fire. Before being cut off, we learned that over 500 people had died. Longowal and Gurcharan Singh Tohra (president of the Shiromani Gurdwara Parbandhak Committee and no relation to the Gurcharan Singh implicated in the death of Surinder Singh Sodhi) had surrendered and been taken away. Bhindranwale would remain in the Akal Takht until his death at the hands of the Indian forces.

The chaos inside the Golden Temple must have been unimaginable. Here, among those who had come to seek solace in our living room, there was horror. There were tears, too, but above all the overwhelming reaction was simply shock. Despite the rhetoric and rising tension, nobody had imagined that the government of India would launch a full-scale attack on the holiest site in all of the Sikh faith.

When the hostilities finally ended on June 6, the official number was 493 civilians dead, but human rights groups put the estimates much higher, with some tallying the fatalities at around 3,000. The Darbar Sahib building had received 259 bullet holes and the Akal Takht was destroyed, its pristine white walls collapsed into a heap of soot and blackened stone. Indira Gandhi, with the kind of cynically manufactured sensitivity that was her hallmark, said, "The necessity now is to heal the wounds inflicted on the hearts of the people."

What an absurd thing to say. There had been several routes to peace and ample opportunities for dialogue. Both Longowal and Bhindranwale had wanted a dialogue with the government, had courted arrest in the past, and were willing to do so again. Failing that, laying siege by throwing a cordon around the complex would have taken time, but surely this too would have been infinitely preferable to the violence that Gandhi decided upon. The destruction was not limited to Amritsar: 38 other gurdwaras across Punjab and in neighbouring Haryana had also been surrounded and attacked. This act was seemingly designed to destroy the centres of Sikh faith throughout the land, to inflict a wound on the entire Sikh population, to snuff the life out of Sikhs and their aspirations in one fell swoop.

Later, we learned that the government of India had code-named the action "Operation Blue Star," a rather pretty-sounding phrase for such an ugly, despicable act. That day, when I grasped the enormity of the attack on our sacred places of worship — on the genocidal challenge to our very existence — I realized that Sikhs would never experience the promised glow of freedom within the Indian state. I was far from the only Sikh to reach that conclusion.

CHAPTER 3

WHEN A GREAT TREE FALLS

O N JUNE 10, 1984, a crowd of British Columbia Sikhs conservatively estimated to be 15,000 strong (some claimed upward of 25,000) gathered in front of the Vancouver Art Gallery, the natural rallying place for all protests in the city. The numbing shock of the attack on the Golden Temple earlier that week had dissipated. In its place was rage and a sense of disbelief: had it really come to this? How could the Indian government kill so many innocent citizens?

One by one, speakers took to the microphone to express their feelings. "To ask Sikhs in Canada to remain silent is like asking them to give up their religion," one young man, Sarbjeet Singh Neel, eloquently put it. He was right. For Sikhs, opposing injustice is a duty, not a choice. And now that an injustice had been visited upon us, it was our obligation to make our voices and our pain loudly and unequivocally heard.

At the art gallery protest, there was a clear sense that the community had to figure out a way to support our brothers and sisters in Punjab. Despite the fact that only the Indian government's version of events was making it through the media blackout in Punjab, virtually every Sikh in Canada had close relatives and personal connections there, and they knew that the situation was far worse than the government was presenting. They knew the number of people killed by the army had been grossly under-reported, no mention made of the fact that most of those dead were innocent pilgrims, including the elderly, women, and children, some as young as six months old. When I was asked to speak, I focused on the need for the community to stand united. I strongly believed then, as I do now, that for Sikhs, the principles and lessons taught by the gurus should be our guide.

After the speeches, the protesters marched down Howe Street, ending in front of the Indian consulate. Placards, some bearing the phrase "We Want Justice!," were held high, as were posters of Jarnail Singh Bhindranwale. In life he was a remotely familiar name for most Sikhs; in death he had become the symbol of resistance to the Indian government's handling of the Punjab situation. The rationale was simple: for years, he had been vocal about the government's disregard for Sikh aspirations, for its callous, at times even inhumane, treatment of Sikhs. Now, the government's disregard of Sikh lives (and the sanctity of the Golden Temple) lay clear for all to see.

Whatever Bhindranwale was accused of was cast into doubt in the eyes of the community. Even if some of it was true, the rationale went, it paled against the atrocities committed by the government of India. For me, that I knew the man — or at least had been in regular telephone contact with him — certainly added a personal dimension. Throughout our dialogue, he seemed to me a man of integrity, someone who walked the talk. Unlike others, such as Longowal, who had capitulated when their personal safety was threatened, Jarnail Singh Bhindranwale had remained true to his word and his cause.

Although the Vancouver demonstration was by far the largest in Canada — B.C. was then home to about 68,000 Sikhs, and by some estimates as many as 40 percent of us came out that day — similar scenes were taking place across the country, notably in Calgary, Edmonton, Winnipeg, and Toronto, as well as internationally. Almost without exception they were peaceful. Considering the shell shock and raw emotions at play in those first days and weeks, this was a credit to the community here and abroad. But all in all, the situation was a tinderbox. News reports were scarce, a result of the continuing Indian government blackout, leaving those who had close relatives in the area — most of us — fearful that lives were still at risk.

As people searched for meaning in the massacre, they wanted to know where to cast the blame. Predictably, there were cries of "Zailu Kutta!" in reference to India's president Zail Singh (kutta means "dog") and "Indira Gandhi Murdabad" — a common call for a politician to abase herself when the public is unhappy. But there was another cry, too, one that would have been unimaginable mere months before: "Khalistan Zindabad!"

LONG LIVE KHALISTAN!

In Punjab itself, the cries for independence remained muted; to declare sympathy for Bhindranwale or the notion of independence was to court retribution from an Indian military that had continued to tighten the noose on Punjab and was now actively trying to root out anti-government sentiment (by then shared by the vast majority of Sikhs). It was partly for this reason that the diaspora became so integral to the events in India: since Punjab's Sikh voices had been stifled, we would have to speak for them. With one brutal strategic blunder, Indira Gandhi and her cohorts managed to make nationalists of the majority of Sikhs around the globe.

Sikh nationalism can be traced back to before the Raj. Banda Singh Bahadur took on the mantle of leadership among the Sikhs after Guru Gobind Singh's death in 1708, establishing the first Sikh Kingdom on May 14, 1710. After conquering the territory of Sirhind, he expanded his reach throughout Punjab for five years, until he finally lost to the Mughals. (He and his son Ajay Singh and 700 of his army were slaughtered on June 9, 1716.) By the late 1700s, after a half-century of brutal repression and persecution, Sikh groups finally extinguished Mughal rule in Punjab for good.[15] In 1799, Maharaja Ranjit Singh unified the Sikh misls (small independent regions) that had previously fought against the Mughals, founding a secular

Sikh Empire that eventually encompassed the entire Punjab. With a government composed of Sikhs, Muslims, Hindus, and Christians, it was radically enlightened for the times. Ranjit Singh's reign spanned 40 years, ending with his death in 1839. His demise heralded the beginning of the end of the Sikh Empire, which dissolved a decade later when the British East India Company started the Anglo-Sikh Wars and brought Punjab under its domain, the last of the Indian kingdoms to be subjugated.

Although the Sikh Empire died with the rise of the Raj, the idea of Sikh independence was not discarded, merely mothballed. It lived on in the collective memory of Sikhs through their prayers. The words "Raj Karega Khalsa," often attributed to Guru Gobind Singh, literally mean "the Khalsa shall rule," and became the rallying cry for Sikh sovereignty during the persecution of the 18th century. Later, in the wake of British dominance in Punjab, the words would become part of the Sikh daily prayer, and continue to be recited today.

Leading up to Partition, there was, as I've noted, considerable lobbying for some sort of autonomous area where Sikhs could "experience the glow of freedom"; the fact that there had once been a Sikh Empire with governing apparatuses, a standing army, and identifiable borders fueled hope that Sikh independence, at least as a concept, could be resurrected. In 1971, the call for an independent Sikh nation — Khalistan — came from a seemingly unlikely source. Having grown dissatisfied with the prospects for real reform in Punjab from the Indian government, Jagjit Singh Chauhan, a London-based medical doctor who had served in the late 1960s as deputy speaker and finance minister for the Punjab Assembly, abruptly proclaimed an independent Khalistan in a half-page advertisement in the October 13 edition of the *New York Times* and asked for United Nations recognition. The ad made a moderate splash — enough that Chauhan was able to get a hearing from a few American politicians and attract a certain amount of Sikh support, financial and otherwise.

After moving back to India for a few years in the late 1970s, Chauhan once again relocated to London in 1980, but not before hoisting the Khalistani flag on March 23, 1980, in Anandpur Sahib. By June 16 of that year, he'd left the country and declared himself President-in-Exile of the Republic of Khalistan. Among his 11-member exile council were Balbir Singh Sandhu as general secretary and Hardyal Singh Thiara, who lived in Vancouver at that time and later moved to the U.S. On April 13, 1981, Balbir Singh Sandhu (no relation) released a Khalistan passport and postage stamp in Amritsar. Never quite out of the picture, but never finding a significant audience for his message in Punjab or elsewhere, Chauhan and a few others kept the idea of Khalistan alive — but barely, a flickering flame.

OUR MISSION

In the aftermath of the attack on the Golden Temple, those of us in leadership roles in the diaspora were in constant contact, trying to formulate a collective response. Since I was fortunate to have my own business I had the flexibility to travel extensively, and I did so, heading abroad to essentially take the pulse of Sikhs internationally, and of their leadership. In effect, our mission was to gauge how much support there was for creating a unified voice to address the human rights crisis in Punjab.

With my friend Avtar Singh, president of a gurdwara in the neighbouring town of Quesnel, I flew to Washington, D.C., to talk with our American counterparts. There, we met with Ganga Singh Dhillon. Dhillon had been head of the Sri Nankana Sahib Foundation, a small U.S.-based group that had been advocating for a Sikh national homeland since at least 1975; as far as strategies went, he unfortunately seemed content to simply align his group with Pakistani strongman General Zia ul Haq — a letdown for both me and Avtar Singh. After hearing his views, and those of other American Sikh leaders, we made plans to continue on to Britain, where the largest Sikh community outside of Punjab was located.

Because of his early and ongoing advocacy for Khalistan, Jagjit Singh Chauhan was seen after the June 1984 attacks as more credible than ever; the "President-in-Exile" was now arguably the most prominent British Sikh leader. Chauhan had visited Canada several times since the early 1970s, trying to drum up support for his cause. I had never met him. In fact, when I had the chance to do so I declined. In 1981, Chauhan was in British Columbia on a North American fundraising trip. Through intermediaries he offered to come to Williams Lake and speak to our gurdwara sangat (congregation) on the subject of Khalistan. Frankly, like most Sikhs at the time, I didn't find his arguments in support of separatism very persuasive. I was also sceptical of his motives in pursuing this path in the first place. His allegedly close relationship with Zia ul Haq and Pakistan's Inter-Services Intelligence, or ISI — and the suspicion that his presence was designed as a lightning rod for Sikh dissatisfaction with India — concerned many of us.

Chauhan had received a lukewarm welcome in British Columbia. Interestingly, his main contact here was the late Tara Singh Hayer, the newspaper publisher. Long before he became a voice for "moderation," followed by his murder in 1998, Hayer was well known as a vociferous critic of India and a staunch Khalistan supporter (until he did a 180-degree turnaround). The *Indo-Canadian Times*, his Punjabi-language paper, routinely featured articles full of heated rhetoric. It was to Hayer that Chauhan turned after finding his mainstream reception chilly. Hayer, in turn, put Chauhan in contact with the Babbar Khalsa, a tiny but vociferous group based mainly in B.C. that advocated the use of violence in the fight for independence, and whose actions would later greatly damage the Sikh community in Canada.

In B.C., with backing from the Babbar Khalsa, some of what Chauhan spearheaded was simply absurd: with Surjan Singh Gill and a few others, Chauhan opened a "consulate" in Vancouver, issuing passports, postage stamps, even worthless Khalistani currency — $5 and $50 bills printed by Tara Singh Hayer's *Indo-Canadian Times*. (Conveniently, the Khalistan consulate office was initially located in the offices of the *Indo-Canadian Times* on Kingsway in Vancouver.) None of this did Chauhan any favours within the larger Canadian Sikh community. But following the Golden Temple attacks, Sikhs in general were much more open to the idea of Khalistan, and to Chauhan. Because he had been arguing for Sikh independence for over a decade, and the idea was relatively new to the rest of the Sikh community, Avtar Singh and I decided to go to England and talk with him.

We met the self-proclaimed president of Khalistan at his London flat along with his financial backer, Ajit Singh Khaira. Chauhan, a slim, soft-spoken man with a long white beard and white dastar, talked to us at length about Sikh history and the roots of independence and, without providing specifics, claimed to have gained international support for the cause of Khalistan. Of this I was sceptical. It did become clear during our talk that, unlike his Babbar Khalsa supporters who were by then advocating for the violent birth of Khalistan, Chauhan fervently believed that change could be brought about through peaceful, diplomatic means. This certainly resonated with me. As former finance minister of Punjab, he was politically very astute. (His affiliation with Babbar Khalsa, it seemed to me, was likely a marriage of convenience to establish a Canadian base for Khalistan advocacy.)

Chauhan repeated an odd story, one that had also been making the rounds in Washington; it had been mentioned to me by Ganga Singh Dhillon, too. The rumour: despite what seemed to be indisputable evidence to the contrary, Jarnail Singh Bhindranwale had not died in the Golden Temple. Rather, Chauhan insisted, he'd escaped the carnage and fled to Pakistan (with Chauhan's assistance), where he was apparently alive and well. To both Avtar Singh and me, the story seemed preposterous. For Bhindranwale to have made his way through a cordon of thousands to the safety of Pakistan was impossible to believe. And really, from what I knew of him through our conversations, it did not seem in character for him to do so: whatever one thought of his means, he always struck me as a man of principle, someone whose commitment was his bond. He had clearly been determined to die fighting for his ideals. To run away to Pakistan would have been, I believed, anathema to who he was.

Still, the rumours persisted and were gaining currency in some circles. And so, after some discussion, Avtar Singh and I decided that we'd go to Pakistan and see what we could discover. Neither of us harboured hope of finding Bhindranwale. But if we could put the fable to rest, that alone would be worth the trip. Since both Chauhan and Dhillon claimed to have contacts within the Pakistani bureaucracy and security apparatus over the years, we asked them to introduce us to a few individuals who could help us when we arrived. Both men tried to discourage us from going. Clearly, they did not want us to discover the truth about Bhindranwale's fate — he had become a powerful, unifying symbol and I suppose they wanted to keep him "alive" as long as they could. Nevertheless, we booked a flight out.

IN SEARCH OF SANT BHINDRANWALE

The next day, July 10, 1984, only a month after the attack on the Golden Temple, Avtar Singh and I boarded a direct flight on Pakistan Airlines from London to Lahore. We took our seats, two amritdhari Sikhs looking more than a little conspicuous in an airplane full of Pakistanis who, during the partition of India only a few decades earlier, would have been our sworn enemies, and we theirs. "Well, Avtar Singh," I said, doing up my seat belt, "it's too late to turn back now." He smiled, just a little nervously.

After we reached cruising altitude, the door to the cockpit opened and the captain emerged. He strolled down the aisle, not stopping until he reached the row where the two of us were sitting. He stared at us — and then, smiling, stuck out his hand. We took turns shaking it.

"We're very glad you're flying with us," the captain said.

"We're glad to be here," I replied. The warmth of the greeting, from the other passengers to the flight attendants to the captain himself, was completely unexpected.

The captain leaned in. "We don't usually serve drinks on Pakistan Airlines," he said quietly, "but for honoured guests, we can make exceptions. What can I get you? Scotch? Gin? A beer?"

Avtar Singh and I smiled at each other. "Thanks for the offer," I said, "but we don't drink." As observant Sikhs, I explained, neither of us consumed any intoxicants, including alcohol.

"Really?" he said. "That's new. In my travels, I see a lot of Sikhs drinking."

Of that, I told him, I had no doubt.

At Lahore airport we were received right on the tarmac by someone I believe was a state security agent and led directly to the baggage area — no customs or immigration formalities. Wow, what hospitality! Throughout Lahore, we were treated like royalty. We took a horse and buggy tour of the city; it was, our driver told us, free of charge. We passed stalls where people were selling sugar cane juice, and they came out to greet us, insisting that we sample their wares — again, for free. We Sikhs were not the enemy, not anymore. We were, instead, local celebrities. Things do change, even if that change comes at the cost of bloodshed. In the ever-evolving dance of allegiances that defines South Asian politics, the enemy of my enemy was thrilled to be my friend.[16]

Still, from the moment we landed we'd been shadowed by the Inter-Services Intelligence (ISI), the nation's equivalent to the CIA or MI5, as well as an Indian intelligence agent, who, after he was "made" by one of the ISI guys assigned to us, was chased out of a gurdwara we were visiting. (Since Partition, many Sikh historical sites and gurdwaras, including the birthplace of Guru Nanak Dev, are now in Pakistan.) In short order, the "clandestine" surveillance was anything but, and ISI agents were openly talking with us, often cordially.

We even shared a meal or two. At lunch one day, during a discussion with one of the ISI agents assigned to us, he asked if we would come with him to Islamabad, Pakistan's capital. Islamabad was at least a four-hour car ride from Lahore; if Bhindranwale had, in fact, bucked the odds and made it across the border — still a ludicrous notion, in my opinion — why would he risk heading farther into Pakistan? West Punjab no longer had any significant Sikh population. But the Punjabi language was still spoken in the region. In the very unlikely event that Bhindranwale was alive, he'd surely want to stay in an area where he could at least communicate in his own tongue. (Punjabi remains the primary language of over two-thirds of people living in Pakistan's Punjab region.)

"Sorry, but why should we go north?" I asked him. "You're not seriously suggesting that Sant Bhindranwale is alive and living in Islamabad?"

Our new friend shifted nervously in his chair. "I didn't say that," he replied. "But in Islamabad, there is a senior official who can, um, shed some light on what you seek."

"Okay," I said. "And who is this 'senior official'?"

"Gian Singh, I am not at liberty to say."

Avtar Singh and I exchanged looks. Something wasn't right. But we had come this far. There was no going back, not until we had reasonably explored any avenue open to us. We talked quietly and agreed to go.

Islamabad is about 400 kilometres from Lahore. You can get close by train, but that route was notoriously unreliable: trains would break down, delays happened frequently. Instead, we agreed to go with the ISI agent in his van. The journey itself was not particularly memorable — but it certainly could have been for us that day. For reasons that were never made clear, our instructions were that if we were pulled over, Avtar Singh and I were to throw on burqas, complete with full mesh face coverings. With our beards and turbans, we were supposed to pass as women! Every time our van stopped at a checkpoint, we had to play dress-up — although, luckily, we were never asked to step outside the van so the checkpoint guards could take a closer look. Finally, after an uneventful drive that took us onto the Potohar Plateau, we arrived in Islamabad.

Lahore had felt familiar, though I'd never visited it before this trip. Its walled inner city was similar to Old Delhi, with narrow streets and labyrinthine alleyways full of people, full of bustling shops — full of life. Even the dialect was indistinguishable from what was spoken in Amritsar, which was only about 50 kilometres away. By contrast,

Islamabad bore no resemblance to the older cities and towns of Punjab. Built on a grid with wide, imperious boulevards, its skyline punctuated by the odd high-rise, the modern (if somewhat sterile) city would have seemed to an exile from Amritsar like the metropolis of a parallel universe.

It was late in the evening when we arrived in Islamabad with our ISI escort. We were housed in a brand new upscale bungalow next to the residence of the USSR ambassador. For breakfast, we were greeted by the "senior official" our ISI agent had told us about. He had nothing substantive for us, aside from confirming that a dozen Sikhs had crossed into Pakistan after the June attacks. Unsurprisingly, Bhindranwale was not among them. Instead of giving us information, the official tried to pick our brains, questioning us at length about the activities of Sikhs in Canada and throughout the diaspora. Some of the names were indeed familiar to us: Talwinder Singh Parmar, Ajaib Singh Bagri, Balbir Singh Nijjar (from Toronto), Ganga Singh Dhillon, and Jagjit Singh Chauhan.

It was a fishing expedition, nothing more. But it wasn't a complete waste of time. It confirmed for both Avtar Singh and me that we could return to British Columbia and, without reservation, report that tales of Bhindranwale's flight to Pakistan were a fantasy, nothing more. It confirmed one more thing, too: Avtar Singh and I would never again want to be put in a position where we'd have to disguise ourselves with burqas.

MADISON SQUARE GARDEN

Our "temperature-taking" trip spanned three full weeks. Unfortunately, we never made it to our final, and most important, destination: Amritsar, site of the Golden Temple massacre, only 50 kilometres from Lahore. It wasn't for lack of trying. At the time, we knew that the Indian government had placed a moratorium on visas being issued to Sikhs from Canada. Still, we decided to take a taxi to the border on the off chance that we might get a sympathetic hearing from a border control guard. Not a chance. We were told, in no uncertain terms, that we wouldn't be let through. (It was only much later that I learned I was personally banned from entering India.)

After being turned away at the border, we traveled to the Dera Sahib gurdwara in Lahore, the historical site where Guru Arjan Dev was tortured and executed in 1606, and met a group of young Sikh doctors. Intent on immigrating to North America, they had crossed the border from India to Pakistan to write pre-entry exams, a hoop they had to jump through to practise medicine in the U.S. and Canada. Prior to crossing, they had been in Amritsar. There, they had witnessed scores of bodies being loaded into dump trucks — casualties from the Golden Temple attacks. Some of the "bodies," one of them claimed, were still breathing as they were carted off. Hearing this, I felt physically ill.

When I returned to Williams Lake on July 27, 1984, I had to hit the ground running. A business, no matter how solid, will not run itself, as I was discovering. As a result, I was unable to attend what would be another seminal event for the Sikhs.

Held in New York City on July 28, 1984, just seven weeks after the Golden Temple attack, the International Sikh Convention at Madison Square Garden was notable for several reasons.[17] First was its size: there were about 5,000 delegates in attendance. Second, it presented an opportunity to build a truly international organization with broad consensus: with delegates from nations around the globe gathered in one spot, the possibility of finding common ground was very real. Third was the incredible passion of those who spoke that day — although in one instance, that passion would cause us nothing but grief.

The main moderator, Dr. Gurcharan Singh, a professor of political science at New York City's Marymount Manhattan College, kicked things off: "I have a message for our Hindu brothers and sisters," he told the audience as video cameras rolled. "Our struggle is for equality and justice and not against Hindus or any other community, whether in India or elsewhere in the world." Maj.-Gen. (retired) Jaswant Singh

(J. S.) Bhullar, a hero of the 1971 Indo-Pakistan War who had worked with Bhindranwale, delivered the keynote speech. Bhullar was one of the convention's main organizers and the one leader almost everyone agreed was positioned to move the Sikh agenda forward; he was clearly going to assume a lead role in whatever might come next. He spoke articulately about the state of Sikhs worldwide, and what it would take to satisfy nationalist aspirations. He, too, struck a conciliatory note, emphasizing a "pragmatic, cool-headed" tack and admonishing that "an emotional approach has never solved any dispute."

There were 25 other speeches, and in almost every one there were references to Khalistan, an idea whose time had clearly come. The speakers had anger, yes. They were frustrated — sure. This was to be expected. But none of them crossed any lines. Except one.

Ajaib Singh Bagri was a member of the Babbar Khalsa. He shouldn't have had the floor, but the group's leaders, Vancouver-based Talwinder Singh Parmar and his right-hand man Surjan Singh Gill, had been denied entry into the United States: apparently both were on an FBI watch list because of their pro-violence views. Bagri's main mission at the convention seemed to be to position Parmar as a viable candidate for worldwide Sikh leadership.

Nobody knew the speech he gave would eventually overshadow all else that was said that day. But it did. Not because it was enlightening or eloquent. Rather, it was notable for one extraordinary sentence. Claiming that 50,000 Sikh youths had been killed in Punjab because of their faith, he said: "I tell you one thing, they have amused themselves, these Hindu dogs. Now it is our turn.... Until we kill 50,000 Hindus, we will not rest!"

There was only scattered applause.

PRELUDE TO A MASSACRE

On Wednesday, October 31, 1984, the sun rose over Delhi as it has done for centuries. Indira Gandhi, India's prime minister, woke, had breakfast, got dressed. The leader of the Congress (I) Party, the "I" standing for Indira, who had remodeled the nation's leading political party in a more totalitarian image, had seen her reign met with controversy: in the south, the Sri Lankan Tamils were becoming restless; in the northwest, Punjab had already exploded. But she remained the recipient of much international goodwill, perhaps because as the female head of state of a developing nation, her optics were seductive. Her married surname didn't hurt, either, even though her husband was not related to Mohandas Gandhi. (Born Feroze Jehangir Ghandy, he reportedly changed the spelling of his name after being inspired by Mohandas Gandhi and joining the independence movement.)

Born on November 19, 1917, Indira Nehru, the first child of India's first prime minister, was a divisive figure. Assisted by her father, Jawaharlal Nehru, she rose swiftly in politics: starting as his unofficial personal assistant, by her early 40s she had become the president of the Congress Party he had led. After he died in 1964, Indira was appointed Minister of Information and Broadcasting in the government of his successor, Lal Bahadur Shastri. Following Shastri's death in 1966, Indira Nehru, known as Indira Gandhi since her 1942 marriage, became India's third prime minister.

In 1975, her rule veered into autocracy; the imposition of a state of emergency, during which she jailed many of her political opponents, was a taste of what was to come. The Sikhs, and particularly the Shiromani Akali Dal, were first among those who opposed the state of emergency. By the time she was ousted in 1977, she had earned a reputation for tight, centralized control and a penchant for ruthlessness. She made powerful enemies, and on October 3, 1977, she was arrested for allegedly planning to murder political opponents.

She was released in December 1978 — something of a spectacle, and one that I witnessed firsthand. My family and I were at the airport in New Delhi that day, about to board our return flight to Canada. A huge crowd had gathered; we were unsure of what was going on. A film star? It was someone famous, that much was certain. In time the immense crowd parted and from it, Indira Gandhi emerged. My mother-in-law, Dalip Kaur, was in awe at the sight of her. Thrilled by the chance encounter, she ventured into the crowd to shake the hand of the woman who would eventually cause so much heartbreak in our lives.

Gandhi's return as a political force resulted in her winning the 1980 general election. In the ensuing four years, she again demonstrated political cunning and a boundless lack of compassion that reached its zenith with the Golden Temple attack in June 1984.

Mere months after the desecration of the Akal Takht, the violence that Gandhi unleashed on Punjab had already begun to be forgotten by a Western media that, on the final day of October 1984, once again came courting. Around 9:20 a.m., Gandhi left her home and began the short walk to her office, housed in a bungalow on the same grounds. Accompanied by her personal secretary, R.K. Dhawan, she was to meet with Peter Ustinov, the actor, who was waiting to interview her for an Irish television documentary. Her hair, with its distinctive streak of grey, was perfectly coiffed. She was wearing a light orange sari and black sandals.

Passing a wicket gate, she nodded to her two bodyguards, both of whom had reportedly just returned from a visit to Amritsar, where they'd witnessed firsthand the destruction wrought by the Indian Army. Satwant Singh, hired only five months before, was a recent addition to Gandhi's security detail, but Beant Singh had worked for the prime minister for a decade and was a particular favourite. As she approached Beant, she smiled, clasped her hands together, and nodded "Namaste." Three shots from his service revolver rang out, followed by a quick, 30-round burst from Satwant's Sten gun. At 2:30 p.m., Indira Gandhi was pronounced dead.

News of the assassination was withheld for about 10 hours. When it was finally announced that she had been killed by her own Sikh bodyguards, events were set in motion that would rival or even eclipse the desecration she had directed earlier that year.

At first, reports of attacks in Delhi seemed alarming but random. Sikhs were being pulled from their cars and beaten; soon, there were reports of "necklacing" (placing a tire around a man's neck, then lighting it on fire). The horror escalated. Women and girls were raped, with their sons, husbands, or brothers forced to watch. They in turn were killed in front of their brutalized daughters, wives, sisters. All because they had the audacity to be born Sikh. The violence would not stop. It was the prelude to a genocide.

Trilokpuri, a lower-class Delhi neighbourhood rebranded in the 1970s as a "resettlement colony for slum dwellers," was perhaps hardest hit. Its 30 blocks, jammed with about 900 single-story homes, were diverse: Hindus and Sikhs coexisted with only the usual rancour born of poverty and cramped space. But on November 1, the day after Indira Gandhi's assassination, everything changed.

As police stood by, refusing to intervene, angry mobs swarmed the streets of the normally placid neighbourhood. They were looking for Sikhs — any age, any gender. Men (mostly unskilled workers, rickshaw drivers, and tradespeople) were dragged from their homes, tied together, doused with kerosene, and set alight, their screams and the smoke from their flesh filling the air. Boys, some as young as two, were not spared. Desperate to escape bloodthirsty crowds, some men tried to cut their hair and beards and pose as anything but Sikhs; but everyone knew who was who in Trilokpuri. Of all the streets ravaged in the ghetto, Block 32 was the epicentre. There, over 350 Sikh men, women, and children lost their lives. On one street.

When the violence stopped four days later, over 3,000 Sikhs had been killed in Delhi alone. Later, Rajiv Gandhi, Indira's son (he was anointed leader after her death), had this to say about the carnage: "When a great tree falls, the earth shakes." It was as cold a statement as could be conceived.[18]

A GREAT BLACKNESS

The pogrom that followed Indira Gandhi's assassination horrified Sikhs worldwide. Along with most, I was sickened by the bloodshed and by the rationale put forth by those who tried to "understand" the events of November 1984. The standard line: these were unplanned acts, the result of a spontaneous outpouring of grief. The real story was far more sinister: evidence subsequently pointed to a targeted and systematic campaign of violence, directed from within the ranks of the Congress Party by a few cabinet ministers.

Anecdotally, so many of the arguments suggesting an uncoordinated paroxysm of violence just didn't hold water. The depiction of the non-Sikh population of Delhi, fueled by grief and dark thoughts of revenge, taking it out on their innocent neighbours ... this explanation is thin, disingenuous, vacuous. It portrays a slice of Delhi's Hindu residents as violently emotional haters, a ridiculous notion in a city where different ethnicities and faiths have lived side by side for centuries.

Massachusetts Institute of Technology political scientist Ashutosh Varshney, who has written extensively about ethnic and religious conflict in South Asia, believes that certain conditions must be met before a claim of "ethnic violence" can be considered. Communities, he writes, must be "organized along interethnic lines" with "interconnections between other communities [being] very weak" or non-existent. The situation between Hindus and Sikhs in Delhi did not fit this definition at all. Specifically, Trilokpuri was hardly a Sikh-only enclave, and there was much interaction between groups before, and after, the pogroms of 1984.

So if the violence didn't erupt spontaneously, was it directed? And if so, who was responsible? Many would be singled out for blame. President Zail Singh, a Sikh by birth, seemed more preoccupied with ensuring the orderly transfer of power from Indira to her son Rajiv; he stood by when his own people were hunted and burned alive. Gautam Kaul, the joint commissioner of the Delhi police (and Indira Gandhi's first cousin), seemed to encourage retribution; addressing a television audience the night of Gandhi's death, he essentially claimed that he didn't have the resources at his disposal to contend with the situation — tacitly granting the mobs impunity.

In this leadership vacuum, men were going up in flames, women were being raped, and children were bearing witness to traumatizing horror. There are many on-the-ground accounts of the violence, and of police and army inaction. In November 2014, 30 years later, journalist Joseph Maliakan from the *Indian Express* remembers:

> I took a few steps into a narrow lane in Block 32 and was horrified to see a huge bonfire of bodies. It dawned on me only later that the police were in Trilokpuri in the afternoon to ensure that the bodies of those killed were burnt so that no evidence was left. In fact all over Delhi, the pattern was the same. The killings began in east, west, south and north almost simultaneously on the first evening and continued till the third. Everywhere the bodies were disposed of by burning.
>
> The massacre was planned meticulously and executed with military precision. The mobs were armed with weapons, kerosene, petrol and other inflammable material. They also had copies of the voters list to identify Sikh homes. The involvement of Congressmen in power in organizing the mass murders was very evident. Also evident was the connivance of Delhi police.

Another account of the Block 32 carnage comes from Gurdip Kaur. To this day, her version of events, which was published in a special issue of *Manushi*, a well-regarded Indian magazine, in early 1985, is so gut wrenching it makes me sick:

> On the morning of 1 November at about noon, the attack started. My husband and two sons ran out and were set on fire. My youngest son stayed in the house with me. He shaved off his beard and cut his hair. But they came into the house. These young boys, 14 and 16 years old, began to drag my son out even though he was hiding behind me. They tore my clothes and stripped me naked in front of my son. My son cried, "Elder brothers, don't do this. She is your mother just as she is my mother." But they raped me right there, in front of my son, in my own house. They were young boys, maybe eight of them. When one of them raped me, I said, "My

child, never mind. Do what you like. But remember, I have given birth to children. This child came into the world by that same path." After they had taken my honour … they took my son to the street corner, hit him with lathis, sprinkled kerosene over him, and burnt him alive.

When the killing finally stopped on November 4, 1984, the official death toll was 2,733 in Delhi alone — a total that likely underestimates the true number. The Delhi Sikh Gurdwara Management Committee estimates the number to be over 14,000 and has created a memorial at Rakab Ganj gurdwara, across from the Indian Parliament, where Guru Tegh Bahadur's body was cremated in the 17th century. This violence would go down as one of the darkest chapters in India's history. Following so closely on the heels of the events of June 1984, it galvanized the diaspora, warning us that Sikhs were no longer safe in the country of our forefathers and giving fresh and vital impetus to the quest for an independent homeland.

CHAPTER 4

ONE BIRTH, MANY DEATHS

THE MADISON SQUARE Garden convention moved the
needle on Sikh aspirations. Proving himself to be as capable
in the political backroom as he was in battle, J.S. Bhullar was
unanimously chosen to be the new group's first secretary general.
Weeks after the convention he was pouring his energy into the
newborn World Sikh Organization.

Bhullar was uniquely positioned to lead the WSO. Born in 1923
in the village of Dhapali, Punjab, he had risen through the Indian
military ranks, eventually becoming a major general whose heroics
in the 1971 war with Pakistan were widely acknowledged. Although
he had spent the bulk of his life in defence of India, after retiring from
the army he came to believe that his nation's treatment of its Sikh
minority had gone from bad to unconscionable, and in the 1980s,
the former military man dedicated himself to advancing the cause of
Sikh rights in Punjab. In this struggle, he joined with Jarnail Singh
Bhindranwale, becoming a key figure in his advisory group. This was
not lost on the delegates assembled in New York.[19]

The mandate for the fledgling group was broad, but so was the
scope of the tactics. In addition to lobbying various levels of government for support internationally, the new group would also work

to stop the desecration of Sikh national monuments, manuscripts, and historical artefacts; after the destruction of the Akal Takht, it seemed clear that when it came to the Sikh faith, nothing was sacred to the government of India, no deed out of bounds. In addition, the WSO would confront Indian depictions of what was happening in Punjab and oversee public relations efforts on behalf of Sikhs around the globe.

Bhullar was also charged with framing the policies for the new group, as well as liaising with the various national chapters that were in the process of forming, especially in regions where there was a significant Sikh presence: in Britain, the U.S., and here in Canada. There was one more order of business. The new organization would channel its efforts to assist and lobby on behalf of Punjab's Sikhs for the peaceful establishment of an independent state, with its own borders: Khalistan.

Aware that the Indian government was engaged in a campaign to discredit Sikhs by equating support for Khalistan with terrorism and extremism, Bhullar astutely identified the next steps as paramount. Noting that emotions were running high in the diaspora, especially among youth, on September 9, 1984, he released a "code of conduct," aimed primarily at young Sikhs:

> *In Punjab, the Indian Government used its own agents and even Government agencies to commit acts of violence and passed on the blame to Sikh organizations. Through a well orchestrated crescendo, the Government tried to soil the true image of Sikhs as well as created a climate whereby it could reasonably justify its calculated attack on the Golden Temple. It is, therefore of paramount importance to be very cautious in our actions and utterances, lest we should fall in the same trap laid down by the Government of India in the Punjab.*
>
> *Any deviation from the code will endanger our reputation as true Sikhs of Guru Gobind Singh and the world will feel convinced of the Government of India's propaganda against the Sikhs.*

The guidelines were both prescient and practical. They included everything from liaising with authorities and respecting local laws to maintaining strict discipline in the face of provocations from Indian government agents — a fear that was well founded, as we shall see. The fledgling organization even entered the political fray, feeling out sympathetic legislators. All of this was part of a strategy designed to challenge the Indian government's version of events, and inject the worldwide Sikh perspective into the discussion. We were on the move. But Gandhi's assassination was overshadowing much of the effort.

Like many in the Sikh diaspora, I was not horrified by the death of Indira Gandhi. Her connivances and calculations — from her abrogating of democracy and jailing of political opponents to ordering a direct attack on the Sikh faith by invading and destroying our most sacred place — had made her a lot of enemies in India and abroad. After the Golden Temple massacre, most Sikhs, myself included, felt that her death was a case of a despot reaping what she had sown.[20]

Yet for those, especially in the West, who didn't know the history of bad blood that had accumulated under her reign, the death of the first woman to ascend to leadership of a major developing power was framed as an outright tragedy. And those who seemed to shrug off her assassination were cast in a sinister light.

True, the images could be difficult to digest: young men in beards and turbans, dancing with glee,[21] handing out sweets in celebration of the violent death of a stately and dignified woman; aside from "the Mahatma," Indira Gandhi was arguably the best-known Indian public figure of the 20th century. Even J.S. Bhullar, who had earlier preached circumspection to Sikh youth, seemed to stumble on this score: although he prefaced his comments on Gandhi's assassination by saying "the death of any human being anywhere is always a sad affair," his take, which essentially boiled down to "those who live by the sword, die by the sword," did not go over particularly well in the West.

One of the most persistently damaging images was traceable to the Madison Square Garden meeting. Ajaib Singh Bagri's call to violence — and cut-and-paste editing that implied the thousands of Sikh delegates in attendance rapturously cheered him on, when only a handful of the 5,000 assembled actually did — blackened the name of the WSO before the organization had even got off the ground. We wanted to launch strategies designed to propel the community forward but were kept on the defence. The only consolation for the Sikhs: had Talwinder Singh Parmar actually been allowed to cross the U.S. border and speak to the attendees, it could have been even worse.

THE LIVING MARTYR

Born on February 26, 1944, in Panchat (also known as Panshta), Punjab, about a 35-kilometre drive from my village of Rurka Kalan, Parmar arrived in Vancouver in 1970, around the time I landed in Williams Lake. Working at L&K Lumber to provide for his wife and three children, he was to outside appearances much like any of us who immigrated to Canada during those years. In 1975 he traveled to Pakistan, rather than India, and took amrit and adopted the Five Ks at a ceremony at Guru Nanak's birthplace, Nankana Sahib.

In the early 1980s, Parmar became a marginal player in British Columbia's Sikh community. As one of the founders of Punjab-based Babbar Khalsa International, one of several groups vying for the spotlight in the growing opposition to India's treatment of Punjab's Sikhs, he had achieved some notoriety both in Canada and in India, where he'd returned to participate in anti-government activities and encourage youth to become amritdharis from 1979 to 1981.

Traveling back and forth between Canada and Punjab, he was detained in Germany in 1983 on an arrest warrant issued by India the previous year, accusing him of murdering six people, including a police officer, in Punjab. But the specifics of the charges against Parmar were vague, and by this point many had stopped trusting the veracity of warrants issued against Sikhs by the government of India. Hearing of his detention, the Sikh community in British Columbia intervened to help plead his case to the Canadian government — and so, in solidarity, the Morcha Action Committee also pressed the government to bring him home. In early July 1984, after about a year spent in German custody, Parmar was allowed to return to Canada. (The government of India's sudden change of heart, dropping his case in Germany, was a bit suspicious.)

His predicament gave him some cachet, adding to his reputation as a devout Sikh who could be taken seriously. He'd certainly worked at this image. Having spent time in India during Jarnail Singh Bhindranwale's ascent, he had absorbed certain lessons from the charismatic spiritual leader, right down to copying his rhetorical style.

But upon meeting him, you sensed a self-serving component to Parmar's piety: his act, I thought, was more P.T. Barnum than Sant Bhindranwale. His claims, often ludicrous, verged on occasion into hilarity — his arms, he bragged, were long enough to reach to his knees, which he claimed was a sign from God that he was an avatar, or reincarnated deity.[22] His followers — a small group that included Ajaib Singh Bagri, Surjan Singh Gill, and a few others — repeatedly spread the notion that he was "The Living Martyr," whatever that entailed.

It was Tara Singh Hayer, the editor and publisher of the *Indo-Canadian Times*, who did more than anyone to promote Parmar. The Living Martyr, dressed in traditional Sikh clothing complete with a metre-long sword, or sometimes with an AK-47 in his hands, would sometimes wind up on the front page of Hayer's paper — until the two men had a falling-out, apparently over a business deal that had soured. Hayer used the parting of ways as an opportunity to rebrand himself as a "moderate," railing against the extreme views of the International Sikh Youth Federation[23] and Babbar Khalsa.

The Sikh community in Canada was small, so it was hard not to know those in leadership roles of the various organizations. I ran into the Babbar Khalsa leader at a few community functions, but I never exchanged more than the usual salutations with him, except once, soon after Parmar returned from his time in German custody in 1984. He had come to Williams Lake to preach his vision at the home of a relative who lived in our area. Curious, I decided to go and hear what he had to say.

About 40 people showed up. He spoke for over 45 minutes without interruption. His speech was obfuscation on an epic scale. He simply made no sense. If you had to identify the gist of his "sermon" — though since it had more to do with self-promotion than faith, you could hardly call it that — it was essentially that Tara Singh Hayer was a bad guy, and that we should all boycott his newspaper. Despite disagreeing with some of his editorial views, I still defended his right to voice them publicly and found it preposterous that Parmar was using his profile to smack down his former ally.

Finally, I had heard all I could stand. I stood up. "Talwinder Singh Ji," I said. "I'm sorry to interrupt. But we've been listening to you for the better part of an hour and you have basically said nothing."

He stared at me, eyes narrowed. This was a man who was used to having his devotees devour his every word.

"Look," I continued, "if you consider yourself a leader in this community, then you should show leadership. Stop complaining about what Hayer's writing about you."

"But you think this is fair?!" he thundered. "By the will of God, it must be stopped!"

"I honestly have no idea if it's fair. But we didn't come to hear a tirade, or to help you settle scores. Maybe you should stick to religion, and leave the politics, and vendettas, alone."

He glared at me. I returned his stare. I knew then that Talwinder Singh Parmar was a vindictive man, but not because I had any inkling of what would eventually be laid at his doorstep. No, what I could see was that if he ever achieved true prominence, his mouth would be a problem for us all.

IT WAS WHAT WAS NEEDED

Bagri's words, an abhorrent call for retaliation and indiscriminate violence, had not only sickened us but had dug a large hole for the community. Instead of moving forward, we were often back on our heels, fighting a rear-guard action against fringe players who sought to define us. It became more imperative than ever to ensure that the organization we were creating had clearly defined goals and was truly representative of Sikh aspirations — and would pursue those aspirations through peaceful, nonviolent means.

Yet we knew, even then, that those who sought to reduce the Sikh community or the growing Khalistan movement to sensationalist storylines about extremism would capitalize on that moment in New York. Within the Sikh community, it was understood that the New York convention had been an attempt by the global Sikh community to come together on a single platform in response to June 1984, but that many who participated had since gone their separate ways. Among the groups that were represented at this gathering, some had come simply to see what ideas would emerge; others were there to push their own ideas and agendas and, after failing to see them take hold, departed unsatisfied.

The Shiromani Gurdwara Parbandhak Committee (SGPC), the institution that had responsibility for all Sikh historical gurdwaras in Punjab, was represented by Manjit Singh Calcutta. Based exclusively in India, and subject to the whims of the Indian state, the SGPC was unable and unwilling to take up the call for Khalistan that resonated so clearly in New York, although almost 30 years later, when it became safer to do so, they would set up a grand memorial to Jarnail Singh Bhindranwale within the precincts of the Golden Temple, right next to the Akal Takht.

The Shiromani Akali Dal, the Punjab political party of Harchand Singh Longowal, was also represented. The Akali Dal, despite their civil disobedience campaign — and the fact that they were championing the implementation of the Anandpur Sahib Resolution, which Gandhi's Congress Party viewed as a secessionist document — had never actually come out in favour of secession. This rendered them out of sync with the Sikh community. They would later split into separate factions within Punjab, some openly espousing independence.

In this context, the Babbar Khalsa representation, one among many dozens of organizations, would hardly have been notable had it not been for Bagri's speech. Bagri and the Babbars were never given a platform at a WSO event in Canada, nor was there any cross-pollination of members or leadership; the lines between the two organizations were clear and substantial. Babbar Khalsa would go on to become a vociferous critic of the newly created WSO (and we of them), yet despite WSO's peaceful working pattern, some journalists found it more convenient to lump the entire community together and reduce it to a caricature.

Our way forward was clear. Advocating for the creation of a separate nation was a reflection of the tenor of the Sikh community at the time. This call for the peaceful transition to nationhood would be the central plank in the convention's emerging mandate. It was what was needed. It was also what was demanded.

By the end of the convention, it was agreed that the new organization be called the World Sikh Organization. Didar Singh Bains, a millionaire from California, would be president, with J.S. Bhullar acting as secretary general. It was also agreed that all of the nations with a significant Sikh presence would set up their own national organizations, each of which would function according to the laws of its country. It was now up to those of us in Canada to create the World Sikh Organization of Canada, and make it over in a distinctly Canadian way.

We wouldn't be building out of a void. The Federation of Sikh Societies of Canada (FSS), which had played an organizing role in the Madison Square Garden convention, was already operating as a national body representing Canadian Sikhs. At the time, the FSS could justly claim to be the largest organization of its kind in the country; after all, it was the only one in existence. Inaugurated in 1980, it was the first nation-wide group to represent Sikhs in Canada, and as such occupies a prominent place in any historical timeline.

A less pliant, more determined mood had taken hold of the Sikh community, both internationally and in Canada. Khalistan, which had never truly been on the table before, was now being openly discussed as not just an option, but the only option — the end game for Sikhs. This was no fringe movement. After Operation Blue Star, and especially the pogroms in Delhi, this was imperative.

The FSS did not seem up to the task. Gopal Singh Brar, who sat on the executive of the FSS, was troubled by the inability of his own organization to truly reflect the needs, hopes, and aspirations of Sikh Canadians. Around the world, Sikhs were tired of hearing about compromise; what they wanted was to stand on the rooftops and shout "There is no justice for Sikhs in India!" in a loud, collective voice.

Part of the reticence of the FSS to press more strongly for what Sikhs were now demanding was simply pragmatic: it was funded by the government of Canada. This left the society vulnerable; funding could be cut off should FSS policies develop in a way that the Canadian government couldn't or wouldn't support. Just as importantly, it left a back door open for Indian government interference. (This was exactly what did happen when, on the December 9, 1985, edition of CBC Television's *Pacific Report*, Jagdish Sharma, the Vancouver-based consul general of India, admitted that he'd complained to the Canadian government about the "secessionist activities of the Federation.")

Having served on its executive, Brar was well aware of the FSS's strengths and shortcomings. Like many others, he was keen to establish a strong and articulate Sikh voice that could be heard in Canada and in international circles, too; this, he believed, could only be done through the auspices of a new group untainted by any compromising associations, untethered from the past. Although he had served hand in hand with the FSS, he thought a new Canadian group that could work toward the WSO International's goals, including support for an independent Khalistan, would be the best way to go.

Because of my activities on behalf of the B.C. community and my support for the FSS, Brar and I knew each other well. He called me over a dozen times to participate in the upcoming All Canada Sikh convention in Toronto. At the time, I was just back from a worldwide trip and focused on running my business. He tapped Vancouver Sikh leaders Daljit Singh Sandhu and Joginder Singh Sidhu to persuade me to attend the convention. I finally gave in and flew to Toronto with Daljit Singh Sandhu and Mota Singh Jheeta, having no inkling that Brar and Inderjit Singh Bal were planning to enlist me to lead the organization.

Brar and I stayed at Bal's house. We got into lengthy after-dinner discussions. Brar sought my input and, after we talked for some time, he made a request: "Gian Singh Ji," he said, "would you help us by taking a lead role on this?"

I told him I'd have to get back to him. This was not a request I could entertain lightly. I was supportive of any move to create a WSO chapter in Canada. That said, I was already incredibly busy — partly with WSO International business. After the Madison Square Garden convention, I'd received a call from J.S. Bhullar. The new organization, he explained, needed an operational constitution. He'd been talking with two other groups about developing a document that could sum up our goals and help guide us. One group was led by Dr. Gurcharan Singh, the eloquent political science professor from New York's Marymount Manhattan College; his speech and manner at the July 28 convention, I'm assuming, had impressed Bhullar. The other group was the FSS; their perspective, I thought, would be interesting in light of their reticence to sanction an independent Khalistan. But because I was on Bhullar's radar (at some point before he was killed, Jarnail Singh Bhindranwale had talked with him about me), he also wanted my input. Would I be able, he asked, to come up with a constitution for the WSO International? It would be a great honour to have my perspective as one of three under consideration. It took me all of two seconds to agree.

As for taking a lead role in the creation of a Canadian chapter, I wasn't nearly so certain. Between Khalsa Enterprises and my existing commitments on behalf of both WSO International and British Columbia's Sikh community, I was stretched pretty thin.

And then there was my family. My daughters Kamaljit and Palbinder were now both students at the University of British Columbia in Vancouver. They, too, had begun to dedicate their time to the community, and through the newly founded Sikh Student Association (SSA), they were helping the FSS to raise the $350,000 necessary to establish a Chair of Sikh Studies at UBC. Palbinder plays a mean tabla; Kamaljit's forte is the harmonium, as well as her exceptional singing voice. On weekends they and other SSA members traveled around the region, going from gurdwara to gurdwara, singing kirtan, or Sikh hymns, and making speeches to raise funds. Naturally, both Surinder and I were proud.

With the business only three years on, we were stretched to the max putting the kids through university. Plus, by this time our family had grown by one, although not in the way you're probably thinking. In 1980 Surinder's 11-year-old nephew, Surjit, had come to Canada to visit. Although he was still very young, after spending time here he elected to stay and live in B.C. But to do this he'd need to be sponsored by a Canadian family. Surinder and I discussed it with the kids, especially our son Harjinder, now age 12. They were thrilled at the prospect of having another brother, and in 1981, we formally adopted Surjit and he became part of our family.

It was a hectic life, to be sure. So when faced with the pressure to pile on even more commitments, I wasn't convinced. I talked it over with Surinder. We went into the pros and cons, the potential demands on my time. I was unsure. Surinder had a different take.

"Ji," she said, "if Sikhs need you, you should do it."

I was surprised. "But you do know it'll mean a lot more travel, and—"

"You wanted to do seva. I think you should follow through. You must."

She was right, as she often is. So I spoke to Brar and Bal, telling them that I might be willing to shoulder the leadership responsibility if it was unanimously decided by the delegates. I have never been a fan of standing for elected office.

The event took place at the Prince Hotel in Toronto on December 1 and 2, 1984. By the end of the first day, I was unanimously chosen by the 135 delegates to act as president. My time in the World Sikh Organization of Canada had begun.

TO SPEAK WITH ONE VOICE

My appointment as president of the World Sikh Organization of Canada was not universally embraced. The Federation of Sikh Societies of Canada, although in my opinion clearly out of step with the evolving mood in our community, continued to attempt to position itself as the only viable voice for Canadian Sikhs nationally.

To be fair, they were trying as best they could to work within the new realities that had come out of the events leading up to and including the Madison Square Garden convention. But the writing was on the wall: there would be — should be — one credible, go-to group that could represent hundreds of thousands of Canadian Sikhs in this specific time of crisis. And the FSS, having played coy on the issue of Khalistan, was not that group. Seeing which way the wind was blowing, some in the FSS lashed out at the fledgling WSO Canada, and at me. In response to a CBC Radio interview I gave soon after being appointed WSO Canada president, Mohinder Singh Gosal, my counterpart in the FSS, tried to downplay our significance, telling one reporter that I was "a king without a crown."

It was, I thought, a rather odd critique, especially considering our past. Since he was based in Kamloops, I'd worked with Gosal and the FSS on a variety of initiatives including raising funds for the Sikh Chair at UBC; he should have known that the last thing I wanted was authority or power. My intention was — and has always been — simply to perform seva, to be of service to my people and our faith. Nevertheless, Gosal and the FSS must have perceived us as an existential threat (which, as it turns out, we were) and tried to convince Bhullar and WSO International President Bains to recognize the FSS, and not us, as the group to represent the interests of our fellow Canadians under the aegis of the WSO International.

1. I joined the Indian Air Force in 1960, age 17; training in Bangalore (2,500 kilometres away) gave me a taste of independence.

2. Surinder's grandfather, Inder Singh Dhaliwal, was the first of the family to move to Canada, in 1904.

*1. My father, Bawa Singh
(1920–1975).
2. From left: my sister,
Harbhanjan Kaur but known
as Bhajno (1938–1995),
and my mother, Chanan Kaur
(1918–2015).
3. Surinder and me at our
apartment in Adampur,
Punjab, 1963.*

4. *Landing in Williams Lake, B.C., 1970.*
5. *I quickly embraced the culture of my new country, but regrettably I also gave up my turban and beard. Here, at the Williams Lake Stampede, 1972.*
6. *On my uncle Sucha Singh's farm in 1975 during a visit back to Punjab. I'm in the back row, right, behind him and his workers.*

1. The Darbar Sahib,
or Golden Temple, is at the
centre of spiritual life for
those of the Sikh faith.
2. A family portrait when I
became amritdhari in 1981.
Front to back, from left: my
mother-in-law, Dalip Kaur
Dhaliwal, and my mother,
Chanan Kaur; our children,
Palbinder Kaur, Harjinder
Singh, and Kamaljit Kaur;
me and my wife,
Surinder Kaur.

3. The Akal Takht, or Throne of the Timeless One, before the Indian Army attack in 1984. It has been the seat of Sikh temporal and spiritual authority since 1606.

4. This photograph, taken by journalist Sondeep Shankar on June 8, 1984, shows the extent of the damage to the Akal Takht. Photos on next two pages are also by Shankar.

1. Sant Jarnail Singh Bhindranwale (standing) shares a dais in the Golden Temple complex with Akali Dal leaders Sant Harchand Singh Longowal (seated, far left) and former chief minister Parkash Singh Badal (with garlands), 1983.
2. Sikh shops burning as a mob looks on in the Chandni Chowk market, Old Delhi, November 1984.
3. A machine gunner in a bunker outside the Golden Temple.
4. Federal and state police enforce curfew before the army action began in June 1984.

1. *At the WSO Canada founding convention in 1984, I was selected ad hoc president.*
2. *WSO Canada convention speakers. From left: Dr. Lorne Greenaway (MP), me, Dr. Amrit Singh (California), and B.C. cabinet minister Robert McLellan.*
3. *With former prime minister Paul Martin.*
4. *The 1985 WSO Canada executive. Front row, from left: Inderjit Singh Bal, Joginder Singh Bains, Balbir Singh Sara, Daljit Singh Sandhu, WSO International President Didar Singh Bains, Gobinder Singh Randhawa, Kuldeep Singh Bhullar, Gopal Singh Brar, and me. Back row, from left: Sajjan Singh Bhangoo, Daljit Singh Gill, Karnail Singh Gill, unnamed delegate, Satnam Singh Johal, Hardev Singh Gakhal, Jasjit Singh Bhullar, Surinder Singh Jabal, Nirvair Singh Sandhu, Parminder Singh Parmar, Balwinder Singh Bola, unnamed delegate, and Harbhajan Singh Pandori.*

Still, in the near term we had to work together — the three constitutions Bhullar had commissioned would be debated in early 1985. By late 1984, my version was complete. With help from my friend Tom Scott, a Williams Lake lawyer I'd known for years, I'd spent the past few months fine-tuning the proposal with an eye toward ensuring that it would be ready not just for the WSO International meeting, but for the WSO Canada founding convention in December 1984.

The delegates approved the constitution and bylaws without much debate. The entire document, including bylaws, spans about 25 pages. But our organizational mandate is summed up in our objectives, presented here in an abbreviated form:

- Work toward the achievement of the objectives of the WSO International
- Promote, preserve, and maintain Sikh religion and identity
- Abide by the dictates (hukamnamas) issued from Sri Akal Takhat Sahib
- Coordinate and promote understanding, friendship, mutual respect, and cooperation among Sikhs and Sikh organizations and facilitate functional integration for service to the Panth as per the ethics of Sikhism (Sikh Rehat Maryada)
- Mobilize resources and serve as a central forum for the purposes of serving the religious, cultural, social, educational, and economic interests of the Sikhs while maintaining full awareness of and respect for Sikh tenets
- Promote the Punjabi language in Gurmukhi script; initiate and encourage research, scholarships, and educational programs concerning the religious, social, cultural, economical, and political role of the Sikhs in Canada; and strive to establish Khalsa residential schools in Canada
- Foster understanding and goodwill towards all nations, creeds, persuasions, and faiths in the international society

- Act as a representative body of the World Sikh Organization International in Canada
- Act as representative body of the Sikhs of Canada, and help resolve differences amongst members and member organizations
- Liaise with government and non-government agencies and apprise them of the interests of the Sikhs
- Encourage, develop, and maintain close relationships with similar and like-minded organizations throughout Canada
- Do all such things not inconsistent with the doctrines and ethics of Sikhism and the law of the land.

It was and remains a non-divisive document, meant to foster goodwill and understanding, as well as ensure that the Sikh perspective receives a hearing. Maybe that's why it passed with so little fuss. But while the birth of the WSO Canada (and the approval of our constitution and bylaws) was cordial and marked by a willingness to cooperate and get things done, the same cannot be said of the WSO International.

The meeting to approve a WSO International constitution was scheduled to take place in Los Angeles on January 12 and 13, 1985. There were several individuals and organizations present, including myself, the Constitution Committee, a number of interested Sikh groups, and the ad hoc governing council.[24] The meeting, at which the three proposed versions of the WSO International constitution were tabled, did not go smoothly.

As we were about to begin deliberations, the meeting was interrupted by members of the Sikh Youth Federation and Babbar Khalsa, both of which basically wanted to dictate the outcome of the proceedings. The two groups had assumed more stridently militant positions since the July 1984 convention; when it came to advancing the Sikh cause, the rest of us were having none of that. (Both organizations would eventually be outlawed by the Canadian government.) To avoid any trap that could be laid we decided to move the proceedings to the home of Lakhbir Cheema, a businessman who had a mansion nearby large enough to serve as a substitute venue; on the second day of the proceedings, we were hosted by Dr. Amrit Singh and his wife, Harjasbinder Kaur, at their residence, which also had ample space to accommodate all delegates. Sikh hospitality was at its peak at both houses.

That was the first hurdle. There were more to come. Soon after it began, the Federation of Sikh Societies of Canada registered its objection to the proposal that the WSO International president should be an amritdhari Sikh who would do seva without pay. (The FSS was arguing for financial compensation.) Another objection? Any document that explicitly advocated for the creation of an independent Sikh state. Since the FSS was dependent on Canadian government funding, it wasn't prepared to be a signatory to any document that could jeopardize those funds — and any constitutional language supporting an independent Khalistan would certainly tick off its bankers. In the end, the head of the FSS, Gurcharan Singh Bal, once a key player, walked out of the meeting with his associate Bakhshish Singh Samagh and into irrelevance.

At Cheema's home, we got down to business. The WSO International constitution was finally approved; it was pretty much identical to the WSO Canada charter I'd submitted, with some minor changes. Well, one major change: unlike the WSO Canada document, the international constitution called for the creation of the sovereign state of Khalistan, to be achieved through peaceful means. The fact that the WSO Canada constitution pledged that we would work toward the WSO International objectives meant that we, too, were bound to support the creation of an independent Sikh state through nonviolent means.

It was a landmark decision, now enshrined in our international constitution. In time, some would seek to hold this against us, using our support of the establishment of Khalistan as a way of categorizing the WSO as an "extremist" group — even though we categorically rejected the use of violence to achieve this end. But it was an honest and accurate reflection of where the community and the WSO were during this time.

Soon after the January meeting, the WSO got to work, and by the spring of 1985 we were making headway in our fight to present the Sikh perspective to various legislative bodies. In the U.S., Ganga Singh Dhillon had made a friend in Jesse Helms, the controversial Republican senator from North Carolina — a relationship that was remarkable in light of Helms' abhorrent long-held views regarding segregation.

Helms, a powerful and influential member of the Senate's Foreign Relations Committee, addressed the Senate on June 12, 1985, just over a year after the Golden Temple attack. "Profound religious conflict on the subcontinent resulted in the formation of the state of Pakistan and the state of Bangladesh, both Muslim countries," he said. "If a just solution to the situation in the Punjab, the homeland of the Sikhs, is not found, a similar process will inevitably occur."

In the same speech, Helms went further, taking on Rajiv Gandhi, Indira's son and India's new prime minister, for threatening to cancel an appearance before the National Press Club if Ganga Singh Dhillon was allowed the same opportunity. "The American people have a right to know about the situation on the subcontinent and the grave conditions affecting the religious and human rights of minorities there," he added in defence of Dhillon. Helms passed away in 2008. If he'd been similarly eloquent regarding his nation's African-American constituents, he might have carved out a prouder legacy.

The senator was just one part of a broad public relations effort. Immediately after the January meeting, the WSO engaged the lobbying services of Jim Corman, a former congressman from California; soon after Corman came on board, former Democratic senator Vance Hartke was also commissioned to lobby on our behalf. In the coming months, a formidable line-up of allies was assembled; all told, within a year, roughly 30 congressmen and senators were willing to take on our cause in the House of Representatives and the Senate.

We were busy in Canada, too. The day after Jesse Helms spoke in the Senate, Lorne Greenaway, the Progressive Conservative member of Parliament for the Cariboo-Chilcotin riding (my MP at the time), raised his voice in our name in the House of Commons. Greenaway, a rancher and veterinarian, was articulate and fair-minded. We'd had many talks about the aspirations of the Sikh community, which by then was growing quickly in the Cariboo region.

As someone who very much viewed representing his constituents as a sacred trust, Greenaway was more than willing to press for Sikh human rights, even if that might ruffle feathers within diplomatic circles and, indeed, his own party. "Mr. Speaker, last week marked the first anniversary of the storming of the Golden Temple," he said in Parliament. "For a year, the Punjab state has been under martial law, and communication has been difficult. Many are concerned that serious transgressions of human rights have occurred and continue to take place in Punjab. Such organizations as the International Red Cross and Amnesty International have been denied entrance to this state. The citizens of my riding are concerned."

Needless to say, statements like those made by Jesse Helms and Lorne Greenaway didn't sit too well with the government of India, nor were they well received by its intelligence operatives and diplomatic corps. Rajiv Gandhi had managed to beatify his mother in death — and ignore the horrifying violence against Delhi's Sikhs that took place in the wake of her killing — but a parallel campaign to demonize the international Sikh community had also woven itself into the Congress Party's strategy. In the run-up to the Golden Temple attack, Indira Gandhi's cohorts had taken great pains to equate "Sikh" with "terror." Back in India, this had worked. Was it now time to export this tactic and apply it elsewhere?

Reports of militant Sikh activity in Canada began circulating soon after Indira Gandhi's assassination. Canada, the Indian government claimed, was at the centre of a large gun-running operation, part of an international Sikh effort to channel weapons from abroad into the hands of Khalistani "terrorists" in Punjab. Although duly investigated, the reports — one suggesting that the small orchard town of Winona, Ontario, was a particular hotspot of terror — were dismissed out of hand by the RCMP and the newly formed Canadian Security and Intelligence Service (CSIS).

The false reports were most often directed to the Department of External Affairs. Because of political considerations — India was, after all, still a Commonwealth nation, and an ally of Canada — the department felt bound to investigate any allegations of wrongdoing, no matter how bizarre. The sheer number of alleged threats, apparently targeting everything from high commissions to the homes of well-known Hindu Canadians, expanded in the spring of 1985, in the run-up to the one-year anniversary of the Golden Temple attacks.

There was a Chicken Little quality to the stories emanating from India. Investigative journalists Zuhair Kashmeri and Brian McAndrew, co-authors of the 1989 book *Soft Target: How the Indian Intelligence Service Penetrated Canada*, have documented how both CSIS and the RCMP wasted countless hours chasing down nonexistent leads. Having been fed so much useless information and coming up empty, they were essentially in the throes of "tip fatigue." India's efforts at demonizing the Sikhs in Canada, it seemed, were backfiring.

Despite the dire warnings, and a certain tension in the air, anyone with a stake in the issue breathed a sigh of relief when the first week of June came and went without incident. For any Sikh inclined to make a violent statement, the first anniversary of the Golden Temple massacre would have been an opportune time. Worldwide, there were protests marking the desecration, but the week passed like any other. As we'd hoped and expected, the community expressed its sadness and anger — but the commemorative actions were peaceful.

For the WSO there was one more major order of business to complete. In the third week of June 1985 we would hold the first official World Sikh Organization USA conference, a forum to get down to the business of electing the WSO USA national executive and nominating U.S. delegates for the WSO International governing council.

The conference was to take place at the Marriott in Berkeley, California, from June 22 to 23. Unlike the WSO Canada's founding convention, it promised to be a contentious affair, marked by political infighting. There were three main candidates: Ganga Singh Dhillon, whose credibility was thrown into question by his preposterous claim that he would "get close to establishing Khalistan within one year"; Didar Singh Bains, a wealthy California orchard owner (the so-called Peach King), whose commitment and dedication were unquestionable, and who had been serving as ad hoc president of WSO International (but who was opposed by the youth wing and the intellectual and professional delegates); and Sulakhan Singh Dhillon, a well-respected PhD who taught comparative philosophy at Golden Gate University in San Francisco — and was, it seemed, the frontrunner, despite having previously played only a minor role.

When the proceedings got underway, it was immediately obvious that the divisiveness that marked the January constitutional meetings had not abated. What a contrast in styles: in Canada, people almost had to be begged to accept a leadership role; in the U.S., it was more like a giant arm-wrestling match, with many different actors vying for positions of influence. It was like old-style Punjab village politics, played out against a New World backdrop.

A BLACK DAY FOR HUMANKIND

Sunday, June 23, 1985, the second day of the WSO U.S. founding convention, was clear and warm. I had spent the night at the home of a friend who was living in nearby Yuba City. It's been a longstanding habit of mine to get up early to do my prayers and meditations — some people like to sleep in, but that has never been my way. After finishing up, I walked over to the dining area to get a slice of toast, a bowl of cereal. Some of the others who had driven down with me were also up and about. Five of us took seats around the kitchen table. Someone turned the television news on.

At Narita Airport in Tokyo, two luggage handlers had died when a suitcase they were transferring from a Canadian Pacific Airlines flight from Vancouver exploded. Another developing story was much more devastating. An Air India Boeing 747 flight originating in Toronto had disappeared from radar screens just off the Irish coast, about an hour from Heathrow, where the plane was scheduled to pick up passengers and fuel before heading to New Delhi.

I later learned that the first reports simply stated "a plane is missing." But by the time I awoke in California, there was consensus. Both the Narita explosion and Air India Flight 182 had been terrorist attacks, likely coordinated and originating in Canada. There were 329 people on board the *Emperor Kanishka*, as the Air India jumbo jet was known, 86 of them children. All were dead. It remains the largest mass murder in Canadian history.

I pushed away my breakfast. I was stunned, sickened. The loss of life was too horrific to believe. But there were other ramifications, too. Even in the first minutes after hearing about the tragedy, I knew this act would be the prism through which those who opposed us would attempt to get the world to see us. June 23, 1985, a black day for humankind, would haunt the Sikh community in Canada forever.

PART II

A COMMUNITY UNDER SIEGE

(1985–1995)

CHAPTER 5

"YOU GUYS DID IT"

I N THE DAYS after the Air India 182 tragedy, many of the victims' families flew to Cork, Ireland, to identify their loved ones' remains. Among the grief-stricken was Kalwant Singh Mamak, a businessman from Sarnia, Ontario, whose wife, Rajinder, was one of the 329 senselessly murdered. A mother and housewife, she was 42 years old.

Like my marriage to Surinder, the Mamaks' union had been arranged. In India and other traditional societies it was a common practice, a custom that cut across ethnic and religious lines. Yet — and I can heartily attest to this — the absence of a "love match" does not mean a lack of love. The death of Rajinder left a terrible hole in Kalwant Singh's heart, in his life, and in the lives of their three children.

He was not alone. Kalwant Singh's flight from Canada to Ireland was a gathering of mourners, all of whom were heading to a common wake. Fathers and mothers died. Aunts and uncles. Grandparents were cut down, and those 86 children would never again run laughing through the snow or eat too much birthday cake.

One would expect such a horrific tragedy to bind those who had suffered so much, to bring Kalwant Singh and his fellow passengers together in shared loss, but this was not universally so. Like me, Kalwant Singh was an observant Sikh. On the plane ride from Toronto to Cork, the glares shot at his turban and beard were acid. "You guys did it, you guys did it," was one unconscionably brutal accusation leveled against him. Says Kalwant Singh: "I had to tell them that I lost my wife too."[25] Imagine.

Many Sikhs died that day. In all, 33 of the 329 people whose lives ended tragically in the skies off the Irish coast were Sikh, including the pilot. But in the flurry of finger-pointing that ensued, this fact has been overlooked.

What was clear was that Kalwant Singh Mamak's loss was amplified by a terrible burden that would be carried by anyone named Singh or Kaur.

RECRIMINATIONS FOLLOW SWIFTLY

After hearing the news of the bombing of Air India 182, I called Gobinder Singh Randhawa, WSO Canada's Toronto-based senior vice-president, and asked him to convey our deepest condolences to the families of the victims and issue a statement condemning the attack.

At first, there was relative harmony in Canada as the Hindu and Sikh communities struggled to address a tragedy that had claimed victims from both faiths. A day after the bombing, a headline in the *Globe and Mail* summed up the mood: "Terror in the Skies: Hindus, Sikhs forget bitterness to unite in grief over loss." In the article, Hindu leader Amar Chand Erry said, "The event has brought us together." Similarly, WSO Canada's Randhawa said, "In grief, all of us are human beings and not Sikhs and Hindus."

United in sorrow, the two communities were also bound by anger. Soon after the bombing, I listened in stunned disbelief as Brian Mulroney, the prime minister of Canada, expressed his condolences for the horrifying loss of life ... to Rajiv Gandhi. This, despite the fact that the vast majority of the victims were Canadian citizens. It was a slap in the face to both Sikh and Hindu Canadian communities and sent a message: regardless of how long you've been here, you're really only part of "us" if you're white.

The snub was keenly felt by Hindus and Sikhs alike, but our common front was already crumbling. Almost immediately after the bombing, an anonymous caller to the *New York Times*, claiming to be from the pro-Khalistan Sikh Students Federation, took responsibility. (In Vancouver, Manmohan Singh, an International Sikh Youth Federation [ISYF] spokesperson, denied the claim, saying, "Why kill innocent people? No Sikh would approve that.")

In Toronto a multi-faith remembrance service held three days after the bombing was meant to highlight the pain felt within Sikh, Hindu, Muslim, and Christian communities; after all, the 329 victims of the Air India bombing had been followers of many faiths. At the service, Swami Premanand, a Hindu priest, used what was supposed to be a unifying occasion to deliver a sermon some felt linked terrorism with the Sikh community. (That he closed his speech by chanting "Long live Mother India" probably didn't help.)

When Gobinder Singh Randhawa attempted to point this out, a group of Hindus accused him and the five Sikhs with him of murder. Remarkably, he managed to remain composed, telling those who had confronted him, "We will be quiet until we can talk to you privately and without interruption."

This toxic atmosphere was unsettling, to say the least. More unsettling still was the arrow of suspicion that was quickly loosed against us by India. Rajiv Gandhi publicly criticized the Canadian government, saying the nation "had not been stern enough with terrorists earlier," which in turn prompted Mulroney to respond in a sharply worded letter to Gandhi — a copy of which was conveniently distributed to Canadian media.

In it, the Canadian prime minister, perhaps stung by home-grown charges of his earlier callousness toward the Indo-Canadian victims of Air India 182, struck back, rhetorically asking what more a democratic society could legally do. And there was more. "In the absence of constructive advice, condemnation of this country's efforts may strike many Canadians as gratuitous," he wrote. "I wish to avoid mutual recriminations as well as interference in India's internal affairs. Clearly, however, the terrorism now implanted on Canadian soil has its roots in the unresolved political tensions of the Punjab."

Touché.

CONVENTIONAL THINKING

Amid this turmoil, the World Sikh Organization remained determined to push forward and elect a leadership. A competent, active, and engaged organization, positioned to advocate for Sikhs around the world, was needed more urgently than ever.

As I noted, in the U.S. the divisiveness that marked the January WSO constitutional meetings had not abated. Considering the potential for serious acrimony, the chairperson would have to be chosen carefully. The organizers were tasked with finding someone whose impartiality would be unquestioned. Since I had no dog in this particular fight — and because I knew the main actors and had been instrumental in helping them set up their constitution and bylaws — I was asked if I would chair the convention. Although I worried it could be like sticking my hand into a wasps' nest, I agreed.

On the convention floor, I pitied poor J.S. Bhullar, who was being hauled back and forth between groups of delegates who were pressing the case for their respective candidates. Bhullar, ever the diplomat, deferred all their pitches to the impartial chairperson — me.

At the risk of overusing the wasp imagery, I was almost swarmed. The intensity of the attack was unnerving, surreal. One approach was almost comical. I was shaking hands with delegates when I was approached by Gurpal Kaur, the wife of Ganga Singh Dhillon, one of the key players vying for the top spot in the executive. She strode over to me, took my arm, and pulled me aside.

"Gian Bha Ji," she said, using the Punjabi word for "brother," a respectful term. "You must make sure that my husband will be president."

"Look, Bhain Ji," I said, responding in kind, "I honestly don't have the power to—"

"I want to be First Lady of the Sikh nation!" she exclaimed.

It was all I could do not to laugh out loud. I didn't have the heart to tell her that it had become clear to me that, even if he should win, there was no real love for her husband among the delegates, despite his exceptional work in helping to establish the Sri Nankana Sahib Foundation, an organization dedicated to securing access to the many historical gurdwaras left in Pakistan by Partition. (Nanakana Sahib is the village where Guru Nanak was born.)

The first day of the convention was acrimonious, due largely to challenges related to sorting out delegate eligibility and establishing the criteria for selecting an executive and national council. Predictably, the mood on the second day was sombre. Much of the talk on the floor concerned the Air India disaster, including speculation as to who might have been behind it. Some raised the possibility that certain fringe actors within the community may have had a hand in it. But there was another suspect: many believed the Indian government was responsible. For years, they had tried to malign the Sikhs. The possibility, however distant, that the disaster was engineered to make pariahs out of us and kill off the fledgling separatist movement was not lost on the delegates.

Eventually, after a bit of horse trading, the delegates reached a compromise. Didar Singh Bains was persuaded to remain on as WSO International president; Ganga Singh Dhillon, who had spearheaded most of the lobbying efforts to date and who'd enlisted Senator Helms as an ally, was named president of the U.S. chapter. Sulukhan Singh Dhillon, who had won over many delegates, agreed to continue working with the organization, but not take an executive role.

With an executive elected and a formal constitution in place, we should have been ready to go all out in an attempt to engage stakeholders and convey the Sikh message to the world. But these were not normal times; a black cloud still hung over the proceedings. As 9/11 would do for Muslims, the events of June 23, 1985, would alter the way Canadian Sikhs were portrayed by the media for decades to come, hampering our ability to press our case against India for its outrageous treatment of Punjab's Sikhs.[26]

A COLLECTIVE CONDEMNATION

After the convention wrapped up, I spent a few days driving back through California, Oregon, and Washington state before finally arriving in British Columbia and eventually making my way to Williams Lake. It was good to be back. By this point, we'd been living in the Cariboo for 15 years. The land, with its rolling green hills, had etched its very presence on my soul. I was home.

In summer in rural Canada, there is a tradition. The small-town rodeo harks back to the days when the first European immigrants made their way across this rugged land, and celebrates that remarkable feat. Everyone gets involved on some level, either as a participant or simply as a reveller.

Each year, for a handful of days straddling the end of June and the beginning of July, our rodeo, officially known as the Williams Lake Stampede, is in full swing — as it has been every year since 1919, when the Great Pacific Eastern Railway completed its line and injected life (and commerce) into what had been until then a fairly sleepy little town.

The town of Williams Lake had always been welcoming, and our lives had become tightly integrated with those of our non-Sikh neighbours. We gathered in their homes, invited them into our gurdwara, and broke bread — or pakoras — together. In March of 1985, when Rick Hansen, Williams Lake's most famous son, began his Man in Motion Tour, the entire Williams Lake population threw its support behind his herculean effort. The Sikhs in Williams Lake were no exception. We were all very proud.

The rodeo week kicks off with a parade through town. This year, at the head of the pack was a clutch of Scottish highland bagpipers, followed by two RCMP officers on horseback, splendidly decked out in their traditional red serge uniforms. Float after float went by. One carried Kelly Fredell, the 1985 Williams Lake Stampede Queen; others represented local businesses and organizations, from a Christian school to the 4-H Club. The Royal Canadian Legion (Branch 139) was applauded by all, Sikhs included — a small irony, since our relationship with the veterans' group would become acrimonious before long.

The Sikh community of Williams Lake had its place in the parade. Our float was beautiful. Covered in flowered garlands, it rolled slowly down the main street of town. Along with the local gurdwara executive, I was aboard, as were several others from our community. As we moved past the crowd, I waved to the many familiar faces and to many unfamiliar ones, too. One in particular caught my eye. A boy, perhaps no more than 12 years old, was smiling at me. I looked directly at him, smiled back, and waved.

He broke out in a huge grin, then put his hands to his mouth to project his words like a bullhorn. "Hey, when are you guys gonna blow the next plane out of the sky?"

I was gutted. Perhaps it was because of the tender age of my accuser. Maybe it was due to the fact that this was the first — but certainly not the last — time I would be forced to bear responsibility for heinous acts outside my control. My head knew it was ignorance, nothing more. But it stung nevertheless. This was the land I was so proud to call home?

Disconcerting though it was, this was just a taste of what was to come. Over the next few weeks the image of the mad bearded Sikh, sword raised and in a sputtering rage, took hold in the public mind. It allowed for easy stereotypes to flourish. As a result, some of the most baseless tales ended up being investigated as if they were plausible. Like all noxious weeds they sprouted easily but were difficult to kill.

In the months after Air India 182, one fabrication in particular stands out. In September 1985, we learned that, deep in the forests of British Columbia, somewhere in the vicinity of the Central Interior city of Prince George, was one of the most formidable terrorist training camps in the world — at least, according to *India Today*, the *Time* magazine of India and one of that nation's most widely read publications. The camp, whose aim was to arm and train Sikhs who'd then return to India to violently establish an independent homeland in Punjab, was allegedly run by a man named Johann Vanderhorst, a South African mercenary. According to the report, this man had advertised for recruits in unnamed Canadian newspapers, offering over $11,000 per month as compensation for being trained in combat and weapons. Apparently, the government of India had obtained photographs of this training facility.

The Canadian media quickly picked up on the story. After all, what a claim: a terrorist training camp in the middle of rural B.C.? In addition to being a truly frightening prospect, it was also every news director's dream — so it wasn't a shock that CTV, one of the nation's two largest television networks, sent one of their national reporters to investigate.

The journalist called me on arriving in Williams Lake. He'd arranged to interview me, so I was expecting him. As is my usual practice, I thought it would be best if we met over lunch at my favourite restaurant, Rendezvous.

We talked for about two hours. I tried to persuade him that there was not one iota of truth to the "terror camp" claim — that it was simply a fake news story planted to make Sikhs look bad. The reporter was unconvinced. "Okay," I said, sighing. "Let's go back to my office. We can sit down and talk a bit more." He agreed.

We drove the short distance to Khalsa Enterprises. I pulled up in front of the office and parked. We got out of my pickup, and I escorted him around to the edge of the 10-acre property, overlooking a small canyon. From here, we had expansive views. Of the city dump.

"There it is," I said flatly.

"There what is?" he asked.

"What you're looking for," I replied, waving my hand at a landscape full of trash. "This is where the Sikhs are being trained."

He was stunned. "Is this true?" he asked.

"Absolutely!" I replied. "If you want to see them in action close up, I could drive you over right now."

The reporter stared at me. Then he broke into a sheepish grin and laughed. At that point, I think the metaphor sank in. The story was rank, as fetid as the garbage rotting in the distance. It was a moment of gentle humour, but over the coming months there would be very few laughs for those of us who were close to "the Sikh file."

It is a terrible thing, to live under a blanket of suspicion. Sikhs aren't the first people to be scapegoated for the acts of a small number of their members, nor will they be the last — ask any observant Muslim how they've fared since 9/11 and you'll hear a similar story. To carry a burden that is not of your own making is exhausting, the weight of despicable acts committed ostensibly by others in your name taking an almost physical toll.

You cringe when some young Sikh hothead says something stupid to the national media. You throw up your hands when an illiterate redneck shoots a guy in a turban — because he's angered by something that happened in, say, Afghanistan or Iraq. There is a psychological residue when you live your life hoping against hope that the next act of violence splashed across the front page has no connection to a man whose last name is Singh. Collective guilt involves the same dynamic as collective blame and, more seriously, collective punishment. The only difference is that the guilt is self-imposed.

"You guys did it." Even if left unsaid, this phrase, like a thought balloon in a graphic novel, seemed to linger over the heads of non-Sikh Canadians, even those who should know better. Our executive director Anne Lowthian, the first non-Sikh to hold this position and someone with whom I worked hand-in-hand at WSO Canada for over 14 years, recently recounted a run-in she had with former Ontario premier Bob Rae in 2005, two decades after the Air India tragedy.

Ann had an appointment to meet with Rae. At the time, he was out of politics. From 1998 to 2003, he had served as a member of the Security Intelligence Review Committee, the agency charged with overseeing the activities of CSIS. By 2005, he was an independent advisor to Deputy Prime Minister Anne McLellan, who was seeking Rae's opinion regarding whether to hold an independent inquiry into the Air India bombing. The meeting did not go well, as Ann recounted to me:

> Bob Rae made me wait over an hour so he could angrily inform me that he believed the organization I worked for was somehow involved in Air India, and then he demanded that I tell the Sikh community to "come clean" and produce the evidence he needed to substantiate his allegations. His direct condemnation of me and the only Sikh organization in Canada that had a proven record of working positively with Canadian officials for over two decades showed the measure of his ignorance... It was the last time I volunteered for public abuse. I left WSO Canada shortly after this incident.

Even for those like Rae who were ostensibly on the left, there was — and continued to be — a rush to judgment when it came to the Sikhs. We were, in the eyes of far too many, the guys who "did it." It was difficult to take, I'll admit. But nothing close to the horror of those orchestrated attacks generated from the country of my birth.

CHAPTER 6

THE LONG ARM OF INDIA

I N APRIL 1986, less than 10 months after the Air India bombing, I was on a plane to Ottawa to meet with officials from the Department of External Affairs. The meeting had been a long time coming.

The mandate of External Affairs is broad. It oversees the diplomatic corps. It makes recommendations regarding how the federal government should proceed with foreign policy. It smooths the way for trade relationships. When it came to India, External (as it's colloquially known) was very aware that entertaining serious complaints made by Canadian Sikhs against Indian abuses in Punjab could threaten the burgeoning trade relationship between the two nations. The fact that both were Commonwealth member states only made the department less enthusiastic about raising Indian human rights violations — of which there were many.

With the help of my member of Parliament, Dr. Lorne Greenaway, I had finally managed to get a meeting with Joe Clark, Minister of External Affairs. (Dr. Greenaway and Tarsem Singh Purewal, president of an Ottawa gurdwara, and no relation to the *Des Pardes* editor of the same name, accompanied me.) The idea behind the sit-down was simple. Since Air India, the Sikh community had been put on its heels. Many of our resources — and untold hours of my time — had been spent simply trying to counteract negative stereotypes. But as occupied as we were in facing down reductionist representations (and those who trafficked in them), we were fully aware of another crucial part of our mandate: to press our government to use its sway with India to ameliorate the human rights abuses committed against Punjab's Sikhs, and by extension against Canadian Sikhs as well.

By now "false encounters," that prettified euphemism for extrajudicial executions, were common in Punjab, and the indiscriminate jailing of Sikh youths under falsified pretences was an everyday event. We wanted the government of Brian Mulroney to act (or at least officially register its disapproval). But to jolt them out of their complacency, we believed we needed to show, as graphically as possible, what had happened at the Golden Temple in 1984.

Toward this end, I'd brought with me a series of 20 photographs taken after the massacre. These photographs were gruesome, horrible; purchased on our behalf, they had to be smuggled out of Punjab because India had taken great pains to censor any unflattering imagery surrounding the attack. In a brutal and unequivocal way, the photos conveyed the scale and nature of the violence wrought by Canada's great Commonwealth ally. I hoped the shock value alone might at least prompt a reconsideration of the Canadian government's line: that the attack on the Golden Temple had been a measured response to an intolerable provocation, and that this was strictly an Indian internal affair.

Arriving at the Department of External Affairs building on Sussex Drive, we were ushered into a modest meeting room. "Minister Clark will be along shortly," an assistant said. "Please make yourselves comfortable." We waited for half an hour, but Clark was a no-show. Eventually, Gerry Weiner, the parliamentary secretary, walked through the door. He was not alone. With him was a clean-shaven South Asian man who looked to be around 40 years old.

"Gian, it's nice to meet you," said Weiner, shaking my hand. "This is John from Montreal, and he'll be sitting in on this — hope that's okay."

There was something odd, too casual, about the way Weiner introduced "John." I decided to poke. "I think that'll be fine," I said, "but John, are you also from External Affairs?"

Weiner and his companion exchanged looks. "John is with another 'interested party,'" said Weiner.

"Ah. Which one?" I asked.

"NACOI," responded John. "The National Association of Canadians of Origins in India."

I'd never before heard mention of "John," but I knew of his organization. In my opinion, its executive had a strong pro-India bias. It did not represent Canadian Sikhs. "Look," I said to Weiner, "somebody should have at least given me a heads-up that we'd be joined by someone else today."

"Yes, well, sorry about that," he said dismissively. "Okay, what do you have for me?"

"Excuse me, but is Minister Clark going to be joining us?"

"The minister is tied up in another meeting. He asked me to attend instead." I glanced at Greenaway, his expression just short of a scowl. It was clear he wasn't happy about this, either.

We decided to continue. Using an overhead projector, I showed shot after horrific shot, providing commentary on each. But the photos, I realized, were not having the intended effect. I suspected that "John" was an agent of the Indian government — of which branch, who could know — and that anything shared with Gerry Weiner would also be shared with the Indian embassy. The trip had done nothing more than tip our hand. I mentioned this to Greenaway and even hinted that he would hear from the Indian high commissioner the next morning — which is exactly what happened. High Commissioner S.J.S. Chhatwal phoned and asked Greenaway for a meeting, and when they got together, diplomatically tried to put forth India's version of events and provide propaganda material.

For myself, I flew back to Williams Lake the next day. By the time I'd dropped my bags at home and driven to work, a message was waiting for me. It was from the local RCMP detachment, asking me to give them a call. Within a half hour, two RCMP officers showed up at my office.

After exchanging pleasantries, we got down to it. "So, gentlemen," I said. "What can I do for you?"

"Gian," one of the officers began, "we were wondering if you were planning on being at the Vaisakhi celebration in Vancouver next week."

"Well, yes, of course. I attend every year. Why?"

The officers looked at each other. "We're here to advise you not to go."

"Why would you do that?"

There was a pause. "There has been a death threat."

"Against?"

"You."

"Me? You're sure?"

"Yes," said the second officer, who'd been silent to this point. "We're sure. We intercepted a call. It was explicit."

"Who from? Who issued the death threat?" I asked.

"We can't say for certain," he replied. "But you are definitely the target."

"How credible is this?"

The men glanced at each other. "Very, I'm afraid," one said.

Although the officers pressed me to skip the Vaisakhi Day parade, I had no intention of staying home. I simply could not live my life in fear. In some respects, this is a matter of faith: a belief that the events of our lives are guided by the hand of God. If I were killed, it was part and parcel of a larger plan. So, yes: a sense of fatalism, embedded in faith, comes into play. But it was also pragmatic. If those in leadership roles could be intimidated into silence, where would that leave us all?

Still, there's certainty and there's certainty. I did not have the courage to tell my wife and family that by attending Vaisakhi celebrations I was possibly gambling away not only my own life but their futures. I wanted to spare them the worry.

In retrospect, I see how that looks, but at the time it seemed the only rational choice. As I mingled at the parade, under the watchful eyes of several dozen RCMP officers who had been alerted to the threat hanging over me, everything must have seemed normal. Accompanied by two undercover officers — they were with me for the entire parade route — I greeted people by name, shaking their hands and smiling like it was just another day. Nevertheless, as I pushed my way through the crowd, there were moments when I scanned the throng, searching for a tell-tale sweat-soaked brow or a hand placed conspicuously in the pocket of an oversized jacket.

Who had issued the death threat? Eventually, I heard through a source that it had been traced to an Edmonton phone, but this wasn't much to go on. It could have been another Sikh group opposed to the WSO's nonviolent approach; it could just as easily have been a Canadian-based agent of the government of India, for whom I, and the WSO, had become a rather large thorn. Considering the threat coincided with my Ottawa trip, this was more likely, in my opinion.

CLOAK AND DAGGER

It's beyond dispute that Indian spies, many of them associated with the embassy in Ottawa or in the consular offices across the country, had been involved in intelligence gathering for years. In addition to providing the usual diplomatic and foreign service functions, the diplomatic corps had two jobs when it came to Sikh expats: to gather information on us and to provide a steady stream of propaganda meant to demonize the Sikhs in Canada. In many cases, India's diplomats were, as one former CSIS operative would describe them, part of a "nest of spies."

Not that cloak and dagger activities conducted under the guise of diplomacy are anything new. Or unique to India. Other nations were doing the same thing; from belligerent states like China and the Soviet Union to allies like Israel, many nations engaged in surreptitious dealings that, in some cases, bordered on the nefarious. But in India's case, the coordination was directed from the very top political echelons.

On April 9, 1981, Giani Zail Singh, the Indian home minister (and eventually president), decreed that the country's Central Bureau of Intelligence (CBI) and the Research and Analysis Wing (RAW), India's CIA, should embark on a bold new mission: to spy on the diaspora in nations where Sikhs were significantly represented. The objective? To undermine criticism of India from the Sikhs who lived abroad by tarring the community at every turn. (Like some others, I was singled out for special treatment over the years. Harkishan Singh Surjeet, a close confidant of Indira Gandhi and a senior leader of the Communist Party of India [Marxist], was sent to Canada to assess Bhindranwale's support among Canadian Sikhs. He dropped by Williams Lake, and we had a rather testy discussion about Gandhi's role in ordering the army to attack Darbar Sahib.)

In Canada, this task initially fell to Davinder "David" Singh Ahluwalia, the Toronto-based vice-consul of India, according to Zuhair Kashmeri and Brian McAndrew, co-authors of *Soft Target*. Seasoned reporters who worked for Canada's two largest newspapers — Kashmeri covered the South Asian beat for the *Globe and Mail*, while McAndrew wrote for the *Toronto Star* — the two journalists connect the dots in their landmark book and lay out a scenario in which a foreign nation, through the use of agents provocateurs and the manufacture of propaganda, manipulates the Canadian government and public opinion, turning both against the nation's Sikh citizens.

Their canvas is broad, the tale sprawling. Coincidences, some with sinister implications, abound. In 1982, Kuldip Samra, a Toronto man who was instrumental in helping Ahluwalia construct his "files" on Canadian Sikhs, was somehow spirited out of the country after killing two people in an Ontario courtroom, where a gurdwara election dispute was being adjudicated; the authors suspected his departure was facilitated by the vice-consul. (Samra was arrested in

India almost 10 years later and extradited to Canada. Convicted of murder, he was sentenced to 25 years in prison.) A protest in Toronto later that year led to a confrontation downtown between two groups of Sikhs, one pro-India, the other against. In the clash, which the authors claim was orchestrated by Ahluwalia, who had intentionally provoked one gurdwara into a rage, a city policeman, Cpl. Chris Fernandes, was shot and seriously wounded.

Other manoeuvres verged on farce. When a couple of Sikhs allegedly burst into consul offices in Vancouver and Toronto and started smashing furniture, reportedly enraged by the attack on the Golden Temple, consular officials called the police — and the news media. But in one case a reporter showed up too quickly and witnessed the embassy staff in Toronto smashing their own furniture in an attempt to make the "rampage" seem more significant than it actually was.

A bit of comedy in the midst of full-on tragedy, I suppose. But there was nothing humorous about being the target of a nation that was obsessed with hiding the truth about their treatment of the Sikhs.

TRUTH IN SHORT SUPPLY

In Williams Lake, I was feeling this discomfort on a personal level. Back in July 1984, when Avtar Singh and I were in Pakistan, we were not surprised we couldn't cross the border into Punjab since it was widely known that Canadian Sikhs were being routinely denied travel visas in the aftermath of the Golden Temple massacre. Soon, it became clear that in my case what was actually happening went beyond any blanket ban.

Since the events of June 1984, we suspected India was compiling a blacklist of Canadian Sikhs who would be disqualified from getting an Indian travel visa. Because of my profile, I was certain that if there were such a list, my name would be on it. I just didn't realize how far the Indian government would go in making things uncomfortable for not just myself but my friends and even casual acquaintances.

Ajit Singh Dhami lived next door to me in Williams Lake. He was a good neighbour, and like any good neighbours, our families had regular contact. We'd wave at each other when we were puttering around in our yards or cutting the grass; when I saw him at the gurdwara, I'd always make a point of greeting him warmly. Williams Lake is a small place. You can't help but know the people you live with, especially if they happen to live on your street.

In 1985, Ajit's father, who lived in Punjab, became seriously ill. Intending to travel back to the old country to visit his dad, Ajit drove to Vancouver to apply for a travel visa. At the Indian consulate he sat across the desk from the visa officer, who greeted him brusquely. There was no pleasant banter while the officer rifled through papers, checking and rechecking the application. Finally, he looked up at my neighbour.

"Is this your house?" he asked.

Ajit examined the photo. "Yes," he said, his eyes narrowing. What on earth was this?

"I see." The officer wrote in his notepad. "And this?" he said, pointing to the adjacent house, "is this the house next to yours?"

"Yes," he responded. "What's this all about?"

"You realize that this is the home of Gian Singh Sandhu, yes?"

"Well, sure, but—"

"Fine. Thank you very much. Your application for a travel visa is denied."

"But my father!"

"Thank you very much."

Because he happened to live next to me, Ajit was prevented from saying goodbye to his father. It was a cruel punishment. But in a very real way, I was the actual target. Was the government of India trying to exert pressure on me by making things unbearable for those who happened to fall into the Venn diagram of my life? I felt sorrow for my neighbour. And a burning anger toward a government that would capriciously try to leverage someone's unrelated tragedy to penalize its political opponents. How many other Sikhs in Canada might be subject to the same callous treatment?[27]

Like many others in our community who were targeted, I was conflicted about being on a blacklist. On one hand, I was incensed: how dare the government of India refuse me entry to the country of my birth? How dare they try to make life intolerable for those whose only crime was that they had the misfortune of living next to me? But there was another, competing feeling, one that was gaining traction in the community. For those of us who were politically active, being banned had become a point of pride.

Ajit's situation was not an isolated incident. Pal Singh Nijjar, another Williams Lake resident, who owned a business located next to mine, was also denied a visa. This time the visa officer's reason for refusal was even more bizarre: someone had accused Pal of being my bodyguard. "But this doesn't make sense! I'm not his bodyguard! Gian doesn't have a bodyguard; he doesn't even need a bodyguard!" Pal protested, upon hearing the reason he'd been refused. The visa officer was unmoved. Denied!

What both stories revealed was that someone in Williams Lake was being paid for information, no matter how scurrilous or untrue. Photos of my house (long before Google maps made accessing these images commonplace), fallacious rumours of bodyguards — who knew what other elaborate fictions were being manufactured by those who mixed among us, ate at the langar, or smiled and shook my hand when we ran into each other walking along Williams Lake's main street? In time, through a conversation I had with CSIS officers, I learned there were at least three Indian informants working in Williams Lake. They were being paid $1,200 per month to provide "intel" — not a princely sum, but a significant payout in the mid-1980s.

To ensure their goose continued to lay eggs of gold — or brass, at least — the informants knew that the information they provided must flow freely and without interruption. The very nature of the "paid informant" relationship meant these people would say almost anything to keep the grift going.

And some nations, I discovered, would do almost anything to keep their abuses under wraps.

In late February 1986, as part of a WSO delegation, I traveled to Geneva, Switzerland, with my colleagues Gopal Singh Brar, Joginder Singh Bains, Jagjit Singh Mangat, and a California-based legal counsel (whose name I have since forgotten) to attend a United Nations conference focusing on human rights. Since we were not representing any specific nation but rather a community whose members were spread around the globe, our legal counsel had arranged to have us participate as the "guests" of a sympathetic nation. (The nation preferred to remain unidentified, for fear of being subject to reprisals from India.)

On February 27, the fourth day of the conference, we hosted an informal reception for all ambassadors at the Résidence Universitaire Internationale. India caught wind of what we were up to and, to steal our thunder, hastily arranged their own reception for the same time. Despite this, over 30 ambassadors (including Gordon Fairweather, who led the Canadian delegation) and their staff showed up to attend our reception.

We were slotted to give our presentation the next day on the atrocities being committed against Sikhs in Punjab. Ready and eager to address the assembly, we had pulled together what we considered to be a comprehensive presentation. But as we were leaving our hotel to go to the conference, about a 15-minute walk from the United Nations Assembly headquarters, we were stopped by four officious-looking men. They produced badges and identified themselves as Interpol agents.

Immediately, we were detained in the hotel — put under "house arrest" is how I'd describe it. While our indignant attorney sputtered and railed against the detention, two of the four officers went upstairs to search our rooms. After an hour, they returned and said we were free to go. I stayed put. I wanted to hear an explanation of why we had been detained.

"Do you know Gurdyal Singh Dhillon?" one of the officers asked.

"Of course," I said. Dhillon was the Indian High Commissioner in Ottawa in the early 1980s, but by then he had moved on to become head of the Indian mission in Geneva. Ironically, he was also a distant relative of Gopal Singh Brar, one of our delegation.

"Well, he has lodged a complaint against you."

"Against us? What for?"

"He claims that you are here to assassinate him."

I didn't know whether to laugh or fume. The fact that we were free to leave, and that our Interpol handlers were smiling rather sheepishly at us, meant that nobody was buying the lie. But the cheap trick had worked. We arrived at U.N. headquarters far too late to make our presentation. At a break during lunch, Dhillon's handlers brought him by — for what reason, I have no idea. Rather than show how upset we were, we decided to embrace our adversary, literally. We greeted him with a traditional Punjabi hug. This must have thrown him, because when I asked him if he had been following orders to have us falsely detained, he actually admitted that it was true.

And then, he complimented us for the good work we'd done on behalf of the Sikh community. All in all, a rather surreal day.

A SETBACK IN BUSINESS

By 1987, my Williams Lake–based forestry business, Khalsa Enterprises, was well established. But we were hardly a large company. Although we had grown to about 70 employees in six years, the sawmill still had no roof — not the best working conditions, I'm afraid, when the mercury dropped to –30° C (as it often did). A reception area, three offices, and a modest boardroom were housed in a 700-square-foot rancher-like building — small, but enough for our needs at the time.

My office was in the back, with a view of the lumberyard and the production plant. A couple of times a day, I'd stretch my legs and take a walk through the plant, spot-checking for quality control. I'd make a habit of stopping by the machine operators for a chat, making sure to recognize those who were doing a good job. How to describe the people I was lucky enough to work with? "Salt of the earth" is probably as good a term as any. We were a tight team and worked together closely. But on the horizon, difficulties loomed.

The lumber industry is cyclical. We had started in a down cycle, and six years later, we were facing another. Plus, at that time interest rates had spiraled out of control, cresting as high as 22 percent. Seeking a better deal, we changed banks from one of the "Big Five" Canadian lenders to a different financial institution, one of the newly created "Class C" banks.

During the downturn, we incurred losses that quickly added up. Our new bank became increasingly concerned that our liquidity ratio — the amount of liquid assets available to pay off debt — was out of whack. To counteract this, we secured venture capital financing, but before the funds could be released the bank was sold. On November 5, 1987, despite having secured an agreement that would have provided funding by the end of the year, we were essentially shut down. (The law has since been changed: Canadian banks are now required to give notice and provide an opportunity to make alternative financial arrangements in situations like ours.)

I was shattered. At the time, it seemed that my life was in ruins. And I was haunted by the fact that my failure was putting so many of my employees, men and women who'd been with me for years, out of work.

This was an incredibly distressing time. Although my eldest, Kamaljit, had graduated by then, two of my children, Palbinder and Harjinder, were still attending university — not nearly as expensive then as it is today, but the tuition and living costs weren't paltry sums. Our house in Williams Lake still had a large mortgage, and as a result our monthly debt was substantial. Plus, I was still dedicating a large portion of my time pro bono to WSO activities. The travel costs alone, all of which I paid out of my own pocket, had been a drain on our diminishing bottom line.

It was at this time that the rumour mill began to grind. My financial difficulties had been a ruse, some whispered; I was as rich as Midas, the owner of vast orchards in the state of California.

Apparently, I was also a big player in West Coast residential real estate, and unbeknownst to me I owned several properties in North Vancouver. People who had once been friendly turned against us and I received threatening letters directed against me and my family. (After recognizing the handwriting of one anonymous coward, I forwarded his name to the local RCMP.)

The only thing that kept us going was our faith, our family and friends, and each other. Surinder's support was unwavering during these times, and I relied upon her perhaps more than she will ever know. Without her, even with my faith to steel me I'm not at all sure I would have had the fortitude to continue.

To find solace, I turned to the words of Guru Arjan Dev:

> When you are confronted with terrible hardships, and no one offers you any support, when your friends turn into enemies, and even your relatives have deserted you, and when all support has given way, and all hope has been lost — if you then come to remember the Supreme Lord God, even the hot wind shall not touch you.

In trying times, you must find perspective. My family was in good health. The love I have for Surinder had only grown stronger as we faced our trials together. Three of our children had gone on to pursue post-secondary studies, and our youngest, Surjit, had more than proved his mettle, helping to sustain the family by working at other jobs during our most vulnerable times. Even in the most difficult moments, we knew we had been blessed.

Thankfully, this dip in our fortunes was temporary. With help from two venture capitalist partners, my friends Prem Singh Vinning and Avtar Singh Sandhu, plus a $125,000 loan from Joginder Singh Sidhu, a close relative, we purchased the remaining assets of Khalsa Enterprises shortly after it closed and I began a new phase in my entrepreneurial life. On December 7, 1987, Jackpine Forest Products Ltd., a company that would eventually manufacture "value-added" wood products for sale to domestic and international markets, was born. In time, it would become one of the largest value-added wood products producers in Canada.

No hot wind could touch us.

A SPY IN THE GURDWARA

On October 22, 1983, Maloy Krishna Dhar and his family landed in Canada. To all who met him, the affable Dhar was exactly who he appeared to be: a top consular official posted to the government of India's Ottawa embassy. To a select few in India's intelligence circles, though, he was known as one of the top spies in that country's history.

Dhar, who had been chosen personally for the position by Indira Gandhi, had come on a mission wrapped in a mission. His true purpose, hidden from others — and certainly from the Canadian government — was succinctly spelled out by his predecessor, Shiva Ramakrishnan, as outlined in Dhar's 2005 memoir, *Open Secrets: India's Intelligence Unveiled.*

After being informed by Ramakrishnan that "Sikh militancy was on the rise," Dhar was instructed to "prepare for another tough battle" by running a rogue intelligence operation independent of the Research and Analysis Wing (RAW) of the formidable Central Bureau of Intelligence. His instructions were simple. "You won't need a detailed briefing," Ramakrishnan told him. "Penetrate the Sikh community, make friends in the gurdwaras and win over important community leaders. Maintain your cover carefully."

With these marching orders, Dhar began his clandestine journey through Canada. It was not an easy one. For one thing, he did not speak Punjabi at all — a huge barrier to overcome if he was to infiltrate the Canadian Sikh community. That changed soon after his arrival, under the tutelage of one of the embassy staff: "Within three months I could read and write the language," he claimed.

Dhar was not operating in isolation. The government of India, consumed with the idea of shutting down "Sikh extremism" in the diaspora, had sent spies to several countries — all part of an effort initiated by, paradoxically enough, one of the more prominent Indian Sikhs at the time: President Giani Zail Singh.

According to *Open Secrets*, India High Commissioner S.J.S. Chhatwal gave Dhar his instructions, which were to:

- Befriend diplomats in the Bangladesh and Sri Lanka missions, in order to influence the Pakistan mission
- Infiltrate certain gurdwaras in Canada
- Cultivate vocal Sikh community assets and assets in the Canadian Sikh workforce
- Cultivate friendly members of Parliament
- Brief Canadian Foreign Office and RCMP staff about developments in India
- Target Canadian media to sell the Indian take on events
- Disseminate audio and videotapes of Indian current affairs, especially atrocities committed by "the Bhindranwale goons"
- Infiltrate the Punjabi media and the broader Asiatic/Indian media
- Improve the *India News* with the help of a new fast printing/copying machine
- Maintain cover

It was a fascinating and comprehensive set of tasks, and this is exactly what he did, starting with the Ottawa Sikh Society's gurdwara on Prescott Highway. I saw him there on a few occasions when I went to Ottawa to address the congregation. Dhar was a small man with a round face, double chin, and aviator-style tinted spectacles — a sort of "blink and miss him" type whose distinguishing feature was that he had no real distinguishing features. Perhaps this helped him in his career as an intelligence agent? I can only guess.

In time Dhar became part of gurdwara life. A competent percussionist well versed in Indian classical music, he made a point of attending almost every Sunday, ingratiating himself by volunteering to play the tabla alongside the singing of the kirtan, or Sikh hymns.

He also added his voice to the chorus of anti-India condemnation rising in the gurdwaras. As he himself put it, he "feigned to share the anger of the Sikh community." And in doing so, he made inroads.

Traveling around the country, going from Vancouver to Edmonton, Calgary to Regina, Winnipeg to Toronto — anywhere there was a sizable Sikh population — Dhar snooped in gurdwara after gurdwara, compiling information, contacts, snippets of overheard conversation, clippings from Punjabi-language newspapers. In British Columbia, he was "granted access" to what he describes as the "extremist-controlled" gurdwaras in the Lower Mainland; he specifically mentioned Vancouver's Ross Street gurdwara, site of much discord between traditionalists and non-traditionalists. (I'm not quite sure who would "grant" him access; the gurdwaras are open to anyone who chooses to attend. It's not like he had to pass some sort of test or produce his credentials at the door!)

On his journeys, he claims his "smooth access" allowed him to identify "targets close to the leaders of the Babbar Khalsa, World Sikh Organization and International Sikh Youth Federation." To an outsider, this may seem like a mighty accomplishment. But really, almost everyone in the community knew who was who in both Babbar Khalsa and the ISYF; at this point, neither of the two groups had yet been banned as terrorist organizations, and so both were free to spread their toxic messages at will. As for the WSO Canada? All you had to do was look at our constitution, or check out the masthead of *The Sword,* our self-published news organ. Our organizational structure was laid out for all to see (even Indian spies). In *Open Secrets,* Dhar claims to have infiltrated the WSO in both the United Kingdom and the United States, but he admits that he made no headway in infiltrating the WSO Canada. In fact, an attempt to get close to one of our leaders backfired in spectacular fashion.

In 1986, Karnail Singh Gill, who then chaired WSO Canada's Public and Government Relations Committee, wanted to travel to India. To do so, he needed a visa, and for that he had to apply through the embassy and, it turns out, Maloy Krishna Dhar. At the time, we had suspicions about Dhar, but it had nothing to do with the fact that he worked at the Indian embassy. Several WSO Canada members in the Ottawa sangat had a feeling that there was something too pat — too perfect — about the unassuming newcomer, despite his prowess with the tabla. On my visits to the Ottawa gurdwara, Ajit Singh Sahota, an active WSO Canada member (and later its president), had made me aware of this, and through me, Karnail Singh Gill as well.

To apply for his visa, Gill turned up at the embassy, where he was greeted by Dhar. They made the requisite small talk, at which Dhar was more than comfortable. After pleasantries were exchanged, they got down to business. Dhar couldn't issue the visa himself, he said. Instead, they'd have to go through another employee whose office was down the hall.

"Will this take long?" Gill asked.

"No, not at all," came the reply.

Gill followed Dhar to another nearby office, where they were greeted by the officer in question. Gill paused for a moment and stared at the guy seated at the desk. He knew this man.

"Hey, Sundar Kumar Sharma!" Gill said. "It's been a long time."

The officer stared at him blankly. "Sorry, wrong guy. My name's not Sharma."

But Gill was certain. "I never forget a face. We were in the same class — the forestry service training program in Dehradun. When did you ..."

The sentence hung in the air, unfinished, while the consular officer fidgeted with some papers on his desk. "Look, I'm sorry, you've got it wrong. My name isn't Sharma, and I've never seen you before in my life."

Gill smiled thinly. "Are you with RAW?" The question remained unanswered — but really, it hardly needed to be asked. It was abundantly clear what Sundar Kumar Sharma was, or who he had become.

My colleague never got his visa. Like me, he was on a blacklist —
although at this point, none of us could confirm this fact. But there
was a silver lining: Sharma's cover was blown. His jig was up.

BLOODIED BUT UNBROKEN

Eventually, even the ostrich yanks its head from the earth. In 1986,
after the government of Canada refused to entertain the possibility
that the Indian embassy and its various consulates across the country
doubled as spy hives, information provided to External Affairs by
CSIS finally moved it to action.

In a very low-key, polite way, Rajiv Gandhi was informed that
four of his "diplomats" were no longer in good standing and would be
immediately expelled: Toronto-based consul general Surinder Malik;
Vancouver-based vice-consul Gurinder Singh; Maloy Krishna Dhar,
who would go on to become the No. 2 man in India's intelligence
service; and, finally, Sundar Kumar Sharma, the hapless agent who
was posing as an Indian visa officer. That last one couldn't have been
a huge surprise. After Karnail Singh Gill blew Sharma's cover, I'm sure
he realized his time here would soon be up.

The expulsions represented a small victory. Since the Air India
tragedy we had continuously been on the defensive. But by the end
of 1986, a year and a half after the bombing, much had shifted. Some
of it was concrete: for example, Khalsa Credit Union, an initiative
spearheaded by 50 Sikhs, was created; today it has six branches
overseeing more than $400 million in assets. Some of it was symbolic:
in British Columbia, Manmohan "Moe" Sihota became the first Sikh
to be elected to any provincial legislature in Canada; and Wally Oppal
joined the Supreme Court of B.C. and later the B.C. Court of Appeal,
after becoming the first Canadian of Sikh heritage to be appointed
a judge.

Despite the interference Sikhs in Canada faced, we were making
headway, slowly and surely becoming a political force to be reckoned
with. We were coming into our own.

THAT'S A LOT OF COINCIDENCES

While Dhar's memoir is a damning indictment of Indian subterfuge, *Soft Target* raises even more troubling questions about India's behaviour, both leading up to the Air India bombing and afterwards. Many remain unanswered. In early 1985, in the months before the tragedy, Indian embassy vice-consul David Ahluwalia met with Talwinder Singh Parmar, the head of Babbar Khalsa, the most militant of the Sikh groups aligned against India. While Kashmeri and McAndrew did not discover the gist of the conversation, the authors believe that Ahluwalia, who knew Parmar was a train wreck in progress, was attempting to raise his profile in order to discredit Canadian Sikhs generally.

The circumstances of Parmar's arrest in India, and his eventual death after he'd already been detained, are widely believed to be yet another "false encounter" orchestrated to stop him from talking about the possible role India's intelligence agencies might have played in the downing of Air India 182 and the Narita explosion.

On the surface, it seems almost impossible to fathom. Why would India involve itself in the sabotage of its own plane? What possible outcome could it want? Theories have been floated: demonizing the Canadian Sikhs is an obvious one, startling even as an accumulation of evidence spilled out over the next few years. The evidence is circumstantial but highly disturbing. Some proponents point to "coincidences" that, when considered in context, raise both eyebrows and questions. Surinder Malik, India's Toronto-based consul general, and his family were supposed to be on Air India 182 — but canceled at the last minute, saying their daughter had a school exam. Others in positions of authority in the Indian diplomatic corps who were booked on the flight never boarded, also canceling at the last minute.

It is, at the very least, odd.

Nobody wants to run screaming down the conspiracy theory rabbit hole. In my life, I've generally avoided the kind of conclusions that can, like so much balled yarn, be spun into socks or sweaters, depending on the knitter. But the possibility of an Indian role in the mass murder of so many Canadians cannot be lightly dismissed — although it certainly was rejected by the RCMP, who decided early on that the sabotage was a case of home-grown Sikh terror, pure and simple.

According to *Soft Target*, over at CSIS a different point of view was taking hold. The more the organization looked into the Air India bombing, the murkier things became. It discovered alarming similarities with an Indian government bombing attempt directed against Tamils in Sri Lanka. After reviewing the evidence — and the parallels — a few of CSIS's rank and file came to a shocking (and shockingly under-reported) conclusion: in order to discredit Canadian Sikhs and the idea of an independent Khalistan, the government of India had likely set up a clandestine network in Canada to commit acts like the bombing of Air India 182.

The actions of the Indian embassy officials in the immediate wake of the bombing also raised a few flags. Almost immediately after the explosion, Surinder Malik went into hyperdisinformation mode, initially claiming that the Sikh pilot, who died alongside the passengers, had received "a package" before leaving Canada; this was quickly proved to be a fabrication. He also provided "evidence" as to the identification of who might have checked bags through, but never boarded, the doomed flights. But how could he know this? And so soon?

Again, at least to some CSIS agents it seemed that this was a continuation of India's modus operandi: throwing out false evidence as fast as they could, for the effect of tainting Sikhs in Canada. That's a best-case interpretation. At worst, the flurry of false leads was designed to throw investigators' suspicions off the government of India.

In 2009, Michel Juneau-Katsuya outlined his thoughts regarding India's use of spies against Canadian citizens. The former CSIS officer and journalist Fabrice de Pierrebourg co-authored *Nest of Spies: The Startling Truth About Foreign Agents at Work within Canada's Borders*, which entertains the possibility that India had ties to those behind the Air India murders. "This is a case in which there is troubling evidence of that country's undercover agents infiltrating Canada's Sikh community and being in contact with the principal suspects of the crime," Juneau-Katsuya wrote.

Although he stopped well short of accusing India of planning and executing the two bombings, some of his colleagues weren't so diplomatic. In 2012, Francois Lavigne, a former CSIS agent who worked with Juneau-Katsuya on the file, issued a particularly damning assessment. "To those who would say that the possibility of Indian government officials being involved in Air India is ridiculous, I would say simply that the Service [CSIS] did possess evidence of that very thing," he claimed in the *Ottawa Citizen*. But, he added, "at the time, in 1984–85, External Affairs were very keen on encouraging commerce between Canada and India, so nothing could interfere with those efforts."

For his part, Juneau-Katsuya cautions against a rush to judgment. Indian involvement in the Air India 182 disaster seems like nothing more than a far-fetched scenario ripped from the pages of a John le Carré novel. Yet he insisted it was at least worth exploring. "Did [India] cross the line, provoke an incident to get Canada's cooperation?" he asked. "We don't know."

Tragically, for the families of the victims, and for the Sikhs in Canada collectively implicated in the crime, this remains true today.

MAJOR FAIL

More than three decades after the destruction of Air India Flight 182 and the explosion at Tokyo's Narita Airport, the culprits behind the attacks remain largely unknown. As a result, there will always be questions dogging us. Who was Inderjit Singh Reyat, the only person convicted in the affair, working with? Was he a patsy? If so, who — or what group — set him up? If there was a conspiracy, how far did it go? We'll never know. But no matter how much time passes, the allegations remain like a jagged and ugly scar snaking across the

Sikh body politic. Like most scars, it has faded with the passing of time but as with all things marked by violence, its presence only diminishes, never wholly disappears.

Still, within the Canadian Sikh community there was hope that the entire truth would eventually come out and that we, a people who had been unfairly held responsible for heinous acts, would finally be exonerated. (The WSO Canada began asking for a public inquiry in 1987, when CSIS revealed they had destroyed 156 audiotapes of alleged Air India mastermind Talwinder Singh Parmar's phone conversations.) Those hopes intensified on May 1, 2006, when Prime Minister Stephen Harper announced the Commission of Inquiry into the Investigation of the Bombing of Air India Flight 182. The news was welcomed not just by the families of the victims and the Canadian Sikh community, but by all Canadians who wanted to know the truth behind the nation's largest mass murder. A definitive finding would at last hang the blame squarely on those responsible. The associative guilt — the collective responsibility — that was our cross to bear could finally be cast aside.

The inquiry, commonly known as the Major Commission (after retired Supreme Court Justice John Major, the judge appointed to oversee it), began its work in June 2006. More than 200 witnesses were summoned and over 17,000 classified materials examined. When the final report was completed in 2010, it ran to 3,200 pages (4,400 if you count the academic studies referenced). Sikh Canadians were naturally interested in having our voice heard as part of this important conversation. As soon as the commission was underway, we applied for, and were granted, intervenor status. I was designated to represent the World Sikh Organization of Canada.

Although its mandate was broad — from identifying how Canada's laws could be amended to thwart terror-group funding to understanding what kind of witness protection should be in place for those called to testify — the Major Commission was primarily focused on determining what had gone wrong in the investigation. Much of this was already known: inter-agency squabbling between the RCMP and CSIS and the latter's evidence protocols. (CSIS erased 325 wiretap tapes after they were transcribed, thereby rendering their probative value useless.) There were a lot of snafus.

Sikhs were less interested in procedural failures, though, and more driven to learn the identification of the suspects. The only way the community could be fully cleared, we believed, was to ensure that the parties who were responsible — all of them — were brought to justice.

Early in the investigation it was decided that Talwinder Singh Parmar and his Babbar Khalsa cohort had masterminded and executed the plot. The conclusion was not baseless; it was likely that Parmar was involved in some capacity. CSIS was on him before the bombings ever happened. He'd been tailed to Vancouver Island, where he met with Inderjit Singh Reyat and another Sikh man who was never identified. They went into the woods, and a sound, described by the CSIS agents who were shadowing Parmar as a "single gunshot," was heard. Much later, RCMP found in this area a blasting cap for an explosive device — likely procured by Reyat, who had earlier purchased explosives to "clear some trees."

There was other evidence, too: several cryptic, coded phone calls made by Parmar (one could have been the actual order to buy a ticket for the doomed flight); the very strange case of Surjan Singh Gill, a Babbar Khalsa higher-up and the self-proclaimed Vancouver-based "Consul General of Khalistan," who inexplicably left the organization a few days before June 23, 1985, possibly because he knew what was about to transpire and wanted to distance himself from the act.

And then there was yet another line of inquiry that implicated the government of India in complicity at the very least.

As mentioned earlier, this was not a crackpot theory advanced only by Sikhs desperate to throw the yoke of suspicion off their own community and place it around the neck of the Indian government. Rather, it was a view that had gained currency even within some corners of CSIS; there was a growing suspicion that Indian officials were not forthcoming about all they knew. Did they see the tragedy looming and choose to avert their eyes? Had the destruction of Air India 182 been preventable?

This was part of our mandate in appearing before the Major Commission. We wanted to expand the scope of thinking (and the list of suspects). This would not be easy. But I had been given an opportunity to speak directly to the commission, and I was not about to waste it. I prepared with great determination.

I was scheduled to appear in early December 2008. To this end, I'd prepared a very detailed "will-say" statement (a précis of what areas I wanted to go into). In late November we struck a deal with the counsel for the inquiry, Anil Kapoor, agreeing that I would be given latitude to present oral testimony "without conditions," albeit within reason. (We had already agreed that a few areas outlined in my testimony would fall beyond the scope of the commission's mandate, but that I would be able to raise all the other points I wanted to make.) I was eventually assigned a slot: Friday afternoon on December 7, 2007, the anniversary of the Pearl Harbor attack. Because it covered a fair amount of ground, my testimony would likely take at least an hour.

In preparing, I'd come across a letter dated February 10, 1988, that I'd received from then solicitor general James Kelleher. In it, Kelleher addressed my concerns about two CSIS officers who had sworn false affidavits during the course of the Air India investigation. I would use this in my testimony, since it spoke to the integrity of the security service. The morning I was to testify, our lawyer handed Anil Kapoor a copy. Kapoor seemed very concerned as to how I would use it in my testimony. But what could he do? I was scheduled to take the stand later that day.

I was called in the early afternoon. I began by briefly outlining the history of Sikhs in Canada, how Sikh religious and cultural traditions were antithetical to violence, and how harmful acts were sanctioned by, at most, maybe two to three dozen people in a community that numbered well over 200,000. I was going to talk about how support for a separate state was not to be conflated with support for terror. I was going to add that the Sikhs in Canada had been subject to threats, harassment, and intimidation from a variety of actors, including Canada's own security agencies. I certainly would have advocated that the inquiry hear from MP David Kilgour and the *Globe and Mail's* Zuhair Kashmeri, both of whom believed that India knew a lot more about what had transpired than it claimed.[28]

I would have done all this and more. But I did not. I was cut off 10 minutes into my testimony — 10 minutes of airtime for several hundred thousand Sikh voices that had been struggling to be heard for over 20 years. We protested, but to no avail. I knew then that the Major Commission would add nothing of value to the discourse. It would not ease the grief of the families of the Air India victims. And it certainly would not ease the suffering of the Sikh community.

In the end, Canadians learned very little that was not previously known. The commission had been neutered from the start. "None of the Terms of Reference calls for an inquiry into the issue of who was responsible for the bombing of Air India Flight 182" was the official line. After 25 years, the government of Canada had come up empty. The Major Commission was, it seemed to me, simply relieved to wash its hands of the whole terrible mess. There would be no justice.

In all, three people were eventually charged in connection with the Air India bombing. After a 19-month trial, Ajaib Singh Bagri and Ripudaman Singh Malik were acquitted of 329 counts of murder due to lack of evidence and, according to Judge Ian Josephson, credibility issues with Crown witnesses. (Although never proved to be connected to the Air India trial, two potential witnesses, Tara Singh Hayer and Tarsem Singh Purewal, editor of the U.K.–based Punjabi-language newspaper *Des Pardes*, were both murdered before the trial got underway.)

Upon receiving a nominal fine for possession of explosives and an unregistered firearm, Inderjit Singh Reyat, the only person ever to go to jail in connection with the bombing, moved to England in 1988. After new evidence surfaced linking him to the Narita explosion, he was extradited to Canada in 1991 to face manslaughter charges. Reyat was found guilty and sentenced to 10 years in jail. In 2003 he received an additional five years after he pleaded guilty to manslaughter in advance of the Bagri–Malik trial, thereby avoiding being charged as a co-conspirator in 329 murders. Reyat was expected to provide damning testimony during the Air India trial, but he was intentionally evasive, earning an additional nine years for perjury. Released two years early, in February 2017, Reyat is now a free man.

Surjan Singh Gill left Canada for Britain shortly after the bombing. He has never been heard from again.[29] Talwinder Singh Parmar, the alleged ringleader of the plot, fled Canada for India, where in 1992 he was killed in police custody. And John C. Major, having risen to national prominence through the commission that bears his name, returned to practise law at the Calgary firm where he worked before his appointment to the Supreme Court of Canada.

Today, more than three decades after the tragedy, the identity of those who committed the bombing of Air India Flight 182 remains a mystery — a wound that never heals.

CHAPTER 7

ET TU, CANADA? ATTACKS FROM WITHIN

IT WAS A Friday afternoon in June 1986. I was sitting in a hotel room.

For some very good reasons, I would rather not have been there. The room was okay: clean and functional, but far from luxurious. It was the kind of room you wind up in when business takes you out of town for a few days, somewhere to drop your bags and sleep. But in this room, which still carried the smell of stale tobacco, I would not sleep.

On the desk next to me was a machine I'd never seen outside of the odd television crime drama. "Okay, do you mind rolling up your sleeve?" asked the polygraph technician. He was in his mid-30s with short slicked-back hair, dressed in civilian clothes. There was a second man as well. Older, also in plain clothes, he was a member of the RCMP unit that was investigating the bombing of Air India 182. His authority was his badge: he had a gruffness to him, a dismissive quality likely cultivated to intimidate. Our eyes met. After what seemed like minutes, he finally averted his gaze.

As gently as possible, the technician attached electrodes to various parts of my body and snugged up a blood pressure cuff on my upper right arm. He then tightened two rubber tubes, one around my upper chest and the other around my abdomen. I became acutely aware of my breath. Too fast? Too slow? Too deep or shallow? In and out. In and out. Finally, more electrodes were placed on two of my fingers.

"There," he said, smiling. "Please make yourself comfortable." Was he serious?

I had nothing to hide, yet my heart pounded. In the room next to this one were two more RCMP. Two rooms. Four officers. For what? I was being recorded, I assumed. In fairness, this location had been my choice. The alternative — undergoing a lie detector test at RCMP headquarters in Burnaby — had been out of the question. If I was seen there, the natural assumption would be that I was an informant conspiring with the RCMP against my own people, or a suspect in the worst mass murder in Canadian history.

I shifted uncomfortably in my chair. Quietly, as if to myself, I recited the Mool Mantar, the opening verse in Sikh scripture: *Ik onkaar satnaam kartaa purkh nirbhau nirvair … One Universal Creator God, God's name is truth. Creative being personified. No fear, no hatred …*

Almost immediately the verse calmed me. The technician played with the machine for a while longer. I assumed he was calibrating it. After finishing, he smiled and sat down beside me. Then, the other officer uncrossed his arms and pulled up a chair. "Okay, let's get started," he said.

"Right," I said.

"Remember: answer all questions truthfully."

"Okay."

"And only 'yes' or 'no.' Got it?"

"Yes."

"Okay then," he said. "Is your name Gian Singh Sandhu?"

A barrage of questions ensued. What was my involvement with the WSO? Why had I become involved? When? Did I know of Babbar Khalsa? How much did I know about them? What kind of contact did the WSO have with them? With the ISYF? So many questions. So much nonsense to dispel.

That I was here at all, in a Burnaby hotel room wired up like an angiogram patient, was testament to two things. First, my poor judgment: no one should ever feel compelled to take a polygraph test. The test is not infallible — just one of many reasons not to indulge the RCMP when they come asking for your "consideration." But questions of poor judgment aside, there was a second reason I had chosen to go through with a lie detector test despite my reservations.

I was there to dispel the suspicion that still hung over the World Sikh Organization of Canada. Like a common criminal, I was here to "cooperate with the authorities." I was tired of men in uniforms dropping by my office in Williams Lake for "a quick chat," of plainclothes officers sitting in unmarked cars at the end of the driveway, waiting and watching. Like so many Canadian Sikhs, I was tired of being treated like an enemy of the state.

My conscience, that ever-present companion, was clear. Truth was on my side. And so, I was here to clear the name of the WSO.

OFFICERS AT THE DOOR

The "visits" began almost immediately after June 23, 1985, with first contact made by two Vancouver-based RCMP Air India investigators. Oddly, I had met one of them a few years before. Although he didn't wear a turban, I knew he was Sikh, a rarity on the force in those days. He had worked on a tragic case involving one of my relatives, a young fellow from Vancouver who, while waiting at a Richmond bus stop after a Christmas party, had been picked up and murdered by bikers in the early 1970s.

The officer's first name was Manjit, but everyone called him "Sandy" — his surname was Sandhu, the same as mine. A small irony, and a reminder that the community, for all its sprawling diversity, is traceable to very specific and commonly held roots.

It was the first of many visits by both security forces. Usually they would call ahead before dropping by my place of work. The CSIS guys were always very courteous. For the most part the RCMP were too, but because of their training — "good cop, bad cop" was often the way they operated — there was a little more edge to their questions.

The differences in approach may lie in the way the two organizations were structured: CSIS is a civilian force, born around the same time as the WSO and staffed mainly by bright young university grads; the RCMP task force guys were drawn from the ranks of criminal investigators. That the two services came from very different perspectives contributed to the lack of cooperation between them, which in turn may have been responsible for fatal missteps in the Air India 182 investigation — an investigation many in the Sikh community feel was woefully incomplete.

In having little choice about entertaining the security forces of our adopted homeland, I was hardly alone. After Air India, this scene played out in Sikh homes and in almost all the gurdwaras across Canada. Most often singled out for special treatment were those of us who had chosen to adhere closely to the requirements of our religion — in other words, practising Sikhs who were easily identifiable by their turbans and beards.

Representatives from the RCMP and CSIS were not shy about simply coming by and peppering anyone with questions. Their interest quickly grew to feel like a form of harassment. And it was intimidating, especially to those newcomers who had never had contact with our country's police services. (In my hometown of Williams Lake, for example, Surinder Singh Dhoot, president of the Western Singh Sabha Association, a local gurdwara, was interviewed twice. In my opinion the second meeting was overkill designed to intimidate. Unfortunately, this was hardly a rare occurrence; we fielded several similar complaints from gurdwara presidents across Canada.)

It seemed that, in the eyes of the Canadian security forces, all Sikhs were guilty — collectively and individually — until proven innocent. Because of this perception, lives were altered in ways that ranged from small to significant. I know of one young woman from Prince George, Manjit Kaur, who wanted to join the RCMP. She jumped through every hoop with ease, passing all the examinations.

After a final four-hour interview, she was assured that she was in. But that assessment was premature. Manjit was denied a spot on the force — apparently because her father-in-law's sister was married to a brother of the spokesman for the International Sikh Youth Federation.

A minor incident, perhaps, but one that unfairly affected the life of a potential young recruit. Considering how few Sikh women there are in the RCMP, she might have been a significant asset to Canada's national police force. We'll never know, and the refusal haunts her to this day. "I still carry that burden," she recently told me.

A more egregious example of the impact that official police interference had on the lives of Sikh Canadians was the case of Balbir Singh, a Punjabi Sikh whose brother, Tejinder Singh Kaloe of Hamilton, Ontario, had been the subject of a 1986 Canadian investigation. Kaloe was charged (and eventually acquitted) of conspiracy to commit sabotage in India. The charges stemmed from hours of taped conversations, some of them between the brothers. According to *Soft Target,* the connection between the RCMP and the Indian government may have been fatal to Balbir Singh: "On July 2, two weeks after his brother was arrested and charged in Canada, Balbir Singh was shot and killed in Punjab," the authors write. The official line? He'd died during a gunfight with "the bodyguards of a local politician."

But the death was suspicious, as was the timing. Had information provided by the RCMP led to an extrajudicial killing in India? Michael Code, the lawyer for Kaloe, approached the Department of External Affairs and raised the possibility that Balbir Singh's death could have been connected to the information-sharing protocols between the RCMP and Indian agencies. He also requested that the Canadian embassy in New Delhi look into what had happened. Joe Clark, Minister of External Affairs, responded. It was, he said, an Indian affair. (Later, when it was revealed that the condition of Singh's corpse indicated he may have been tortured, Code said that the Department of External Affairs "sloughed it off.")

Politics followed us around the world. On October 21, 2003, Bhupinder Singh Liddar was appointed Canada's first consul general to the newly established office in Chandigarh, Punjab. The Kenya-born Sikh had worked as a research assistant on Parliament Hill since 1976, and he expected questions around his appointment to arise. Sure enough, on November 3 Joe Clark questioned the posting in the House of Commons, and the following January CSIS denied Liddar security clearance. He challenged the decision, and after a two-year hearing process, received the clearance necessary for his job as Head of Mission. In a public statement, Foreign Affairs Minister Pierre Pettigrew apologized to Liddar and a Security Intelligence and Review Committee report criticized CSIS for "purposefully" misleading an inquiry into Liddar's case and for drafting a "fundamentally flawed and biased" report halting a diplomatic appointment. Liddar was ultimately appointed and served as Canada's Deputy Permanent Representative to the UN Environment Programme, based out of the Canadian High Commission in Nairobi, from January 2006 to July 2009.

These are only three of many instances where Canada's security agencies overstepped their own lines. Across the nation, people were harassed and questioned; phones were wiretapped. Sometimes, wiretap warrants were granted on the flimsiest of pretences — or, in certain cases, abetted by fraudulently submitted information. In 1987, Thomas D'Arcy "Ted" Finn, the first director of CSIS, paid the price for this pattern of behaviour. He was forced to step down after it was revealed that affidavits filed in support of wiretapping warrants granted in the investigation of an assassination attempt on a visiting Indian politician contained numerous falsehoods and errors.

Within the Sikh community, the feeling was that this investigation had taken on elements of a witch hunt. The times themselves added to our troubles. Even if Air India had never happened, it was a difficult period for anyone with a beard and a turban. And in the new Canada, the one I fell in love with, there were more beards and turbans than ever before, a result of policy changes that had their genesis in the ironically titled "White Paper on Immigration" of 1966. The new Canada was to be multicultural, inclusive, a land where abilities mattered more than skin colour. But this was a seismic shift and so, while the surface changes were dramatic and immediate, the subterranean effects rumbled on for a long time. The shift spawned resentment and occasionally violence, as well as an entire comedy genre: although it seems inconceivable today, "Paki jokes" were shared widely and told even in polite company.

NO MATTER HOW HARD WE TRIED

At the heart of Canada's response to Air India was the minister responsible for External Affairs. Charles Joseph Clark was born on June 5, 1939, in High River, Alberta, about 65 kilometres south of Calgary. As a young man he was drawn to journalism — his father was publisher of the local *High River Times* — but soon after entering the University of Alberta in Edmonton, he discovered his true calling, eventually becoming president of the Young Progressive Conservatives. It proved to be a springboard to a serious political career, first as a behind-the-scenes advisor to long-time PC leader Robert Stanfield, then as an MP, and eventually as leader of the Progressive Conservative Party. In June 1979, at the age of 39, Clark became the youngest-ever prime minister of Canada.

It was a brief reign: Clark's minority government famously came to an end about nine months after it assumed power when, due to the Conservatives' inability to compromise with members of the centre-right Social Credit Party, a vote of non-confidence was called. With three of his own MPs not available for the motion, Clark's government was defeated.

But Clark's political story was not over. In September 1984, the Progressive Conservatives, now with Brian Mulroney as their leader, swept back into office. In this new government, born mere weeks after the events at Amritsar, Clark was named Secretary of State for External Affairs.

One of Clark's first official acts, in early November 1984, was to represent Canada at Indira Gandhi's funeral. While there, he was briefed extensively by Congress officials on the situation in Punjab, and gravely warned about the actions of "Sikh extremists" in Canada. India was in mourning, nerves were frayed, emotions were redlining — it would have taken a special kind of statesman to not be affected by such a scenario, and Clark was not that statesman.

While Clark was being feted, carnage was rampant, as we have seen. Throughout India Sikh men were run down and "necklaced" and women were gang-raped, sometimes by up to 20 men. Clark said nothing — not a single word — about the roughly 3,000 innocent Sikhs slaughtered in Delhi alone during the time of his visit. This just confirmed his limitations. And by extension, perhaps, his regard — or disregard — for Sikhs generally.

From where we sat, it seemed that Clark swallowed the official Indian lies whole. With Indira Gandhi's death, we felt that his sympathies had been aroused and, convinced of the righteousness of the Indian government's case against Canada's own Sikh citizens, he was exhibiting an eagerness to entertain with utter seriousness almost any memo issued by India's High Commission, no matter how fatuous. After June 23, 1985, this became only too apparent.

Less than a week after the Air India disaster, External Affairs presented a prime ministerial brief on "Sikh extremism." The backgrounder provided an overview of the core issues that had roiled Punjab, and identified domestic Canadian Sikh groups that had been singled out for their "violent potential." To be fair, there were violent elements within the Canadian Sikh community: the case of Inderjit Singh Reyat, whose involvement in both the Narita and Air India bombings would eventually be borne out by his own testimony; the near-fatal ISYF attack in spring 1986 on a visiting Indian cabinet minister, on Vancouver Island;[30] and the brutal February 1985 beating of Ujjal Dosanjh all clearly speak to this. Considering the climate in the immediate wake of the Air India disaster, it would have been close to irresponsible for External Affairs to not try and draw a bead on potentially violent Sikh groups.

But not at the expense of the truth. In the brief, WSO Canada was described as "a lobby group [created] to appeal for support in democratic countries for Sikh independence and function[ing] as an international umbrella organization which aspires to represent the interests of various Sikh groups throughout the world." Fine — if a little wordy. But then the characterization took a sinister and entirely fallacious turn: "While the WSO is ostensibly a nonviolent organization, its membership includes several radical Sikh factions. One of its executives, Jaswant Singh Bhullar, has endorsed guerrilla war."

What? This was news to us — as it was, no doubt, to Bhullar, who had never advocated guerrilla war. But this was just the kicker; lies and innuendo riddled the whole description. The WSO wasn't "ostensibly" nonviolent; we were and are nonviolent. And which "radical Sikh factions" did the WSO supposedly include? If by radical, External Affairs meant that the WSO included members who were dedicated to the peaceful establishment of a Sikh homeland in Punjab, then by all means, the entire organization and its membership were radical. It's not like we hid our support for an independent Khalistan. It's in the WSO International charter.

We had come out for Khalistan, and in no uncertain terms. We were also explicit in saying that, should Khalistan come to pass, the WSO would support only a peaceful transition to independence. Unfortunately, we failed to clearly articulate what, exactly, Khalistan would look like if and when it was achieved.

Part of the problem was the term itself. Coined in the early 1970s, "Khalistan" took hold of the Sikh imagination, but in a way that had very little to do with the kind of state many wanted. A more apt name would have been azad Punjab ("independent Punjab"), a term that encapsulated two important concepts: that Punjab would have autonomy, and that it would be a territory based on a region, traditions, and language, not solely on faith or ethnicity. (As noted earlier, there was historical precedent, too. Azad Punjab was the territory name chosen by the Sikh All Party Committee when they presented their demands for independence to British parliamentarian Stafford Cripps, who'd been sent to secure Hindu and Muslim cooperation in the Second World War in exchange for independence after the war.)

The concept of azad Punjab harkened back to the early 18th century and Maharaja Ranjit Singh, the last real emperor of independent Punjab. This cosmopolitan Punjab society and government, with its mix of Sikhs, Hindus, Muslims, and even a few Europeans (and atheists!), enshrined gender equality, freedom of religion and the promise of economic advancement. The literacy rate among women and girls was almost universal. In Ranjit Singh's Punjab, people were no longer subject to the perils of state oppression and the cycles of violence that had marked previous decades.

This was the ideal upon which we sought to model Khalistan, and which we should have set out more explicitly. I may be biased, but to me the closest model to the ideal of Khalistan — or azad Punjab, rather — is Canada, a place where inclusiveness and freedom of thought, expression, association, and religion are enshrined in practice and law.

In this way, the kind of manoeuvring orchestrated by Joe Clark directly contravened all that Canada stood for. Buried in Clark's backgrounder, something ominous was at play. Even at this early date, immediately after the Air India tragedy, it was clear that under Joe Clark's leadership, External Affairs had begun conflating support for Khalistan with extremism — and, by implication, with an embrace of violence and terror.

This was hardly a surprise. It had become obvious that in its dealings with Canadian Sikhs the department was relying heavily on reports generated from Indian sources. This coziness led to directives coming, often as not, straight from the top. On April 1, 1987, in a signed letter marked SECRET, Clark urged Benoît Bouchard, Minister of Immigration, to reject the refugee status application of Punjabi Sikh claimant Santokh Singh Bagga, based on "information received from the Indian High Commission." This "information" implicated Bagga in an alleged assassination attempt on Rajiv Gandhi (later found to be false, with Bagga being allowed to stay in Canada).

Two months later Clark was at it again. Since the events of 1984–85, human rights abuses in Punjab had swelled to such a degree that Sikhs with the means to do so joined an exodus for countries willing to grant refugee status. Germany took 10,000, the United States 8,000, tiny Belgium 5,000, and France 4,000. Canada accepted 6,000, prompting the Secretary of State for External Affairs to ask his immigration minister to slow the flood. Specifically, Clark asked Bouchard to reconsider the refugee status of several Sikhs who had been granted entry by the ostensibly independent Immigration Appeal Board: "I found it most disconcerting to learn that a number of Indian Sikhs were recently recognized as refugees," Clark wrote. "Of considerable embarrassment is the fact that information on these decisions was initially received by my department from the Indian government."

There were many other cases of interference by External Affairs. The initiative by the Federation of Sikh Societies of Canada and Sikh Canadian students to launch a Sikh Studies chair at the University of British Columbia was opposed by Clark's department on the grounds that it could offend India. Clark himself intervened, opining that since Hindus were the dominant group in India, any chair created by UBC should reflect this. But the Sikh community in B.C. was much larger, and had a far more extensive history, than the Hindus, and the funds to establish the chair had come from Canadian Sikhs. (After a flurry of negative press coverage, External Affairs was forced to back down. But not before they managed to help change the name of the chair from Sikh Studies to Punjabi Studies.)

Efforts by the WSO Canada to press our case directly to External Affairs — to be heard by Clark — initially went nowhere. According to *Soft Target,* in a particularly frank disclosure Clark's press secretary, Bill Chambers, admitted that the attempt was futile. "Canadian Sikhs are not going to get a meeting with External Affairs Minister Joe Clark, no matter how hard they try," he told the *Kamloops News* in December 1986.

This attitude was not confined to Clark's department. On occasion, the Canadian government's attempt to influence the Sikh community took on an almost comical air. One of the more ludicrous attempts was the creation of the National Alliance of Canadian Sikhs, or Sikh Congress. Overseen by Multiculturalism Minister Gerry Weiner, who helped fund the project with a $130,000 grant, the Congress was a transparent attempt to create out of whole cloth a pliant, government-directed counterbalance to the WSO Canada, likely to appease India. Not surprisingly, it failed miserably. Did the Mulroney government actually think that, by establishing and funding a group so clearly out of touch with the real interests of the Sikh community, it could mute our legitimate voices?

In February 1986 we faced an especially low blow. In a memo to the RCMP and CSIS, H.G. Pardy, director of External Affairs' South and Southeast Asia division, uncritically forwarded a letter purportedly circulated by the WSO Canada. This letter stated that a hit squad had been assembled to assassinate Rajiv Gandhi within four months, with approval of Lakhbir Singh Rode, leader of the ISYF, along with Talwinder Singh Parmar from Babbar Khalsa, and Gian Singh Sandhu of WSO Canada.

The letter was unsigned and not issued on WSO Canada letterhead. Instead, it was marked with an odd circular stamp containing the words "World Sikh Organization of Canada." This was not a logo we'd ever used. The letter was beyond bogus. Nobody within CSIS or the RCMP took the threat seriously. But External Affairs apparently did. And they seemed intent on making it as hard as possible for the WSO, or indeed any legitimate representative of Canadian Sikhs, to press our case to those in power.

Conducting advocacy work became increasingly challenging for WSO Canada. Meetings were often canceled, sometimes at the last minute. People we'd known and worked with for years were suddenly unavailable. We were being shut out. How completely would soon become evident.

JOE CLARK'S NO GOOD, VERY BAD DAY

Despite the stonewalling and interference, we at the WSO Canada knew that External Affairs wasn't the only game in town. As a classic advocacy group we existed to press our case to influencers, whether in government, media, or the private sector. Since Air India, much of the focus of that advocacy had changed. On the defensive as an organization and a community, we were now effectively fighting on two fronts: mounting rear-guard actions to counteract the negative stereotypes and outright lies being spread about us, and continuing to move the WSO and its causes forward in a positive way.

Since 1986, holding community dinners had been a WSO Canada tradition, allowing politicians and others to experience the community firsthand. In February 1988, one of the first of the year was scheduled to take place in Winnipeg. The guest of honour was Manitoba's NDP premier, the late Howard Pawley. As with any WSO Canada dinner, there was a lavish vegetarian spread. (It's not widely known, but devout Sikhs do not generally eat meat. Yet with everything from pakoras to puri on the menu, we've found that even the most avowed carnivores can find more than enough to stuff themselves!)

It was part of my duties as president of the World Sikh Organization of Canada to attend these functions. And I looked forward to them. They gave us the opportunity to interact with key players in a relaxed, non-pressure-cooker environment. I found these dinners to be a much more effective forum than, say, sitting across the desk in a ministerial office.

The banquet hall buzzed with anticipation. But Pawley was late. The minutes ticked by; a half-hour passed. Where was he? The WSO Canada officials, myself included, paced nervously, occasionally looking at our watches. Someone placed a call to Pawley's office, but it was after normal business hours in the age before mobile phones, and there was no response. A second half-hour passed. It became clear that Premier Pawley and fellow politician Gary Doer, who'd also agreed to attend, were not going to show. But why?

By the time dinner was served we knew. Earlier one of our local representatives, Kabal Singh, had sought me out. In his hand was a letter that he'd managed to get through Manitoba Legislature back channels. The letter was dated December 7, 1987, several weeks earlier:

Dear Premier Pawley,

I am writing to you concerning possible invitations to you or members of your government to attend functions organized by members of the Sikh community. The majority of these invitations are valuable in ensuring that your government is kept informed of developments in the Sikh community and that the community is encouraged to participate fully in Canadian life.

There are, however, three Sikh organizations which exist largely to advocate the creation of an independent Sikh state, known as "Khalistan." These three organizations are the Babbar Khalsa, the International Sikh Youth Federation (ISYF), and the World Sikh Organization. Some members of these organizations have also engaged in or promote violent activities aimed at Indian interests in Canada and elsewhere. The activities of these organizations have been a significant irritant in our relations with India. The government of India has taken particular exception when elected officials attend functions sponsored by these organizations ...

I would appreciate your cooperation in avoiding events and activities which could be perceived as supporting the Sikh organizations mentioned above or their objective in the creation of an independent Sikh state.

The letter, issued on his official letterhead, was marked SECRET and signed Joe Clark.

Pawley was not the only recipient. In all, it was sent to seven premiers across Canada — in every province that had any substantial Sikh population. So you can probably imagine our surprise when the next day Gary Doer walked through the doors of the Winnipeg gurdwara where the WSO Canada executive was meeting.

A man of enormous integrity, Doer apologized for not attending the previous night; further, he also expressed regret over the "circumstances" that led to his decision, implying that he was a victim of political pressure exerted by Clark and Pawley. But Doer did more than apologize. He vowed to bring the matter up with his NDP caucus and press our case to his fellow "Dippers." He was, as always, true to his word. (Most Manitobans would agree: in 1999, Doer became premier of the province, then won re-election twice.)

But the impact of the letter was inarguable. Forget about Indian travel bans and capricious visa denials by clumsy foreign agents. This hit close to home, from home. In a clandestine manner, the External Affairs department of our own government was now compiling a blacklist. The WSO Canada was the only legitimately mainstream representative of the Sikh community, with about 22,000 members, representing around 70 percent of Sikh Canadians (including associated gurdwaras), and we were on that list.

As soon as we heard about the letter, we knew we had to challenge it — to get it out there and use it against External Affairs before our access to the heads of seven provinces was cut off. But how? We decided to go to the media.

After June 23, 1985, the mainstream media had hardly been a friend to Canadian Sikhs. In my home province of British Columbia, our two newspapers of record, the *Province* and the *Vancouver Sun*, were (and still are) owned by the same publisher. At their best, they took pains to frame internal Sikh conflicts for what they were: power struggles over the financial control of some gurdwaras, notably Vancouver's massive 19,000-member Ross Street gurdwara, North America's largest. But juxtaposed against these articles were tales of "moderates" fighting pitched battles against the violent reactionary forces of the "fundamentalist" and "extremist" factions that wanted to reshape the entire community in some 17th-century mould. The "moderates" were clean shaven and "modern," just like Bollywood film stars, representing for non-Sikh Canadians a palatable (if soon to be dated) paradigm: the "assimilated other." The "extremists"? Well, frankly, they all looked the same. Bearded, turbaned, foreign, darkly dangerous. Exactly like me.

Although much of the coverage of internecine battles like the Ross Street power struggles had been slanted, there's no doubt that the community at times behaved stupidly, childishly, violently. This did the image of Sikhs in Canada no favours. But even when we were openly opposed to groups that truly existed on the fringe, our media-assigned role as a reactionary organization in this "moderate vs. fundamentalist" canard was difficult to shake.

The national print media was more balanced, with the *Globe and Mail* being perhaps the most meticulous chronicler of Canadian Sikhs post–Air India. The CBC, Canada's national broadcaster, also produced some excellent work; in particular, a 30-minute segment airing on the television newsmagazine *Pacific Report* delved deeply into Indian propaganda, as well as the intimidation tactics used in Canada by its consul general. But the tenor of CBC's coverage shifted over time, to the point that some reporters built stories without allowing parties an opportunity to respond to accusations against them, myself included.

Particularly disturbing was an emerging motif in stories conflating support for an independent Khalistan with the pejorative catch-all "extremist." The nightly news wasn't the only place this was happening. Many non-Sikhs seemed to regard support for an independent Sikh nation as a classic ipso facto: "If one is for Khalistan, then one is necessarily an extremist," a logical fallacy that often went unchecked and inflicted enormous damage on our community and our cause.

This association of Sikhs with extremists was ridiculous and would never be tolerated in any similar situation. Was everyone who voted for the Parti Québécois an "extremist"? If they threw their support behind the Bloc were they secretly simpatico with the methods employed by the FLQ? Because they longed for the same ends, were the hands of millions of law-abiding citizens in la belle province automatically stained by the blood of Pierre Laporte?[31]

Clear and obvious parallels drawn from their own country's recent history were staring these reporters square in the face, yet they remained blinded by their own preconceptions and facile categorizations. (The Sikh community locked horns in a courtroom with some news outlets and reporters, winning some battles, abandoning others. WSO Canada launched a lawsuit for libel against CBC over the report *Samosa Politics*, which, in our opinion and based on sound legal advice, was libelous. After spending about $200,000 pursuing the case against the deep-pocketed national broadcaster, the organization decided the cost was becoming prohibitive and we mutually agreed to drop the case.)

So by 1988, the Sikh community had what we would call a rather complex relationship with the media. But we were not blind to their uses. Just three days after the dinner fiasco, we ensured that the "SECRET" letter Joe Clark had sent to the premiers was not so secret anymore.

When the media came calling, I pulled no punches, calling Clark's manipulations "a direct violation of the Canadian Charter of Rights and Freedoms." The allegation that members of the WSO Canada had engaged in violence was particularly galling. What evidence did Clark have? If he was in possession of such damning information, he had a duty to reveal it.

Clark's case was bogus. I issued a challenge to that effect. "If any one of us in the WSO is guilty of something, go ahead and charge them. But don't accuse the entire organization," I told the *Globe and Mail*. I went further, pledging that if there was evidence to the contrary, "I will resign. But if Mr. Clark cannot prove it, let him resign." This was not simply a case of me sticking up for the WSO. Our right to free speech was under attack. Our right to advocate for the peaceful separation of Punjab from India. Our right to be ourselves.

That Clark was simply doing India's bidding was recognized by other ethnic organizations as well, and everyone from Croatians to Italians rushed to our defence. Most editorials across the country came down on our side. "Clark needs to be reminded that Canadians are free to go wherever they want and associate with whomsoever they like, without interference from authorities, as long as they do not break the law," fumed the *Windsor Star* in an editorial titled "Joe Clark: Speaking for Gandhi?"

The Opposition was ramping up for attack. Liberal leader John

Turner called the letter a slur on the Canadian Sikh community. MPs Sergio Marchi and Robert Kaplan, who both hailed from ethnic communities and likely felt empathy for us in response to Clark's slights, attacked him in Parliament. Watching it all unfold was moving. We had been knocked so far off balance in the months after Air India, our outreach had been so painstakingly slow, our public image so stained by cowardly allegations and the racism of the day — to finally see umbrage stoked on our behalf was exhilarating.

As the story progressed, we found out who our true friends were. There were those who opposed us — David Peterson, the Liberal Ontario premier, indicated he'd acquiesce to Clark's request (though he later reversed his decision) — and those who supported us by dismissing the letter out of hand, notably Alberta's Don Getty and Bill Vander Zalm in British Columbia. In defending himself, Clark stumbled badly. He acknowledged that the WSO charter sought to establish Khalistan through nonviolent means. But, he added, the WSO's "objectives are incompatible with Canadian policy."

As February turned into March, the battle shifted to Parliament. On March 10, a landmark day for Sikhs in Canada, our case took up the majority of the business of Parliament. Sergio Marchi, MP for York West, moved that "the Government provide Parliament with all relevant information that led to its aforementioned communication with the Provinces and provide the Canadian Sikh community with a full, public opportunity to defend its honour and integrity." Marchi also insisted the government issue a full apology to Canadian Sikhs, and indeed to all Canadians.

That was just the beginning. Clark was also attacked by everyone from British Columbia MP Nelson Riis, one of the more visible long-time NDP representatives, to David Kilgour and Alex Kindy, who at the time were Progressive Conservative MPs in Brian Mulroney's government. Clark was on notice.

We were overjoyed. Never before had our concerns been so front and centre in the nation's political chambers. We were no longer a bunch of bearded ethnic guys to be talked down to and discarded.

We were a community of 250,000 Canadians with divergent views and aspirations, but also with many shared dreams — and now, an inkling of what could be done when we mobilized effectively. It was a turning point: in a sense, it signaled our political awakening. And in a roundabout way, we had Joe Clark to thank for it.

By the middle of May 1988, pummeled from the Opposition benches, Clark had had enough. In response to a letter sent by Liberal MP Herb Gray, he wrote that he believed the World Sikh Organization of Canada was "committed to peace and non-violence." But it was, he reiterated, still his wish that others distance themselves from us. His political boss, Brian Mulroney, did not grant it. In a letter to the WSO Canada around the same time, he wrote:

> As Prime Minister of Canada, I am delighted to extend my warmest greetings and sincere best wishes to the members of the World Sikh Organization of Canada.
>
> The Sikh community in Canada represents an important component of this country's multicultural structure, one which we, as Canadians, are proud of. Ours is a nation that has been strengthened by the cultural and ethnic diversity of its peoples. By celebrating your role in Canadian society you are helping to unite not only the people of your community, but the people of Canada as well.
>
> On behalf of the Government of Canada, may I wish the members of your community continued health and prosperity.

By the late 1980s, partly as a result of our "trials by fire," we were becoming more politically astute. Our banquet format — education wrapped in naan with a side dish of ethnic politics — was gaining traction, and politicians of all parties were now clamouring to hear our concerns and give voice to our perspectives. Our June 22, 1990 dinner in Calgary was a landmark, attracting all the federal Liberal leadership candidates (except Paul Martin), each jostling for a spot to speak at the dinner.

Jean Chretien, Sheila Copps, John Nunziata, and Tom Wappel

— the Liberal Party "A-team" at the time — all took turns wooing attendees. In my capacity as president of WSO International I was also invited to speak. It was, I must say, a rather surreal experience. Years before, we likely would have been shunned. Now, seated before me were some of the nation's highest-profile MPs, all of whom would figure in a future cabinet, and to a man (or in Ms. Copps' case, a woman) they were lobbying me to describe them as "friends of the Sikh community" in my speech.

We had come a long way since I had felt compelled to take that lie detector test.

PART III

A PARALLEL TACK

(1995–)

CHAPTER 8

OF TURBANS AND TURNING POINTS

AT FIRST GLANCE, most eyes probably fixed on the familiar: the red serge jacket, the midnight blue jodhpurs with the classic yellow stripe. From any distance, the ensemble was instantly recognizable as the dress uniform of the Royal Canadian Mounted Police. But there was more to this colourful calendar, sold mainly in Winnipeg bars, than what initially greeted the eye.

Against all contemporary expectations, this cop was bearded, and that beard was long and luxuriant — very "Founding Fathers," or so some must have thought. On his feet were oversized, effete golden shoes, the toes curled into crescent moons. He carried a sword. Perhaps most jarring of all, though, was that in place of the traditional brown Stetson, this deeply tanned cop wore a glorious dastar, or turban, as it's commonly known. Underneath the photo ran the caption "Is this Canadian, or does this make you Sikh?"

When I first saw that hateful image, I didn't know how to respond. Should I be saddened? Angry? Disgusted? Should I feel victimized? Should I laugh? No. There was nothing laughable about intolerance. Worse, beneath the overt racism was a layer of irony so thick you could cut it with a kirpan. The man pictured in the calendar wasn't even Sikh. Rather, he was a white imposter in brown makeup posing as one — specifically, as Baltej Singh Dhillon, the first turbaned Sikh to serve in the RCMP.

Today, almost 30 years after the brouhaha, the debate seems almost quaint. "What," children might now ask, "was the big deal?" At the tail end of the 1980s, though, the possibility that the RCMP uniform would have to be amended to allow observant Sikhs to serve in our national police force was a very big deal indeed.

Turbans in the RCMP would prove to be a critical issue for Sikhs and for all Canadians. For religious minorities, it was about inclusiveness — being able to remain true to our religion as we practised it, without being barred from participating in Canada's national institutions. But it ignited a firestorm between those who favoured the way things have always been and proponents of "reasonable accommodation," a relatively new catchphrase that would become a cornerstone of law and workplace protocol. It was minority rights versus white privilege, the "new" Canada versus the old.

For Sikhs, indeed for most non-white people in Canada, the 1980s were a difficult time. As I noted, even in polite society there was much hand-wringing about Canada's shifting ethnic makeup, but a small group took it much further. From violent attacks to the ubiquitous Paki jokes, "turban" had become "target" in the minds of a few. Ultimately, I processed these slights in the context of what I had learned about Canadians since my arrival in 1970: the vast majority of my fellow citizens were generous and thoughtful, compassionate and welcoming. The reactionary and racist elements, though present, were in the minority — although in some quarters, such as the rank and file of the newly created Reform Party, they were perhaps overrepresented.

Really, there was little we could do to diminish outright racism. As the cliché goes, you can't legislate tolerance. But the country had a relatively new Charter of Rights and Freedoms, and a canon of law was being written in response. Perhaps there were ways to give progress a little nudge.

WAR OF THE WORDS

By this time in our advocacy role, the WSO had experienced some landmark successes, both in Canada and the United States. In attempting to expose the Indian government's treatment of Punjab's Sikhs, we'd spent a lot of time and resources persuading Canadian MPs to open their minds and entertain our perspective on events taking place in India.

During this same period, my role in the WSO had changed — expanded, actually. I'd already spent two two-year terms as WSO Canada president. In 1989, I'd been elected president of WSO International and my time was increasingly spent on issues that took me beyond our nation's borders. Yet, Canadian concerns were still front and centre: the sheer number of Sikhs in Canada meant they would always occupy a significant amount of the global organization's attention.

During my stint as head of the WSO Canada, we'd made a fair bit of headway. Some MPs were on board very early on. My own member of Parliament, Lorne Greenaway, had been very vocal in defence of the Sikh point of view, even though this often put him at odds with his own Progressive Conservative party. (Greenaway had been an outspoken defender of the Canadian Sikh community during question period, and had even gone so far as to rip up a Canada–India treaty in Joe Clark's office.) As we've seen, others like Liberal MP Sergio Marchi were willing to raise our issues in the House of Commons. Closer to home, in British Columbia we'd always had the ear of Social Credit premier Bill Vander Zalm. By the time the 1980s rolled into the '90s, we had begun to assemble a coalition of support that cut across ideological lines.

We'd been busy south of the border, too. In 1986, as a result of the lobbying already conducted on our behalf, we went one step further and organized a luncheon and dinner for U.S. congressmen and senators to press our case in person. The U.S. congressional overtures took place in an actual seat of power: at the House of Representatives

Restaurant in the United States Capitol building. Didar Singh Bains hosted both gatherings with me; by this time, he had served a year as president of the World Sikh Organization International.

We arrived five minutes early for lunch, only to find that we might leave hungry. As you'd expect there was a well-composed menu featuring a variety of entrées, from the "Capitol Special" (broiled ham steak with pineapple sauce, creamy mashed potatoes, and buttered green beans, for $3.25) to the "Low Cholesterol/Low Salt Luncheon" — presumably for those politicians who had spent too much time rooting around in pork barrels. But there was not a single vegetarian option. To his credit, after learning of our needs the chef threw together a fabulous non-meat dish for us.

Lunch was a success; between bites, we managed to raise some good points and a general awareness of what we were facing. That evening, Didar Singh and I went to dinner at a nearby restaurant with several congressmen and a few senators. The dinner was arranged by our two paid lobbyists, former congressman Jim Corman and former senator Vance Hartke. All in all, there were maybe 20 of us.

I sat next to Hartke. The senator was comfortable in the company of his fellow politicians and thought nothing about putting his former colleagues on the spot. "Say," he asked one senator sitting directly across from us, "what goes through your mind when you look at him?" He pointed to me.

The senator — I've forgotten his name — looked directly at me. He was a large man, with a dour disposition. "When I look at him," the man began, in a Midwestern drawl, "I see a guy who looks just like Ayatollah Khomeini, and whose activities are like Yasser Arafat's."

I was startled, shocked. That I'd just been compared to a despotic Iranian mullah and the leader of the militant PLO — based on my physical appearance — was simply incredible. We'd certainly faced our share of stereotyping in Canada, but it was rarely so blatant. "Senator," I began, "we Sikhs have lived in North America for close to a century. What have we done to be compared to two of the most vilified leaders in the world?"

He stared at me for a long beat. "Because," he said slowly, "you have failed to tell us who you are."

It was a ludicrous explanation, but also a wake-up call. I knew then that our public relations battle would be long and arduous. But I also realized that straight talk with men in positions of power, in informal settings where everyone felt free to say what they meant, was the best way forward. (In time, it would become the template for the now-traditional WSO dinners.)

We were slowly gaining experience speaking truth to power (or, at least, dining with those who wielded it!). All of this would serve us well as we attempted to become an even stronger voice. But there were missteps, too, in the years to come. On a personal note, one sticks out.

On July 12, 1987, I'd been invited to attend a breakfast meeting with Prime Minister Brian Mulroney in Quesnel, a 90-minute drive from my home in Williams Lake. I'd been asked to present a brief on Sikhs in Canada, and I had done my homework. What no one was prepared for was a minor eruption in the news cycle.

Earlier that day, a boatload of Sikhs had landed in Nova Scotia. They were claiming refugee status, and their argument was compelling but provocative: they claimed that India was not a safe place to be a Sikh, and they were therefore asking to be accepted as refugees.

My eventual position would align exactly with theirs. But on that day in Quesnel, the news was just breaking and all of us were in the dark regarding the details (including Mulroney, until he was taken away for a private briefing). Before I delivered my brief to the prime minister, my MP, Lorne Greenaway, introduced me to the prime minister in my official capacity as president of the World Sikh Organization of Canada. Considering what was going on, the media were keen to get my reaction to the refugee situation.

All the assembled reporters wanted to know my stance on what should be done with "illegitimate refugees." Since I was representing the WSO Canada and, by extension, the Sikh community, anything I said would have to send a clear signal that, above all, we as Sikh

Canadians believed in and would uphold the laws of the nation. But with few details about the refugees' arrival and their claims, I could hardly speak with any depth.

I decided to issue a general statement: "My position is that all legitimate refugees should be allowed," I said. "However, if anyone is proved to be illegitimate" — I paused here, to gather my thoughts — "then they should be sent back to their country of origin. No one," I added, "should be allowed to circumvent the system." I thought this was a fair assessment. I was about to get an education in the use and misuse of the sound bite.

The CBC was even-handed, running a clip of me declaring that "no one should be allowed to circumvent the system." CTV, on the other hand, edited all the context out of my statement, deciding to run an abbreviated clip that completely eliminated the first part of my statement altogether. What remained was a complete mangling of context. I watched aghast as the words "They should be sent back" and nothing more came out of my mouth — a rather harsh assessment of the refugee crisis, especially coming from a leader in the Canadian Sikh community.

This clip gave the impression that I was in favour of summarily shipping all Sikh refugees back to India, a notion that understandably riled up many Sikhs. In the aftermath, I received a large number of abusive and threatening phone calls. More than this, though, I was humiliated. How could I have been so naive? Then and there, I vowed to make certain that I'd be much more careful when talking on the record.

We in the WSO Canada worked overtime to turn this one around. With the support of the Vancouver-based Khalsa Diwan Society, a Sikh organization that has operated in B.C. since 1906, we immediately arranged for legal counsel to fly to Nova Scotia to represent the refugees and arrange for their release.[32] Eventually, the news moved on. But we learned the lesson: when doing advocacy work, everything you say must be carefully thought out and meticulously planned and coordinated. Winging it is not an option.

We would not forget these lessons when the case of Baltej Singh Dhillon exploded.

THEY FINALLY GET THEIR MAN

Born in Malaysia in 1966, Baltej Dhillon immigrated to Canada in 1983 at the age of 17, joining his brother after their father passed away. His introduction to the Canadian dream was decidedly non-glamorous: up at dawn during the summer to pick berries and trying to fit into a culture that was as foreign to him as he was to it. Dhillon's first day at school was memorable, to say the least. "Someone slapped a sticker on my back that said, 'Go home, Paki,'" he recalled years afterward.

Like so many new arrivals, Dhillon had big plans. At first, he wanted to become a lawyer, setting his sights on criminal law. He was advised to help smooth the way by first getting some relevant volunteer experience. To this end, he spent two years with the Block Watch program in Surrey, B.C., as a volunteer and as a paid summer employee, along the way becoming exposed to the enforcement side of the law. It captivated him completely.

Lawyering was out; policing was in. Dhillon's future career choice was set. But there was a complication. He was an observant Sikh. His faith required that, regardless of which police force he joined (he was considering the Vancouver police and the RCMP), he would have to be allowed to wear a turban.

At the time, there were no turbaned Sikhs on any Canadian police force. (In 1986 the Toronto Police Service had broken ground by allowing Balbir Singh Nijjar to wear a turban in his job as a document server, but no amritdhari Sikhs were employed as actual law enforcement officers.) At Canada's national force, newly installed commissioner Norman Inkster, in the position since the fall of 1987, wasn't keen on changing the uniform requirements to accommodate Sikh officers. But after being persuaded that to exclude Sikhs from service would likely be a violation of their Charter rights, he changed his tune. Plus, the RCMP had hardly been a model of integration. To his enduring credit, Inkster realized that to reflect the new Canada this would have to change.

The WSO Canada had actively lobbied for changes to the RCMP uniform code to allow for the inclusion of observant Sikhs. In 1986 Dr. Surat Singh Bath, Iqbal Sara (the first Sikh lawyer to practise in Vancouver), and I met with James Kelleher, then the solicitor general, to press the case for a new policy. We argued that, human rights aside, it was clear the RCMP investigation of the Air India disaster had been hampered by the simple fact that the force (and CSIS, for that matter) employed almost no Punjabi speakers. Kelleher was very much open to our suggestions and agreed to look into the matter. Time was not on our side. In 1989 he was replaced by Pierre Blais; now, any changes to the uniform had to be approved by him, and he would not be moved to action.

But Blais would not have the luxury of putting things off forever. It wasn't long before Dhillon was accepted into the RCMP training program. At some point during his training, he was asked if he'd be willing to make a few minor accommodations to ease his way onto the force. Would he shed his turban, cut his hair, shave his face? "It was my dream job," he later said, "but it was not enough to abandon everything that ultimately defined who I was." He refused.

The times, they were changing. Despite the implications, Inkster viewed Dhillon's application favourably, and by March 1990 he had amended the uniform requirements to allow Sikhs to serve. He petitioned the solicitor general for the required government approval, but instead of aligning with the force, Blais did nothing for months. This debate polarized much of Canada, pitting supporters of minority rights and freedom of religion against those who felt that some Canadian traditions should be sacrosanct.

Although he never considered himself a trailblazer or craved notoriety, Dhillon was the right applicant at the right time. It was obvious. Upon first meeting him, I knew he was an exceptional individual, soft-spoken and with a gentle demeanour. If those opposed to the possibility of a turbaned Sikh RCMP were expecting a wild-eyed zealot, they would be disappointed. In this debate, Dhillon always exhibited calm and quiet resolve. His was a voice of reason.

While Pierre Blais fiddled, the debate burned. In 1989, as part of their convention platform, the Reform Party resolved that they would ban any religious attire in the RCMP. (Stephen Harper, who would serve as prime minister from 2006 to 2015, was the fledgling party's policy head at the time.) A petition opposing the uniform made the rounds; floated by Kay Mansbridge, Dot Miles, and Gen Kantelberg, three Calgary sisters who called themselves the Defenders of RCMP Tradition, it eventually gathered over 200,000 signatures. Calgary Progressive Conservative MP Bobbie Sparrow hitched her star to this wagon, presenting the petition in Parliament and arguing against any relaxation of the RCMP dress code.

The mainstream arguments against turbaned Sikhs in the service were usually steeped in preserving the cultural status quo. According to this line, allowing such a change in the RCMP uniform would disrupt an important part of Canada's heritage and damage a symbol that helped define us as a nation. On the surface, it was a relatively compelling position. But the RCMP uniform had never been an immutable symbol. In fact, it had been in a state of transition almost since it appeared in 1867. The "hat" worn by the first North West Mounted Police was actually two hats: a spike-topped, white cork pith helmet was worn along with the more casual blue pillbox forage cap, until both were officially replaced by the classic tan Stetson around the turn of the last century. Prior to Dhillon's application, the last change to the "red serge" was by far the most radical: in 1974 the dress uniform was adapted to allow female members to wear a skirt and leather pumps (updated finally in 2012 to the pants and boots that are standard issue for their male counterparts). So much for long-standing, unchanging tradition.

There were other, lesser arguments. One went that since Sikh marriages were often arranged, apparently any accommodation to the uniform could be interpreted as supporting that custom. The safety card was played: a criminal could unravel a turban and use it against a Sikh officer, so for their own well-being observant Sikhs should be barred from the force. And so on. But the subtext that underpinned the objections was always the same: how dare these brown guys come to "our country" and tell "us" that "we" had to change to suit them?

We had anticipated, and were prepared to counter, all of these arguments when the Mulroney government finally approved the changes required and enacted an administrative order allowing the use of religious headgear and other articles of faith by RCMP officers of Sikh background. It was a happy day on August 30, 1990, when Baltej Singh Dhillon was accepted into the RCMP, becoming its first observant, turban-clad Sikh officer. But not the final twist in this tale.

A lawsuit was launched in 1994 to effectively reverse any changes to the force's uniform and, if successful, put an end to Dhillon's RCMP career, as well as that of another Sikh who had enlisted after Dhillon was hired. Bringing the suit was the Lethbridge RCMP Veterans' Court Challenge Committee, consisting of former RCMP officers John R. Grant, Kenneth E. Riley, and Howard S. Davis, and joined by Kay Mansbridge, one of the sisters who made up the Defenders of RCMP Tradition. Their lawsuit was built around a novel argument, to say the least — highly unconventional and, I'll admit, a long way from what we were expecting.

HOSTING AN INTERVENTION

Enacted in 1982, the Canadian Charter of Rights and Freedoms was only 12 years old by the time of *Grant v. Canada (Attorney General)*, as the Lethbridge lawsuit became known. The Charter may have been a new addition to Canada's legal scene, but it was already making its mark.

The Charter was enacted to protect Canadians from governmental infringement of their rights, to prevent the "tyranny of the majority," so to speak. But the tactic used by the plaintiffs in *Grant v. Canada* was entirely different. The claim filed was unorthodox, bizarre — but also interesting. In their suit, the plaintiffs claimed that allowing RCMP officers to wear a visible faith symbol contravened their Charter right to receive police services from an officer who was not visibly aligned with any specific faith. In other words, they wanted freedom from religion, at least when it came to those who served in the RCMP.

It was a clever gambit. Their challenge wasn't about trying to stop someone from exercising their rights. Rather, it was about asserting the right of the citizens of a secular state to have an impartial national police service, one that was free from religious taint. (This argument still has currency in Quebec.)

Considering how young the Charter was, it could have been the beginning of an epic legal battle. But the government did not rise to the bait (or challenge, depending on your perspective). Its response to the lawsuit? It deemed this a matter of administrative authority, nothing more. In issuing a legal administrative order allowing turbans in the RCMP, the government was simply conducting government business — which they were allowed and required to do. The plaintiffs had no standing to contest the move.

The position concerned us. Not because it might be wrong, but because the defence arguments centred on a point of administrative law, and not on what we identified as the core issue. For an observant Sikh, the turban wasn't simply a religious symbol like, for example, a crucifix. It was an article of faith, and a fundamental part of being Sikh. To bar an observant Sikh from becoming an RCMP officer was a direct infringement on our ability to freely practise religion. To allow turbans in the RCMP was necessary in order to protect Const. Dhillon's right to freedom of religion.

But we knew these important arguments would not be made unless we made them. So for the first time, the World Sikh Organization of Canada, on behalf of all Sikh Canadians, applied to be an intervenor.

The way intervenor status works is like this: Through petitioning the court, you let them know that you've become aware of a case that could have implications that will extend beyond the interests of the litigants. Because those litigants may take positions that do not reflect the interests of the broader whole, you request the role of intervenor to represent perspectives unlikely be heard during the course of a procedure — and as a result, may not be considered by a judge when rendering a verdict. The intervenor advocates for those whose interests could be damaged in a judgment. Interventions are normally sought when an interested individual or group believes that the case is of national importance and the decision rendered by the court could have far-reaching consequences.

The court accepted our application, and our legal team went to work preparing our arguments. They were meticulous in the preparation of the briefs. I say this not only as someone who helped with the strategy, and who would be called to give testimony during the proceedings, but also as a proud father.

Palbinder, my younger daughter, was just 24 years old when Baltej Dhillon became an RCMP officer. Specializing in human rights law after being called to the bar in 1991, she naturally gravitated to advocating for Sikh issues. This was the first legal case in which she would officially represent the WSO Canada (along with her senior co-counsel, F. Andrew Schroeder). To say that Surinder and I were proud would be to short-sell our admiration. As the first female amritdhari lawyer in Canada — our daughter wears a turban — she was breaking new ground every time she walked through the courthouse doors.

But I digress. On January 25, 1994, almost three and a half years after Baltej Singh Dhillon had been accepted into the RCMP, *Grant v. Canada (Attorney General)* finally got underway in Calgary Federal Court. The hearing took place over 10 days, 8 in January and the rest in April, when oral submissions were held. During that time, I got to take stock of our allies and adversaries. They had the opportunity to return the favour.

We weren't the only group that had been granted intervenor status. The Alberta Civil Liberties Association, Sikh Society of Calgary, Alberta Inter-Religious Coalition, and Canadian Human Rights Commission were also represented. An expert in Sikh history, New Zealand professor Dr. William McLeod, testified about how the turban had evolved into a true article of faith and was not just a religious trapping. This informed view deftly countered other evidence given, including a submission by a (clean-shaven) Sikh RCMP officer who claimed that this was not the case. (It may not have been — for him.)

As for those who were aligned against us, the "Defenders," the three Calgary sisters whose anti-turban petition had acquired so much traction, were invested enough in the outcome that they were present for the entire proceedings. Occasionally, we exchanged pleasantries. Despite the heated nature of the debate, a very Canadian sense of decorum and civility prevailed in the courtroom.

I was called to give testimony, partly to contest the claim, badly fumbled by the government lawyers, that the Five Ks were optional for observant Sikhs. I started with an overview of the importance of the Five Ks, a primer of sorts. But then, uncharacteristically for me, I decided to tell a story of a personal nature, about a time in my past, when I, like Dhillon, was asked to make a choice between practising my faith and advancing my career.

On May 7, 1971, long before I struck out on my own with Khalsa Enterprises, I was employed by Merrill and Wagner, a local sawmill. My job was "stickering" lumber in the yard for drying, which involved placing several small "sticks" at regular intervals between sheets of stacked lumber to help dry the wood. My supervisor knew I was ambitious and wanted to be promoted (or at least move on to a better position). But he had been putting me off. One day, he called me aside.

"Gian," he began. "We've always been honest with each other, right?"

"Absolutely. What's on your mind?"

He paused. "It's your turban. Well, your turban and your beard."

"Okay …" I knew where this was heading.

"I know it's religion and all that, but it's holding you back. Really it is."

"I don't think so," I said.

"Well, I can guarantee it," he said. "I could promote you tomorrow — if, well, you would just get rid of that."

He pointed at my turban. But he also pointed at me — not just the physical me, but who I was at my very core. He didn't realize that what he was asking wasn't as simple as buying new shoes or putting on a swanky suit. He wanted me to disavow who I was at my most elemental level. He wanted me to not be me. And I complied.

I looked at the faces in the courtroom. With that story, I think the real importance of the turban finally landed.

WE BREAK FOR LUNCH

During the proceedings, all the players, or at least their representatives, were present, save one. Where was Dhillon? We'd spent a lot of time with him prior to his RCMP application; for the trial, we'd spent a lot of money and effort to prevent an outcome that, were it to come to pass, would mean that he would once again have to choose between his faith and his job. But he was never called to court, and he never appeared. There was no prepared statement delivered on his behalf. Even though the fight was right, and we would have undertaken it in any case, there were some in our organization who felt that we'd been used.

After all the evidence was given and all the arguments presented, we had to wait for the judge to render a verdict. On the way out of the courthouse, I passed the three Calgary sisters. We shook hands, wished each other well. Then out of the blue, I blurted, "Do you want to go for lunch?" They looked at each other, then at me. Almost in unison they said, "Yes, we'd love to."

We chose a restaurant across the street. Dr. McLeod, the expert witness, joined us. We ate and talked for over an hour and a half. The sisters were still convinced of the rightness of their cause. In time, it became clear to me that their actions were not based in racism, but were motivated by a sincere desire to protect their beloved force from hasty, ill-considered modernizations. (Kay Mansbridge, in particular, had deep ties to the force. Her husband had been an RCMP officer, and both her son and son-in-law were serving at the time.) But it was clear they'd absorbed our perspective, too.

As we were leaving, one of them said, "You know, Gian, I wish we'd done this a long time ago. It could have saved us so much time."

"And money," another quickly added.

We all laughed. Still, it was another lesson. Bridges can be built across even the most roiling rivers. Legal challenges were fine, but the best way forward was to talk things out. I absorbed this too.

For the Sikh community, the path to mainstream acceptance was now clear: in situations where there was a collision between tradition and the right to be reasonably accommodated, we would first try to sway the hearts and minds of our fellow non-Sikh citizens. But if all else failed, as long as our positions lined up with the Charter we could effect change through legal challenges. By twinning our policies to the Charter — and therefore, to other groups that would also be invested in seeing the spirit of the Charter prevail — we would never again be fighting alone. No matter the outcome of this particular trial, the community had turned a corner, and learned a lesson, one that would in time take us from simple single-issue advocacy to more complex, universal cases.

A COMPLICATED BALANCE

Madame Justice Reed, the judge in *Grant v. Canada*, delivered her verdict on July 8, 1994, almost half a year after the case began. As we expected, the gist of the ruling had little to do with religious freedoms and much to say about the ability of government agencies to enact procedures they deemed necessary:

> *There is much evidence which shows that there is a strong public interest in having a police uniform which is devoid of any symbolism which identifies the allegiance of the officer to a particular religious group.*
>
> *There is evidence that the alleged religious requirement that Sikhs wear a turban is not as categorical as some assert. Indeed*

the application form which a Sikh member must sign on joining the RCMP requires that officer to wear other headgear.

The Commissioner based his decision to allow the turban to be worn as part of the RCMP uniform on his understanding that not to allow such would discriminate against Sikhs and, in any event, the wearing of the turban would operate as a demonstration and an acceptance of the present day multicultural nature of Canada.

These are laudable objectives. The only question for the Court however is whether there is a constitutional barrier to the Commissioner acting as he has done. On the basis of the jurisprudence as it exists and the particular evidence which was put before me, I cannot find such a barrier. The plaintiffs' claim will accordingly be dismissed.

We had "won" — at least, the plaintiffs had not prevailed. Actually, there was more to it than this. Without our intervention and the interventions of our allied groups, the sincerity of our own beliefs could have been roadkill on the way to a verdict.

In her judgment, Madame Justice Reed had erred on an important point, however: the Five Ks were categorically articles of faith, and not merely symbols — this had been established by a Supreme Court of Canada decision in 1985. But the upshot was that Dhillon would keep his beard, his turban, and his job. More importantly, the previously closed doors of the RCMP had been pried open. Long denied the opportunity to serve our country in this prestigious capacity, Sikhs who could pass RCMP muster could now freely wear the red serge and the dastar.

The case was not over. Despite the trial judges' ruling, the plaintiffs launched an appeal to the Federal Court of Appeal. WSO again intervened, and this time we got the chance to set the record straight. The Federal Court of Appeal agreed with our view that administrative law issues aside, Constable Dhillon's right to wear his turban on the job was protected by the Charter. Nevertheless, it was not until the Supreme Court of Canada denied the plaintiffs' request to appeal the Federal Court of Appeal decision to our highest court that the issue of turbans in the RCMP was finally put to rest. At least in the courtroom. Convincing the public would take much longer.

The legal win was heartening, yet the situation continued to bother me. I knew that after being accepted onto the force, Baltej Dhillon had not had an easy go of it. His first posting in Quesnel, not far from my home in Williams Lake, got off to a rocky start. The mayor had written to RCMP headquarters, asking that they not post him to Quesnel; in the bars, people booed when he entered. He finally found his place within the force, or so I'd heard. But his symbolic value to the Sikh community had diminished in some quarters. His stock had gone down in my estimation, too.

I felt bad about this. Recently, I called him up and asked if he'd like to grab lunch. (You're likely sensing a pattern here.) He agreed. Since we both live in Surrey now, we met up at one of my local favourite spots. Over chaat, dal, and paneer, we talked. I asked him why he'd left us hanging in Calgary so many years ago. He replied that he'd been instructed by an RCMP lawyer to steer clear of the whole thing because, as the case was framed, it had nothing to do with him; it was against the government.

I was still disappointed, especially by the fact that he'd never really acknowledged the role the WSO Canada had played in fighting for his rights. But in retrospect, Baltej Dhillon had endured much. A lesser man would have bent under pressure, or cut and run. He did not. He persevered. He has prospered. He deserves our respect.[33] He has mine. Another lesson.

CHAPTER 9

ADVOCACY BROADENED

THE RCMP TURBAN debate was a watershed for the Sikh community and, if read broadly, for other minority groups, too. The right of Sikh RCMP members to wear turbans — a victory for the new Canada over the old — suggested the beginning of the end of European-origin dominance, a new era in which multiculturalism would prevail.

Not everyone was thrilled by this. Especially not those in the Royal Canadian Legion, our next large-canvas battlefield.

Founded in 1925 to advocate on behalf of Canada's veterans of the First World War, the Legion is perhaps best known for two things: their annual poppy campaign, the proceeds of which go to further a variety of good works; and the maintenance of local Legion branches. Some branches, like the nostalgic Billy Bishop (Branch 176) in Vancouver's Kitsilano neighbourhood, are popular watering holes — writers, artists, and hipsters mix with veterans over pints in the memorabilia-stocked room. For Canadian musicians, playing a gig at the Legion is a rite of passage, even today.

The Legion has deep roots, but it is also a place of tradition; the sacrifices made by many of its members demand a level of propriety. In the 1990s, some Canadian Legion branches enforced a dress code, ensuring that a little decorum be observed. For men, this meant removing their hat when they entered. It was a show of respect, of deference to those who had served and to the memory of those who had died in service. But in some branches, decorum and tradition would clash with cultural respect and understanding.

The first incident of a turbaned Sikh being barred from a Legion function occurred in 1987, when Raminder Singh, an Edmonton resident, was prevented from attending a Christmas party with his wife. On January 24, 1990, the Alberta Human Rights Commission ruled that the Legion discriminated against Singh because of his religious beliefs and ordered it to change its dress code. The Edmonton branch issued a statement in response, saying they would "keep their dress code requirement as is."

Turbans were again in the news in 1991, again in Alberta, when Ram Raghbir Singh Chahal, president of the WSO Canada, was refused entry to a Lethbridge Legion because he refused to remove his dastar. The Alberta Human Rights Commission again intervened, and two years later the matter was settled in a memorandum of agreement: an apology from the branch, as well as a written commitment to modify its house rules to allow for the wearing of headwear.

But the issue was far from dead. The next conflict began as a conciliatory gesture that quickly soured. For the 1993 Remembrance Day ceremonies, the Newton Legion in Surrey, B.C., invited five Sikh war veterans to take part, one of whom, Lt.-Col. (retired) Pritam Singh Jauhal, received 13 medals from the British Army. But when the men arrived, they were refused entry because they were wearing turbans. Jauhal asked to speak with the branch's president, Frank Underwood. He mentioned the invitation and tried to explain the significance of the turban to observant Sikhs. His words, Jauhal later informed me, "fell on deaf ears."

Astutely, Jauhal realized that this issue was doomed to play out again and again. There were 1,700 Canadian Legion branches across Canada; trying to force change one Legion at a time would be like playing a massive game of whack-a-mole — exhausting, and likely futile. No, the issue was national in scope. The target, then, would have to be the Royal Canadian Legion Dominion Command. The means of attack? The media.

Jauhal approached me to help his campaign. Immediately, we threw the weight of the WSO Canada behind it, issuing one press release after another; I myself appeared several times in print and broadcast interviews, pressing his case. We had much on our side — including Underwood, whose ineptitude with the media was such a contrast to the image of Lt.-Col. Jauhal, composed, dignified, rational, and resolute. Realizing they were engaged in a public relations battle they could not win, the Dominion Command reversed their long-standing national "no headgear, no exceptions" policy on November 28, 1993, finally allowing for Sikhs (and Jews who wear the kippa, or yarmulke) to be admitted.[34]

The Legion had backed down in the face of the pre-internet equivalent of a social media shaming. The only thing left was for the rank and file to approve the change through a national vote. But months after, when the vote was cast, members decided against allowing accommodations, staining the reputation of the organization for years to come.

Immediately after the vote, we issued a joint statement with the Canadian Jewish Congress, condemning the outcome and expressing sadness, not anger. This was the first time the WSO Canada had worked at such a high-profile level with an advocacy group from another faith community. It was another turning point. And like the slow drip that in time becomes an ocean, the moral force of our arguments in favour of religious accommodation was growing.

A SUBSTANTIAL SETBACK

The early 1990s was a busy time, for the community and for me and Surinder. After opening in 1987, Jackpine had built slowly, mainly because the lumber market was mired in another of its cyclical slumps. The playing field was altered by changes in the provincial government's forestry policies. Previously, only lumber producers were offered timber licences, but in 1989 producers of value-added forest products became eligible too. This would be to our advantage, as Jackpine had switched from sawmilling (processing logs into lumber) to manufacturing a host of secondary and tertiary high-value wood products, such as finger-jointed studs, joists and rafters, specialty housing components, and doors and windows.

This expansion marked a complete revitalization of our company. Revenue from sales in our first year had been $300,000; by 1993, that number soared to $26 million. We looked beyond our borders and the often-protectionist U.S. market and made inroads into Asia. In time, half of our production was slated for Japan.

By the mid-1990s Jackpine had become a huge success. Some credit goes to Premier Bill Vander Zalm. His championing of small business may have put him at odds with the so-called Club 20 — a small group of British Columbia power brokers who had tradition-ally called the shots — but it endeared him to those of us who were banking on our entrepreneurial skills.

Soon, though, all of this would go up in smoke.

In March 1993, I was in Ottawa attending a WSO Canada meeting when I got a call from Rick Jones, Jackpine's vice-president and CFO. "Gian, I know you're heading to Toronto tomorrow, but I need you to cut short your trip," he said. His voice was shaking. I knew something was very wrong.

"Rick, what's the matter? What's wrong?"

He took a deep breath. "It's gone," he said. "It's all gone." Jackpine, he blurted, had burned to the ground.

I arrived in Williams Lake around midnight. Rather than going home, I drove directly to the plant site. There was nothing to salvage. The site was a smouldering pile of char and ash and twisted metal. I was devastated, almost numb. In these times, your faith is your life preserver, but under this kind of duress, even faith can only comfort you so much. The only consolation I could grasp was that nobody had been injured.

We were insured, but stupidly the plant and all our equipment was covered only for cost — not replacement value. To get the business running again, Surinder, my partners, and I would have to come up with more than half of the funds to rebuild.

Things looked so bleak. But we knew the kind of upside Jackpine could deliver. Between us all, we committed to going forward yet again. We would rebuild. And we did, though it took a year and strong doses of both risk and patience. When we finally reopened, Jackpine was stronger than ever: it grew into a success story in the value-added sector of the forest industry, touching $100 million in annual sales revenue.

FINDING OUR VOICE

By the time of the Jackpine fire, I'd completed my second and final term as WSO International president. The WSO had matured into a much more effective human rights advocacy group; we had ambitious goals and took our concerns to the highest forums. In June 1993, for example, we presented a submission to the World Conference on Human Rights in Vienna. The presentation, by two leading WSO members, Karnail Singh Gill and Sajjan Singh Bhangoo, was a rundown of human rights abuses by India and a plea for the Sikh right to self-determination. India was not amused. (They actively sought to discredit us, trotting out Manmohan Singh, who would become India's prime minister, to absurdly claim: "There are no ethnic people in India. My government recognizes no such category … India is an open book. There are no violations of human rights in India.")

We continued our lobbying efforts in Canada as well. In 1992, this paid off handsomely when we arranged for a parliamentary delegation of Liberal MP Derek Lee, Progressive Conservative MP Barbara Green, and the New Democratic Party's Svend Robinson to visit Punjab and hear what was going on for themselves.[35] There, they met with Sikhs whose sons had been killed in false encounters or jailed on flimsy trumped-up charges. Upon their return to Canada their reports, particularly Lee's and Robinson's, amounted to an indictment of India's treatment of its Sikh citizens. Even Green, whose party included a faction that had traditionally been sympathetic to India's side of the conflict, would not support a whitewash. "There is a need for an objective review of the situation in the Punjab by a reputable outside agency such as Amnesty International or a United Nations working group," she wrote. "Canada should continue to urge India through the United Nations to allow Amnesty International in, but any review should also examine the human rights abuses by militant groups."

Svend Robinson was especially resolute in his defence of Sikhs. When he was confronted by an Indian government official who tried to diminish Indian culpability for human rights abuses in Punjab by raising Canada's treatment of its First Nations people, Robinson pulled no punches. "Don't play that card with me," said the MP, whose hosts likely did not know about his long-time support of aboriginal rights. "Canadians acknowledge we have a problem, and there are men and women of goodwill trying to address this. You," he said, "will not even acknowledge that a problem exists."

In Canada and abroad, we were finding our voice. We had become more politically involved and more savvy, too. But this hadn't happened overnight. Newcomers often feel that, because they are new to a land, they haven't yet earned the right to involve themselves in nation-shaping mechanisms. That view is often shared by those who have been here for a generation or two longer.

But things were changing. Sikhs, both new arrivals and those who traced their history back generations, were becoming politically involved. That stage had been set decades before by Naranjan Singh Grewall. Like many Sikhs, Grewall had made his mark in the lumber industry. In 1950, he became the first Sikh elected to public office in North America, and marked another milestone when he was elected mayor of Mission, B.C., the first Sikh mayor in Canadian history. In the 1990s, the floodgates really opened. We've already encountered Moe Sihota, the Duncan, B.C.–born Sikh who in 1986 became the first Canadian of South Asian descent to be elected to the legislature; in short order, he would be promoted to Mike Harcourt's NDP cabinet, another first. Another Sikh politician came up at the same time, winning his seat in Vancouver-Kingsway that same year. In the 1993 Liberal party rout, Harbance Singh ("Harb") Dhaliwal was elected in Vancouver (and would eventually go on to become the first Sikh cabinet minister) and Ontario's Gurbax Singh Malhi became the first turbaned Sikh member of Parliament. Though Ujjal Dosanjh was a divisive figure within the Sikh community, he unquestionably broke political ground, becoming the first premier of Sikh heritage in Canada before jumping to the federal Liberal party to sit as an MP, and as minister of health in Paul Martin's short-lived cabinet.

As with other immigrants, the post-1970 wave of Sikh immigrants often settled in centres where they could see something of themselves reflected back. As a result, Sikhs became concentrated in certain areas, from which a power base emerged. In Ontario, Brampton's Sikhs banded together politically, throwing their collective weight behind candidates who would give their concerns a sympathetic hearing. In B.C., where the majority of Canadian Sikhs lived, cities like Abbotsford and Surrey became centres of Sikh political influence. If you want votes in Surrey, where today the population comprises over 20 percent Sikhs, you have to acknowledge this.

In these cities, the Sikh community set up gurdwaras, restaurants, clothing stores, and greengrocers selling foods not normally found on the typical "Canadian" roadside diner menu. In these places, the sight of observant men and women in turbans became more commonplace, especially after 1984, when the community increasingly took refuge in faith after the Golden Temple massacre. The turban, once a symbol of apartness, was becoming something else: a symbol of political muscle, of a community that could no longer be taken for granted or denied.

The kirpan was another matter entirely.

Our right to wear the kirpan set off a raucous debate, pitting claims of public safety (no matter how unfounded) against religious freedom. It was a nasty fight and it isn't over yet: as recently as 2016, after the implementation of metal detectors at NHL arenas we had to forge an agreement with the league so that observant Sikhs could attend hockey games.

Instances of the misuse of the kirpan are rare in Canadian history. As Dr. John Spellman once noted, the fact that it has been misused only a handful of times in over 100 years shows the incredible restraint of Sikhs in Canada. The last highly publicized event took place in 2010, when lawyer Manjit Mangat, himself a Sikh, was stabbed by a kirpan-wielding assailant outside Brampton, Ontario's Sikh Lehar Centre.

Of the Five Ks, the kirpan is the most demonized article of Sikh faith. There is much confusion about it. Often wrongly described as a knife or dagger, the kirpan is, in fact, a representation of a sword. Usually less than eight inches long, it reminds Sikhs of their duty to stand up for the defenceless — to protect those in need not physically but metaphorically. It derives from one of the two kirpans worn by Guru Hargobind: sword of piri (spiritual power), which was never to be used except for the blessing of food, and sword of miri (temporal power), which was only to be used in self-defence or the defence of others. The sword of spiritual power, retained as an article of faith for Sikhs, is the one worn today — which explains why instances of its misuse are rare.

For amritdhari Sikhs, the wearing of the kirpan is not optional. It is part and parcel of being a devoted, observant follower of the faith. I have worn it every moment, everywhere I go, even to bed or into the shower, since I became amritdhari in 1981. As with the other Sikh articles of faith, it is a potent distillation of a message that was first heard over 500 years ago, one that for many Sikhs resonates fully and forcefully today. Yet none of this matters a whit to airport security officials.

As early as 1985, the WSO had been working with the Sikh community to allow for the wearing of kirpans in settings where it had been prohibited. The first incident that came to light nationally was when Grade 12 student Suneet Singh Tuli (he went on to co-found DataWind, a world-renowned software company), was banned from wearing his kirpan to school by the St. Albert School District just outside Edmonton, Alberta. Happily, on April 19, 1985, in an Edmonton court, Justice Wachowich delivered a precedent-setting judgment granting an interim injunction restraining the school board from suspending or expelling Tuli from school if he wore his kirpan.

Many cases followed. The first case I personally worked on involved Amritpal Singh Shergill (he would later become my son-in-law after marrying my daughter Palbinder). Then a University of British Columbia student, he was told his kirpan violated the no-weapons policy of campus housing. To rectify this, I called UBC president David Strangway and explained the situation. To his credit, Strangway grasped what was at stake and immediately resolved the issue.

Other interventions were handled similarly. For example, when my friend Avtar Singh (who traveled with me to Pakistan) was called to jury duty in Quesnel, the attending sheriffs forced him to remove his kirpan before he could enter the court. Then they locked his kirpan in a lunch bucket. So there he sat, in the jury box, with a lunch pail on his lap; it would have been laughable if the underlying issue wasn't so important.

During a break, Avtar Singh called me and told me what was going on. In response, I wrote a letter to the judge, Justice H.A. Callaghan, and couriered it to Avtar Singh so he could present it the next day. My argument? It was pretty simple: *If your Honour wants this jury member to be fully part of these proceedings, he'll need to be at peace with himself — and the only way for him to do so is to be able to wear his kirpan, one of our five articles of faith.* The judge allowed this.

Another barrier to the kirpan's emancipation loomed. Dozens of cases of Sikhs with kirpans being refused entrance to airplanes cropped up all across Canada. Eventually, they wound up in court, adding to the canon of law. In one decision in which a Sikh was prohibited in 1996 from flying with his kirpan, the court ruled against the complainant and the Canadian Human Rights Commission and in favour of Canada 3000 Airlines, saying (among other things) that because of the nature of air travel — there is no access to emergency services at 30,000 feet — to allow any object on board that could do more damage than a dinner knife was an unreasonable request. (In my view the complainant, Balbir Singh Nijjar, was pushing the limits of reasonable accommodation by insisting he be allowed to carry his foot-long kirpan on the flight.)

In response to this uncertainty, and in consultation with Transport Canada and the aviation industry, the WSO Canada devised a reasonable accommodation policy accepted by the airlines, the government, and the Sikh community. Sikhs would be able to board flights with a kirpan, as long as the blade itself did not exceed four inches in length — effectively the length of the dinner knives already used aboard most commercial flights. The kirpan accommodation in airlines was broadly implemented, but in the new world order after 9/11, we quickly realized that such accommodations would not always be forthcoming — though patience and legal acuity have taken us a long ways toward universal acceptance of the kirpan. With the help of the WSO legal team, kirpans up to six centimetres are once again allowed.

And so began our first Supreme Court of Canada intervention. *Multani v. Commission scolaire Marguerite-Bourgeoys*, a landmark 2006 Supreme Court case, pitted the right of a Sikh high school student in Quebec to wear a kirpan against the security concerns of his school administration.

Weighing the safety of other students against young Gurbaj's right to freely practise his faith, the court ruled in the student's favour, thereby considerably moving the yardstick of religious freedom. While we were elated at the unanimous decision of our highest court, the victory was bittersweet. By the time the court case had made its way through the legal system, Gurbaj Singh had already finished high school. Forced out of the publicly funded francophone school system, he switched to a private English-speaking school that did not ban

1. When Minister of External Affairs Joe Clark sought a premiers' boycott of WSO functions, the issue reached the House of Commons. On March 10, 1988, a motion to debate was moved by MP Sergio Marchi, pictured speaking at the 1989 WSO convention, and seconded by MP Nelson Riis.

2. WSO function in 1985. From left: me, Maj.-Gen. Jaswant Singh Bhullar, and WSO International President Didar Singh Bains.
3. In Quesnel, B.C. From left: me, Avtar Singh, and then prime minister Brian Mulroney, 1987.
4. From left: Abbotsford guest, Harjinder Singh Sandhu, me, Bob Rae, and Surinder Singh Jabal at a WSO community dinner in 1989.
5. From left: B.C. MLA Russ Fraser, Premier Bill Vander Zalm, Lillian Vander Zalm, and me in 1988.

1. Khalsa Enterprises, 1987.
2. From left: Jackpine Forest Products management Steve Knowles, me, Rick Jones, Prem Singh Vinning, Peter McLaughlin, and Avtar Singh Sandhu.
3. Shift crews like this were key to Jackpine's success.

4. Back row, from left: members of Jackpine senior management Ron Bhalla, Brad Forster, Rick Jones, Neil Vant, and Peter McLaughlin. Front row, from left: Surinder, my mother, and me.
5&6. Flames destroyed our business in March 1993; employees worried whether the company would rebuild.
7. An aerial view of the rebuilt Jackpine, 1995.

1. *At a 1995 WSO parliamentary dinner, activist Jaswant Singh Khalra presented proof of more than 25,000 killings in Punjab. Two months later, he was abducted from his residence in Amritsar.* 2. *From left: WSO's Gopal Singh Brar, a member of the WSO legal team, me, Gordon Fairweather (head of the Canadian Human Rights mission), and Jagjit Singh Mangat at a 1986 UN human rights conference in Geneva.* 3&4. *WSO Canada has recognized Baltej Singh Dhillon, the first RCMP officer to wear a turban, and Ajit Kaur Tiwana, the first female Sikh RCMP officer.*

5&6. Balbir Singh
Sandhu (above right)
declared himself
General Secretary of
Khalistan. In 1981,
he released "official"
passports, stamps,
and currency.
7. After 38 years on
the Indian government
blacklist, Surinder and
I finally reached the
Delhi airport on
April 26, 2016.

1. From left: Amarjit Kaur with son Harjinder Singh; daughter Kamaljit Kaur with Hardip Singh and Manraj Kaur; Surinder Kaur with me; my mother, Kartari Kaur; Harneet Kaur and Amritpal Singh with daughter Palbinder Kaur; son Surjit Singh with Sukhwinder Kaur.
2. Order of British Columbia inductees, 2002.
3. I pose with Surinder, my "Dogwood" on proud display.
4. In 2002, Premier Gordon Campbell and Lieutenant Governor Iona Campagnolo presented me with the Queen's Golden Jubilee Medal.

1&2: The Gurmat Gyan Sewing Training Centre and Computer Training Centre now fill our home in Rurka Kalan (that's Surinder holding the sewing machine).

3. Jaswant Singh Khalra was memorialized at the 2017 Walk for Reconciliation in Vancouver. Back row, from left: his daughter-in-law Itinderjit Kaur and his son Janmeet Singh stand with Minister of Indigenous Relations and Reconciliation Scott Fraser. Front row, from left: Perry Bellegarde, National Chief of the Assembly of First Nations, me, and Chief Dr. Robert Joseph, ambassador for Reconciliation Canada.

his kirpan. (He's now a high-profile public speaker and was recently invited to speak at the prestigious annual conference of the Canadian Institute for the Administration of Justice.)

The ruling affirmed Gurbaj Singh's right to carry the kirpan in a school environment, but perhaps more critically, the arguments presented by WSO Canada's legal counsel helped the court to conclude that any blanket prohibition of the kirpan was unlawful, since these kinds of prohibitions erroneously presumed a safety risk and ignored the actual meaning of the kirpan and its significance to Sikhs.

The *Multani* decision has had a significant impact on Canadian jurisprudence and is one of a trilogy of leading cases on religious accommodation released by our highest court. WSO would also play a significant role in the second case in this trilogy.

COMMON CAUSE

Another watershed test occurred in 2004. At first blush, it seemed to be simply a case of property rights, a small dispute confined to the interests of residents of a Montreal condominium complex. But much more was at stake. At the heart of the dispute was an issue of faith, or more precisely, of belief. And this is where, in the matrix of interests that overlaps many faith communities, we in the World Sikh Organization of Canada found ourselves — for the first time — as an intervenor in a case that had nothing directly to do with Sikhism.

Some background first. The condo in question, managed by a company called Syndicat Northcrest, had a clause in its contract for purchase prohibiting the building of any structures, temporary or otherwise, on balconies. (Although each balcony was reserved for the owner/occupant of the connected unit, the balconies themselves were jointly owned by all owners, a common practice ensuring that structural problems, such as a leaking roof, are a shared responsibility.) This stipulation was hardly unusual; many, if not most, strata agreements have a similar restriction.

However, four of the condo owners were Orthodox Jews for

whom the observation of Sukkot, an eight-day celebration harkening back to the Old Testament and commonly known as the Feast of the Tabernacles, was a critical part of their religion. One element of observing Sukkot requires that Orthodox Jews build a sukka, a temporary hut topped with organic material (branches or fronds), in which they take their meals. Some even sleep in the hut for the duration. After Moïse Amselem and a few others erected sukka huts on their balconies, the Syndicat Northcrest was not impressed, demanding that they take them down, citing all manner of reasons — from fire risk purportedly caused by the temporary structures to breach of contract to diminished property values for the adjacent condominium owners. Amselem et al. were not swayed and a protracted legal battle ensued, ultimately ending at the Supreme Court of Canada.

When it came to reasonable religious accommodation, Syndicat Northcrest wasn't entirely tone deaf. They offered a compromise, which included allowing a communal sukka that could be built in the shared garden area; but the homeowners rejected this on the grounds that their personal religious beliefs required them to each set up their own sukka.

By the time we got involved, the case was in appeal — an earlier Quebec court ruling had found in favour of Syndicat. One of the issues raised in the appeal was the lower court's undue reliance on expert testimony. Rather than focusing on Moïse Amselem's own religious beliefs to determine whether a violation of his religious freedoms had occurred, the court had preferred the expert testimony of someone presented by the Syndicat to be knowledgable of the Jewish faith. In other words the lower court had decided that an expert knew more about what Amselem believed than he did himself! This course of action was clearly flawed — for the WSO, it was the reason we had become intervenors in the first place.

The crux of the matter wasn't that some objective truth or unassailable edict had to be unearthed or divined for justice to prevail. Rather, the real argument was whether or not the defendants sincerely believed that their faith required them to erect sukkas, and that the construction of these huts had to be done on an individual basis.

Sincerity of belief. For faith communities, it's an incredibly important concept. The stakes for Sikhs were high. As with most religions, Sikhs follow a divergent system of practices. A clean-shaven Sikh, for example, though not amritdhari, has no greater or lesser claim to the religion than, say, I do. My beliefs require me to adhere to the Five Ks; the beliefs of others who consider themselves Sikhs do not. They may hold to their beliefs as sincerely as I hold to mine.

This was a critical litmus test for minority groups that would set a precedent. The kind of testimony provided by Dr. McLeod in the RCMP turban issue, in which he and others were called upon to determine for the court what the bona fide religious practices of a faith entailed, would no longer be part of the equation. Instead, the decision would come down to whether or not there was a basis in faith for a particular belief or practice (that is, it wasn't simply made up) and that those adhering to the practice or precept sincerely believed it was necessary to their faith.

The WSO was not alone; other faith communities and advocacy groups had also applied and been permitted to intervene in this case. In court, we sat next to representatives from the Evangelical Fellowship of Canada, the Seventh Day Adventist Church, the Ontario Human Rights Commission, and the B'nai B'rith.

When the judgment was rendered in favour of the Orthodox Jews — and their right to practise their faith according to their beliefs — it was a victory on two fronts for Sikhs. First, we would no longer have to call on "experts" to validate the practice of our religion to any court. And second, we had for the first time made truly common cause with an array of faith organizations. It was a powerful testament to cooperation and the first time that a religious group had participated in a legal action (at their own cost) to support the religious rights of members of another faith community. We were breaking ground, and we hoped that our intervention would lead the way for more religious organizations to publicly advocate for the rights of others.

With this success, we saw how we could impact social change on a much broader level. This was a powerful realization, inspiring a significant switch in tactics. We no longer viewed the protection and promotion of Sikh interests in isolation; the context for our struggles was broader, our coalition potentially vast — and it included some groups that once would have had a difficult time making alliances with us, and us with them. The concept of standing up for the beliefs of others was not a foreign one for Sikhs. After all, our religion had been founded on such ideals. Freedom of religious expression and equality of religious beliefs are enshrined in our core values. The Sikh scriptures are a compilation of the teachings of our Sikh gurus as well as 30 teachers from other faiths who shared the same beliefs in gender equality, religious equality, and rejection of caste and race divisions. Indeed, our ninth guru, Guru Tegh Bahadur, was beheaded for his unwavering commitment to the Hindu people's right to freely practise their faith.

In some instances, reaching out beyond our own specific interests was fairly simple. For example, when Hamish Jacobs, a 19-year-old Lethbridge, Alberta, high school senior, wanted to wear a kilt, the traditional dress of his ancestral home, to his graduation ceremony, his principal refused. The WSO Canada stepped in to help and issued a press release in support. This sparked an avalanche of publicity, and the original decision was overturned. This result aligned with our own views supporting cultural expression. For us, this was a no-brainer. We felt that it was important to add our voice to his base of support. (Which, by the way, grew exponentially after he made an appearance on *The Late Late Show*, hosted by fellow Scotsman Craig Ferguson.)

What we chose not to advocate for was also important. In 2009, members of an Alberta Hutterite group launched a Charter challenge. The case revolved around the Hutterite prohibition against being photographed. This was in conflict with the Alberta government's stipulation that anyone wishing to drive a vehicle requires a driver's licence with a photo for identification purposes. In our opinion the Hutterites were sincere in their beliefs, but we understood that, in this case, to not submit to photo I.D. could have serious repercussions for broader society. Since our position would have likely placed us on the opposite side of the Hutterites — and this was not where we wanted to be — we opted to sit this particular fight out. (After losing their first two court battles in Alberta, the provincial government appealed to the Supreme Court of Canada, which decided 4–3 in the government's favour.)

We had long ago recognized that our fate aligned with the Canadian Charter of Rights and Freedoms.[36] As I mentioned before, Sikh principles are inherently consistent with the Charter. Thus, this extraordinary document became our lodestar, guiding us in the decisions we took and the causes we chose to support. This path was not without its perils. We were inspired to take a stand for gravely important issues we knew were principled and in line with the Charter, knowing they would cost us dearly in our own community. This was certainly the case when the World Sikh Organization of Canada threw its weight behind Bill C-38, the 2005 bill legalizing same-sex marriage throughout Canada.

At the time, this move was controversial. Predictably, many of the more "traditionalist" voices were united in opposition. Even among the governing Liberals, the issue of gay marriage was divisive — although in the end most supported the bill, along with the Bloc Québécois and the NDP. The Conservatives, led by Stephen Harper, voted against the bill, and Harper himself said that if he became prime minister, he'd try to reverse the act in a free vote in Parliament. (After assuming power he did try, meekly, by asking for a House of Commons vote on whether the issue should be reopened. He was soundly defeated.)

In the faith communities, there was a solid front of opposition, with the Catholic church leading the charge against — no small matter, since about 40 percent of Canadians consider themselves part of that flock. (The Vatican got involved in the debate, imploring Catholic MPs to vote their conscience, not the party line.) There was some faith-based support for the bill. The United Church was on board, as were some Jewish synagogues. It wasn't exactly a crowded party.

Unlike with some other faiths, there is no specific condemnation of homosexuality, and no specific references to homosexual acts, in the Guru Granth Sahib, the Sikh scripture that represents the collective spiritual wisdom of Sikh gurus. The Akal Takht (temporal authority for Sikhs) was asked by some Sikhs to weigh in on the issue of same-sex marriage. The Akal Takht's jathedar (leader) Joginder Singh Vedanti ruled that same-sex marriage could not be performed in any gurdwara, and issued an edict to Sikh parliamentarians not to support it.

Vedanti's ruling was controversial. We knew that the edict had missed the mark, and that it was likely issued without full information about the same-sex marriage legislation. Under the act, no religious leader would be compelled to perform a same-sex ceremony; the Supreme Court of Canada, in an earlier ruling, had made this clear. For us, the issue was equally clear. This was a human rights matter flowing from the interpretation of the Charter. To not support Bill C-38 would be a betrayal of our guiding principles.

Personally, I had no trouble supporting the bill. None. Neither did anyone else at the World Sikh Organization of Canada — although all were aware of the potential for blowback. At this point, we had seen the power of the Charter of Rights and Freedoms in action; we knew firsthand how it ensured the rights and freedoms of all Canadians, regardless of ethnicity, religion, gender, or sexual orientation.

The Charter completely aligns with Sikh values. But the implication by the Akal Takht that gurdwaras would be forced to perform same-sex marriages needed to be challenged. To ensure that there was no confusion about the practical application of the bill, I wrote the following in my capacity as WSO Canada senior policy advisor:

> With the utmost of respect for the Akal Takht, the passing of legislation in Canada to allow for same-sex marriages has no bearing on the conduct of marriages in gurdwaras. The bill will

be debated in the Canadian Parliament, and as understood so
far, will simply allow equal rights of marriage to gay and lesbian
couples. The focus of this bill is the right to a legal marriage …
it does not in any way affect the rights of religious communities
including Sikhs to perform marriages in any manner they wish.

In the same release, Ajit Singh Sahota, then president of the WSO Canada, added, "We as Sikhs have an obligation to support the rights of others to live according to their own conscience."

Some were, let's say, highly unenthusiastic about our position. In one gurdwara, I was prohibited from speaking; interestingly, some of the so-called "moderate Sikhs" tried to use my support of same-sex marriage like a club against me. (The irony of these self-proclaimed moderates attacking the "fundamentalist" for supporting the right of gays to marry must have escaped them.) Shockingly, threats were made against WSO president Ajit Singh Sahota's life and mine. We tried to dismiss them — they likely came from hotheads, small men who were brave only when positioned at the other end of a telephone line or sitting at their computer — but they were unsettling nonetheless. We weren't alone in facing a backlash. Liberal MP Navdeep Singh Bains, an exceptional young man, was also demonized by some. His defeat in the 2011 election may have been due in part to his principled stand on Bill C-38.

The WSO lost a few members over the issue, there's no question. But we also gained a few younger professionals who now saw the WSO Canada for what we already knew it to be: a progressive advocacy group willing to go to bat for all Canadians in pursuit of equality. In time, as the controversy surrounding the decision to back gay marriage rights faded, more came around. Even my wife, Surinder, who is pretty conservative on the whole, backed me on this. That meant a lot. Yet even though many disagreed with my perspective, I knew that the community could handle this kind of debate. We were maturing rapidly. We didn't need our sensitivities salved. We didn't need coddling.

THE REAL MISSION

Our decision to support gay marriage in Canada remains one of our bolder moves. But on the horizon there were plenty more battles to join and alliances to make that once would have been unthinkable. Several legislative attempts at "combatting terror" or enshrining "traditional Canadian values" (whatever these may be) have been floated over the past decade, to the detriment of our fundamental civil rights. Some, like 2015's Bill C-75, the Oath of Citizenship Act, seemed intent on targeting one particularly vulnerable minority, in this case Muslim women who wear the niqab, in order to curry favour with the Conservative's support base. Had this bill passed and become law, it would have forced anyone taking the citizenship oath to "reveal their face" during the actual ceremony (even though their identity had been previously confirmed).

Although Muslims and Sikhs may not always have seen eye to eye philosophically, in the world since 1984, and particularly since 9/11, more has held us in common than divided us. As Sikhs, we too had been demonized in the past, and forced to pay the collective bill for crimes committed in our name. The fact that the last attempt at this bill was introduced by Conservative MP Tim Uppal, a practising Sikh, was personally distasteful to me, and to many other Sikhs. For the Harperites, wedge issues were their bread and butter; to blunt criticism that they were aligned against minority groups, why not trot out a brown guy in a turban to lead the charge? Another cynical move from a government that had a history of outdoing itself on that score. (Perhaps I too am being overly cynical, but that's how I saw it. Who knows, maybe Tim Uppal did believe in the proposed bill.) The WSO Canada advocated against the proposed law, reaffirming our commitment to religious freedom for all people, Muslim women being no exception.

In 2015, WSO was again the only intervenor from a different faith community that came to bat at the Supreme Court of Canada, this time on behalf of the Catholics. In what would become known as the Loyola decision, we supported the right of the Catholic high school to teach the Christian portion of the mandated "Ethics and Religious Culture" curriculum, in accordance with the boundaries of its faith. This was the third time my daughter Palbinder presented arguments in front of the Supreme Court of Canada as the lead counsel for WSO. *Loyola High School v. Quebec (Attorney General)* was eventually decided in the high school's favour. Our participation in the *Loyola* intervention allowed us to build even stronger bridges with Christian advocacy groups.

WSO also broadened its work with the First Nations communities of Canada. Our participation in the Truth and Reconciliation Commission (TRC) and Reconciliation Canada's inaugural Walk for Reconciliation in 2013 resulted in a remarkable show of interfaith understanding when Navneet Singh, a survivor of the 1984 genocide against the Sikhs, was honoured as a representative for all victims of genocide around the world. Sukhvinder Kaur Vinning, a bright and energetic young woman who served as our executive director, also orchestrated a poignant video called *It Matters: The Legacy of Residential Schools*, which broke new ground and was featured at TRC's national events. WSO also helped launch a young adult initiative called Through Our Eyes: Changing the Canadian Lens that focused on building bridges of understanding between Indigenous and non-Indigenous young adults.

And we worked against Bill C-51, the Anti-Terrorism Act, with its clause about criminalizing support for "terrorism offences in general" — a broad and problematic phrase that in our view had the potential to make things like supporting, say, Nelson Mandela and the African National Congress's fight against South African apartheid rule a potentially criminal act. Our position, in line with that of the Canadian Bar Association, questioned whether C-51 provided a reasonable balance between public safety and the right to free expression.

These were not just Sikh issues, ethnic issues, religious issues. They were Canadian issues. We now truly understood — not just intellectually, but in a visceral way — that our mission was about all of us. We were jumping into a variety of conflicts that on the surface had little or nothing to do with the Sikh community per se, from advocating on behalf of disabled veterans' pension rights to producing educational videos casting light on the trials of First Nations for the TRC.

In all, by 2017 we had allied ourselves with everyone from the Canadian Jewish Congress to the Croatia National Home. Most recently, along with several other organizations, WSO has been granted intervenor status in a case that once again has the potential to profoundly impact religious freedom in Canada. At issue is the right of the Law Society of Upper Canada to refuse to allow law school graduates of Trinity Western University to be admitted to the bar. This controversy arises from the fact that all students of the small, Langley, B.C.–based Christian university must sign a Community Covenant, a document that pledges they will avoid "sexual intimacy that violates the sacredness of marriage between a man and a woman." The Covenant, the law society argues, violates the rights of people who are not heterosexual. (Although lesbian, gay, bisexual, and transgendered students are not barred from attending TWU, they must abide by the Covenant, even if legally married.) Our legal argument factum is being prepared as I write, and the case will be heard by the Supreme Court of Canada in late 2017, with a decision coming sometime in 2018.

We fought — are fighting — these battles not because we were Sikh but because we were Canadian, with a history in Canada stretching back well over a century. We had come so far that our past, long ignored by others, was being recognized: in 1999, a 46-cent stamp commemorating the Sikh centennial in Canada was issued, and in 2014 a stamp recognizing the *Komagata Maru* tragedy was also released. This was not a bone thrown to the Sikh community; it was, rather, a part of Canadian history that had been overlooked. We were a part of this country. We would no longer be overlooked.

CHAPTER 10

THE SIKH COMMUNITY TODAY

"**F***CK YOUR TURBAN."

In September 2016, the posters, featuring a bearded Sikh man in a glorious orange dastar, were found in several locations around Edmonton's University of Alberta campus. "If you're so obsessed with your Third World culture, go the f*ck back to where you came from!" the posters said. Hash tags? #Non-Integrated. #Invasion.

The posters seemed to have been put up by ImmigrationWatchCanada.org, a racist anti-immigration group that operated out of Vancouver. The group first made news in 2014 when they produced a flyer illustrating how Brampton, Ontario, had changed: two photos graphically revealed how the city had gone from happy and civilized (read: white) to a place where strange and unpalatable people (read: Sikhs) roamed free.

But when asked if they were behind the University of Alberta action, a spokesman denied it, even though the group's web address was prominently displayed: "We do not support flyers taking on a strictly vulgar and emotionally charged narrative!" they huffed in response. For the shock troops of the anti-immigrant movement, irony is just one more foreigner at the party.

To some, it must have seemed that we had traveled through a wormhole in time, finding ourselves back when Paki-bashing was in vogue and white fragility had not yet been named. But immediately after the posters came down, to counteract the negative energy and drain the moment of any lingering toxicity, Sikh students at the U of A (acting in coordination with WSO Canada reps) organized a turban-tying campaign. The initiative was widely embraced; soon, hundreds of non-Sikh students had demonstrated solidarity with the Sikh community by wearing a turban for the first time. At one point, the turban-tying became a bona fide internet meme: months later, a video of Dan Curtis, the mayor of Whitehorse, Yukon, went viral. He was having his turban tied — and then enthusiastically (if awkwardly) dancing bhangra.

The reaction was heart-warming, and an indication of how far we'd come as a community and a nation. This was not a return to the 1980s, a time of great difficulty for us. No. The nation had changed. In the years since the Air India disaster and the resulting firestorm of disapproval aimed at Canadian Sikhs, this country has evolved. Multiculturalism isn't just a nice phrase to be trotted out by politicians seeking the so-called ethnic vote. It has become a true cornerstone of Canadian values, one that today is embraced almost universally. Multiculturalism is now part of our core, as critical to our sense of shared identity as universal health care and international peacekeeping. It is who we are.

We have all changed. In my time in Canada, I have seen the most extraordinary things, shifts that would have seemed impossible to a new immigrant in the '70s. In British Columbia, Sikhs account for about 4.6 percent of the entire population (2011 census). With 104,720, Surrey has the highest number of Sikhs concentrated in any one place outside of Punjab, a fact that is more than evident to any observer passing through.

When I arrived in 1970, there were hardly any Sikh politicians holding office anywhere. And there were no visible Sikhs involved, not even on a provincial or local level. The turban back then would have been like "vote repellent," I'm sure. Today in Parliament there are 18 Sikh MPs; 5 of them wear the dastar, with 4 appointed to Prime Minister Justin Trudeau's cabinet. (In keeping with Trudeau's gender-inclusive cabinet and caucus, Bardish Kaur Chagger is the first female house leader in the Canadian House of Commons; that she is also Sikh is a matter of pride for the community as well as for all Canadian women.)

The two most visible Sikhs in Parliament are Defence Minister Harjit Singh Sajjan and Minister of Innovation, Science, and Economic Development Navdeep Singh Bains. Both of them are dignified and natural on the world stage, inspiring pride in all Sikhs across Canada and around the world. That feeling is amplified manyfold for our family: Harjit's sister, Amarjit, is married to my son Harjinder. I've known Harjit since we helped smooth the way for him to wear his turban while serving in Bosnia and Herzegovina. Over the years, I've watched this shy young fellow grow and mature into the man we all know today. He is both an exceptional person and someone I am proud to call a part of our family.

And although Sajjan has arguably the highest profile, he is just one of many Sikhs, both observant and secular, who are making a mark. In the judiciary, I've mentioned Justice Wally Oppal, the first Sikh Canadian appointed to the County Court of Vancouver and to the Supreme Court of British Columbia. In law enforcement, Kashmir "Kash" Singh Heed, former B.C. Liberal cabinet minister, was the first Sikh police chief in Canada. In politics, Sarabjit Singh Marwah, former vice-chair and COO of Scotiabank, Canada's third-largest bank, was the first Sikh to be appointed senator. And just as this book was going to press, an achievement occurred that I never imagined I would see in my lifetime: a person of Sikh heritage elected to lead one of the country's main political parties. On October 1, 2017, I was proven wrong when Jagmeet Singh was chosen leader of the federal NDP with more than half the votes on the first ballot. This is the Canada I crossed oceans to join.

The evolution is everywhere. In sport, former defensive lineman Nuvraj Singh Bassi was the first turbaned player in the Canadian

Football League. And in design and film, Waris Ahluwalia, a dastar-wearing Sikh, shot to fame in the 2006 Spike Lee film *The Inside Man,* and since then has appeared in films like *The Grand Budapest Hotel, The Darjeeling Limited,* and even the indie film *Rosencrantz and Guildenstern Are Undead,* where he played the very non-Punjabi role of "Hugo Pepper."

Toronto funnyman Jasmeet Singh, whose YouTube handle is "Jus Reign," is cracking jokes, largely at the Sikh community's expense — an ironic twist and a barometer of progress, considering the tone of the punch lines the last time we were the focus of comedy routines, back in the 1980s. (Though being made to remove his turban while passing through San Francisco's airport security in 2016 was a pretty stale joke.) Rupi Kaur, also from Toronto, has seen her debut poetry collection, *Milk and Honey,* sit on the *New York Times* Paperback Trade Fiction Best Sellers list for over 56 weeks, reaching the No. 1 spot and selling more than 1.5 million copies. Canadian Sikhs are even jumping on the hip-hop bandwagon: Abbotsford's own Saint Soldier (real name: Amrit Saggu) pumps out rhymes for a mainly Sikh fan base while paying tribute to his roots. Not to be outdone, Toronto YouTube sensation Lilly Singh (also known as ||Superwoman||, aptly named given that she is a comedian, rapper, and author) has received a People's Choice Award, MTV Fandom Award, and two Teen Choice Awards.

Sikhs have even made their presence felt in Canada's national game — in broadcasting, if not yet en masse on the ice. Who can forget Harnarayan Singh of *Hockey Night in Canada* (Punjabi edition), and his reaction to the winning goal by the Pittsburgh Penguins' Nick Bonino in the first game of the 2016 Stanley Cup finals? "Bonino! Bonino! Bonino! Bonino! Bonino! Booonnnnniiinnnooooooo!" may go down as the most gloriously exuberant play-by-play call in the history of North American sports. It may be a stretch to say that he put the "colour" back into "colour commentary," but man, talk about passion!

At this juncture, the Sikh community is — well, frankly, it's a bit of a misnomer to call it a community at all. In truth, it is many communities, a sprawling and diverse group of people with a spectrum of beliefs and practices, political affiliations, and lifestyle choices. And diverse attitudes, too. When the WSO Canada decided to back same-sex marriage in Canada, we were clearly outside our own mainstream. But now, just a few short years later, things have changed remarkably. You know you are in a new era when the oldest Sikh organization in North America, the Vancouver-based Khalsa Diwan Society (founded in 1906), partners with the LGBTQ group Sher Vancouver and invites them to participate in the 2017 Vaisakhi parade celebrations.

There are still challenges ahead. The abhorrent South Asian and Middle Eastern practice of honour killings is still not unheard of. Those predisposed to seeing Sikhs in an unfavourable light are pleased to point this out, though the practice is certainly not confined to Sikhs. But this horrible aberration is universally condemned by all right-thinking people, regardless of faith or ethnicity.

Much more problematic is the involvement of Sikh youth in the drug trade, especially in British Columbia's Lower Mainland. Beginning in the 1990s, a gangster mentality took hold of some young Sikh men, and hard-core murderers and drug dealers like Bhupinder "Bindy" Johal and the Dosanjh brothers committed acts of brutal violence, blackening the reputation of the B.C. Sikh community. Today, the problem is ingrained; year after year we wring our hands at the number of Sikh youth killed in targeted drive-by shootings.[37] I was recently dumbfounded to hear some listeners to a Punjabi radio talk show call in with praise for Johal. Many public meetings have been called to address this difficult dilemma, attended by Sikh and non-Sikh alike. There are no easy answers here, I'm afraid. (No simplistic conclusions should be drawn either: drug violence is hardly confined to Sikh youth. In Edmonton a similar problem exists for the Somalis. African-American and Asian street gangs have been a problem in many Canadian urban centres, and the bloody Mafia turf disputes and biker wars in Quebec have been a stain on that province.)

The political climate is worrying, especially in the United States and parts of Europe. In Canada, not so much. There will always be people whose perspectives don't align with your own; to me, this is a sign of a functioning democracy. Generally, Canadians are more inclined to be understanding than our neighbours to the south, though a recent Quebec mosque shooting, in which six Muslim men were murdered by an anti-Islam zealot, is a heartbreaking exception to prove the rule.

The kind of us-versus-them discourse unleashed in the U.S. since the 2016 presidential campaign frightens me, especially when it comes to the treatment of Muslims and other minorities. But make no mistake: racists are hardly sophisticated, even about their racism. To many racists a brown guy with a turban is symbolic of every slight directed against them, from 9/11 on. It's informative that the first American "Muslim" murdered in retaliation for the World Trade Center attack was Balbir Singh Sodhi, a Sikh gas station owner from Mesa, Arizona, who was shot to death on September 15, 2001, by a guy whose rationale was, "I'm a patriot and an American … I'm a damn American."

Brown guy + turban = target. This sad equation has been written several times in the past decade, from the 2012 murder of six Sikhs at a gurdwara in Oak Creek, Wisconsin, to — unbelievably — the shooting of Balbir Singh Sodhi's brother Sukhpal in California almost a year after Sodhi himself was gunned down. Much of this violence (not all) is misdirected; Sikhs, so visible and vulnerable, are the stand-in for the intended victims. The only light in this dark pattern: this shared danger has strengthened the ties between Sikhs and Muslims, once bitterly divided by India's partition. In our struggle, we see theirs reflected.

SEVA ABOVE SELF

The World Sikh Organization went through its own struggles. All three of the major WSO organizations outside of the WSO Canada faced significant threats from India. After serving two terms as president of the WSO International chapter, I stepped down in 1992. The international branch still exists on paper, at least, with Calgary resident Ram Raghbir Singh Chahal listed as president, but really it's not much of a player. The United Kingdom's branch was shaky from the start; Britain's ties and its historical relationship to the government of India allowed the group to be infiltrated easily, assuring its demise almost from the get-go.

In his book *Open Secrets*, Maloy Krishna Dhar revealed that the American branch was also targeted for Indian infiltration from the beginning. But the real assault against them may have been internal: there was always a power struggle in the U.S. branch, a divide between everyday Sikhs driven to play a grassroots role in the community and those from the professions (lawyers, doctors, academics, et cetera) who believed a position on the executive was their inherent right. This was not a part of the Canadian experience at all; in fact, this kind of power struggle directly contravened the idea of seva, or service. (At least, it did for me.) Despite the fractious nature of its politics, the American branch lingered for quite a while, but by 1998 most members abandoned it to form the World Sikh Council (USA). Today, it has morphed into the well-run, professional American Sikh Council, primarily based in gurdwaras. And that's just one of perhaps a half-dozen national Sikh-American organizations, all representing some segment of Sikh society.

As a contrast, the World Sikh Organization of Canada has remained both vibrant and vital, attracting new members and a dedicated team of volunteers. I've often thought about why we managed to survive and thrive while the other branches did not. One reason is that Canada's peculiar demographics forced us to coordinate across a vast geographical footprint and form allegiances across the nation, ensuring a broad perspective. Another is having a shared cause, which required us early on to pool our energy and talents.

Overall, though, I think it comes down to the WSO's organizational culture, which values the group's interests above those of its leaders, regardless of whose hand is on the tiller. There are no stipends, no perks of office; everyone, from the president to the board members, travels on their own dime. This makes working for the WSO Canada less appealing to the corporate vulture types, since being a leader in our group is an expensive proposition, not likely to appeal to those seeking a cash cow they can milk at will.

As a result the World Sikh Organization of Canada remains a vibrant part of the community. Today, our mandate is broad and inclusive: to promote and advocate for human rights protections for everyone, regardless of race, religion, gender, sexual orientation, or ethnicity. Toward this end, we cooperate with like-minded organizations, whether faith-based or secular.

The World Sikh Organization and the Sikh community still face challenges. On occasion, gurdwaras have been defaced, and wearing the kirpan, in particular, still poses problems in some regions. Specifically, legal traditions and attitudes remain a challenge in Quebec (where, as in France, the cleave between the secular and the religious is codified in law). Legal challenges continue. And though my daughter Palbinder has moved on to the judiciary (more on that in a moment), new paths in human rights jurisprudence are being blazed by Balpreet Singh Boparai, the WSO Canada's full-time legal counsel, and many volunteer lawyers throughout the country.

A longstanding WSO Canada policy is to not allow senior executives to serve more than two terms, or a total of four years. This has paid huge dividends for the organization, which continually reinvigorates itself, making room for fresh ideas and approaches as it drives toward its objectives. Today, 30-year-old, Montreal-born Mukhbir Singh is serving his second term as its ninth president, injecting the WSO Canada with a youthful energy that serves us well. (For a full list of WSO Canada presidents, see Note 1 on page 223.)

Much more remains to be done. But we have the will, the record, and the resources to ensure that we move forward.

WHERE ARE THEY NOW?

Does Khalistan still matter? To many, certainly. But this was and remains an issue that must be decided by those most affected by the change it would auger: the people of Punjab. Those of us in the Western hemisphere (particularly in Canada) who enjoy our freedom and liberties remain committed to supporting the wishes of Punjab's Sikhs. Our goal was always to speak up for those who couldn't — or wouldn't dare, for fear of reprisal and persecution — and if their voices were raised in favour of the formation of an independent Sikh nation, it was, and would be, our duty here in the West to aid them. But realistically, the chances of any significant movement toward a self-governing Khalistan during my lifetime are highly unlikely.

After the Golden Temple attack, there was a wellspring of popular support for an independent homeland. A hot passion raged in the wake of India's shameful desecration of our most sacred place, but that fire to create a place of safety and self-purpose, which once burned so bright, has largely died down. Support has cooled both here in the diaspora and in Punjab. The embers are there, smouldering still — it would be a mistake to think they have died out entirely. The tinder that is India's crass, cynical, and harsh treatment of its Sikh minority is still plentiful and bone-dry. All it would take is an inciting incident to spark the flames once more.

I will always remain an advocate for the right of the people of Punjab to chart their own destiny. State boundaries are, after all, little more than coincidences of history manufactured by people at a particular point in time to suit their purposes. Circumstances change.

Mine certainly did. After the devastating fire at Jackpine, we rebuilt — at a cost of $3.6 million above the $2.4 million insurance settlement. Situated on a 10.6-acre parcel on the north side of Williams Lake, the rebuilt plant was state-of-the-art, with a complete finger joint line, steam dry kilns, moulders, and planers — the equipment required for a modern high-tech processing facility. In time, we expanded, adding value-added and engineered-wood products manufacturing plants at a cost of $30 million: the Jackpine Engineered Wood Products plant on a 178-acre site in Williams Lake; Burnaby, B.C.–based Redwood Value Added Products; and J.P. Doors and Windows. The Jackpine Group of Companies was the 12th-largest lumber manufacturing plant in the province of British Columbia by volume and the 17th-largest exporter of softwood lumber products to the United States. At its height in the mid-2000s, the group provided over 300 jobs in B.C., with annual sales touching $100 million.

During this run, we overcame many challenges, prospering along the way. But as with so many other small- and medium-size businesses, the financial catastrophe in 2008 hit us hard. The collapse of the U.S. housing market was the final nail. Despite our previous success in diversifying our markets globally, by the time Lehman Brothers went down for the count, 85 percent of our products were shipping to the United States. After the subprime fiasco, our losses were significant and unsustainable: an $8 million shortfall in 2007 was followed by a disastrous $13 million loss the following year.

At the time, the banks we were dealing with were headquartered in the U.S. They, too, felt the sting of the collapse, with one having to be bailed out by the Obama administration and the other by Warren Buffett. We had a variety of projects in the planning stages. As far as any new financing went, our bankers said we were on our own. We could have pursued other means of finance. If I had been 10 years younger, I would have gone for it. But after consulting with Surinder and my partners and the bankers, we decided to shut down operations.

Soon after, Surinder and I left Williams Lake and resettled in Surrey, where our two daughters and their families already lived. Our son Surjit also moved his family to Surrey to be near us. Emblematic of yet another Canadian migration — from rural to urban — we became part of the British Columbia Lower Mainland's active multi-cultural community. The diversity of this region is a testament to the acceptance we have all experienced as new Canadians in a society that has time and again proved itself willing to accept newcomers and, with them, change.

Like many other immigrants from a wide variety of backgrounds, our family tapped into the Canadian dream. After spending time as an elementary school counsellor, our daughter Kamaljit, our eldest, went back to university and got her PhD in counselling psychology;

Dr. Sidhu now runs her own practice, masterfully juggling it all while raising three wonderful children with her husband, Hardip, a high school counsellor. Palbinder, the lawyer (our second oldest), married Amritpal, a registered psychologist and they too have three children. As if being designated a Queen's Counsel (Q.C.) was not enough, in June 2017 she had the extraordinary distinction of being welcomed to the B.C. Supreme Court. The family was invited to the private investiture ceremony of Madame Justice Palbinder Kaur Shergill, and no one was more proud of her accomplishments than this old man in the corner fighting back tears.

Our son Harjinder completed a PhD in computer science and worked as a university professor at York University for a few years, but eventually left teaching to found or co-found several technology start-ups, most recently in the field of artificial intelligence. Along with his wife, Amarjit, a Harvard graduate, and their two boys, they now live in Seattle. Our youngest, son Surjit, went into business with me, as I mentioned; of all our kids, only he knew the extent of the difficulties we faced during our bleakest financial times, when Khalsa Enterprises was forced to close. Surjit worked with me until we pulled the plug on Jackpine. Today, he works for a Vancouver-area lumber mill and also lives in Surrey with his wife, Sukhwinder, and their two children.

After Jackpine closed, I couldn't remain idle. Almost immediately, I set up my own management consulting business; today, I advise resource companies on all aspects of business management (start-ups to turnarounds) from strategic planning to achieving peak efficiencies. Thus far, Skeena Sawmills of Terrace, B.C., has been the most challenging resurrection (and the most gratifying and successful). My consulting business occupies much of my time, but even today I remain WSO Canada's senior policy advisor. Pretty much every day I devote at least two hours to various WSO issues, liaising with the current executive and, I hope, providing guidance and wisdom gained through almost a half-century of service, over three decades of which were spent with the WSO. As I've told my wife, it sometimes seems like I'm married to the World Sikh Organization for life (along with Surinder, of course!). Not bad for a 74-year-old ...

I'm not someone whose ego needs to be stroked on a regular basis. Honestly, I derive my most immense satisfaction from setting goals and getting results. But I have to admit that I was incredibly honoured in 2002 when I received the Order of British Columbia for, among other things, my charitable work and the leading role Jackpine played in introducing new technology and innovative products and providing jobs for people from diverse backgrounds (we worked with many Indigenous groups). It is the highest civilian recognition given by my home province, and I felt proud to be chosen, even as I remembered that there are many, many people in this world who have done much more than I have been able to do. For them, I am thankful.

Honours like the Order of B.C. are meaningful, yet in the grand design what matters is how we spend the time we are allotted here on Earth. I hope I am lucky enough to continue to do my part, however small. It has been a very fulfilling gift, to be able to help out in my modest way.

Looking back, it's easy to say I have no regrets — easy, but perhaps too simple. There were missteps, certainly. Our failure to articulate a solid vision of what an independent Punjab might look like. My media interview gaffe on the refugees, which for a time put me at odds with some in my community. Business decisions. There were other moments I'd like to have back, too. The weight of one episode I carry still.

In 1995, to raise awareness of human rights violations in Punjab, the WSO Canada invited Jaswant Singh Khalra, a Punjab-based lawyer and human rights activist, to speak at its annual parliamentary dinner and to share information about abuses in the region. Khalra had uncovered a motherlode of disturbing evidence: his meticulous documentation of 2,097 illegally cremated Sikhs found in three mass graves in Amritsar was explosive. His desire to share it with those of us in Canada was an impossibly brave act, since the Indian government was certainly aware of his crusade. There would be consequences.

(Sources within Punjab had informed us that, when Khalra returned to India, he would almost surely end up dead.)

After Khalra delivered a riveting speech in June 1985 before dozens of parliamentarians, we raised with him the danger he was now in and advised that the best route for him would be to apply for refugee status; returning to India could be tantamount to suicide. I still recall his response: "I know I may be killed, but I have a job to do and I don't think I can do it sitting outside of Punjab." He returned to India in July of that year; on September 6, he was abducted from his house in Amritsar by a Punjab police team headed by Superintendent of Police Ajit Sandhu. He was never seen again.

We later learned that he died by beating and gunshots on October 27, 1995, his body thrown in a canal. His death was orchestrated by the head of the Punjab police, K.P.S. Gill, a man notorious for his role in numerous disappearances and killings in the region.[38]

It is a small measure in the face of Khalra's great sacrifice, but the WSO Canada has memorialized his crusade for truth. In 2011, the WSO Canada and the Human Rights Law Network in Delhi launched the Khalra Centre for Human Rights Defenders, its aim to protect those, like Jaswant Singh Khalra, who risk their lives to speak out against injustice.

Jaswant Singh Khalra's sacrifice continues to resonate. Amnesty International featured him in its campaign to promote the 50th anniversary of the Universal Declaration of Human Rights. His story is part of the Canadian Museum for Human Rights. The Indigenous Reconciliation Walk 2017, held in Vancouver with over 70,000 Canadians participating, recognized his contributions and sacrifice by accepting his son, Janmeet Singh, as an honorary witness, Squamish Chief Ian Campbell bestowing a blanket on him. Walking hand in hand, and listening to the painful stories of my Indigenous sisters and brothers, reminded me of the suffering the Sikh community has experienced in India. I wish India had the courage to establish its own Truth and Reconciliation Commission.

The memory of Jaswant Singh remains strong with me. I wish I'd lobbied him harder to stay in Canada. We all should have. Knowing his character, I doubt we would have succeeded. But if we had, perhaps his widow, Paramjit Kaur, could have been spared the agony of raising their two children on her own.

A HOMECOMING

In 2016, after learning that my name had finally been removed from India's travel ban blacklist, I returned to Punjab for the first time in 38 years. But truthfully, I had never entirely left. Years ago, Surinder and I dedicated some funds to open Gurmat Gyan, a computer training centre located in our family's house in Rurka Kalan, the village where I was born. On the same ancestral lands, we also sponsored a sewing school, which was coincidentally slated to have its grand opening during my visit. I attended, along with my wife and our daughter Kamaljit, always at our side in times of both happiness and sorrow. We also had the pleasure of our daughter-in-law Sukhwinder and our granddaughter Manraj joining us for the occasion. I was overjoyed: to actually see an idea take root and flourish, to see a decent thought made concrete, is an extraordinary thing. I was so happy to provide the young kids from my old village with opportunity, a way to move forward. It's gratifying to know that the girls and women who have gone through our sewing school are now self-employed or employed by others. I hope the confidence gained from completing this education will reward them throughout their lives. I only wish that my mother, who passed away in 2015, had been there to see it. She would have been so proud that a school had been opened in her home, giving opportunities that she never had growing up in Punjab at the turn of the last century.

The house itself is still there, although to accommodate the computer classes and a sewing training centre, it has changed — grown in purpose, if you like. As I wandered through, absorbing memories, drinking in the past, there was much to take in.

The last time I was here, I found my father in the guestroom. I had arrived in India just a couple of days earlier. After visiting my sister Bhajno and some other relatives, I returned home late in the afternoon and found him lying on the bed. I leaned down and embraced him. He felt small, fragile. I looked to my cousin Mohinder Singh Sahota, who had been sitting with him when I arrived. Mohinder looked worried.

"Dad, are you feeling okay?" I asked.

He barely responded.

"He hasn't been feeling well all day," my mother said from the bedside.

My dad tried to say something, but nothing came out. He grasped at his chest and his eyes opened wide for a moment. Mohinder bolted out the door to fetch the doctor, and they came back quickly, but by the time they returned Dad was gone.

Although almost four decades had passed, this scene came back vividly as I looked in on the spot where my father passed away. The room seemed haunted by his presence, but then again, old family homes are almost always storehouses of memory, both warm and painful.

Much was different now. After Dad died, my mother had come to live with us in Williams Lake, clearing out much of the furniture from our home. She, too, was now gone but a few reminders of her still remained, including an armoire in the living area. I opened its doors.

Inside were some things that must have had value to her. There were a few copper pots, some bowls, a rolling pin — essentials for the making of a modest life. There was an old radio that I remembered from when I was a teenager; it was my window to a world that, in time, I would explore and embrace passionately. There were also several blankets and throw rugs that Mom had woven by hand. Most were rotting. They had served their purpose, and were changing back to their elemental state, the condition to which we must all eventually return.

I closed the armoire door, perhaps for the final time. I am older now. My time here no longer stretches to the horizon, that endless highway. But when my final passages are written, I would like to be remembered for this:

He was just.
He was principled.
He loved his family.
He served his people.

ACKNOWLEDGMENTS

Pleasure and pain come by Your Will, O Beloved;
they do not come from any other.
Whatever You cause me to do, that I do, O Beloved;
I cannot do anything else.

—Guru Arjan Dev, Sri Guru Granth Sahib, page 432

I T'S BEEN ONE HECK of a challenge to weave together the strands of my life from growing up in a rural Punjab village to serving in the Indian Air Force; then flying over the Pacific Ocean to land in Canada, the best place in the world; and then immersing myself in business, community service, and human rights activism for over 40 years.

Reflecting on these experiences as I put together this book has been so revealing and gratifying. None of it would have been possible without the support of loved ones and a team of dedicated colleagues and volunteers. I am the luckiest, most blessed person to have worked with hundreds of them. Together we experienced many challenges while always working to make the future brighter for the next generation, and the next. Thank you, all. I apologize for not being able to name every individual here.

SURINDER KAUR, the bedrock of my life, who understands what is important to both of us jointly, deserves heartfelt gratitude for putting up with me for over half a century. My life support in everything, my daughters KAMALJIT and PALBINDER and sons HARJINDER and SURJIT persuaded me to write this book, then encouraged me and provided invaluable critiques throughout the process. I would be remiss if I did not also recognize the support of my sons-in-law, HARDIP and

AMRITPAL, and daughters-in-law, AMARJIT and SUKHWINDER, for enriching our family.

I will forever be grateful to GUY SADDY, who helped me to weave my personal life into the overall theme of this book. He has probably come to know me better than many lifelong friends. JOHN BURNS offered overall guidance, editing, and sage advice that helped bring out the best in me, and the design and layout of this book in its current form would not have been possible without the help of their tireless colleagues at ECHO Storytelling: CATHY SMITH, ELENA JANSSEN, ALISON SMITH-CAIRNS, ADAM STENHOUSE, and finally TRENA WHITE for her assistance in creating a publishing strategy.

DAVID KILGOUR (human rights activist and nominee for the Nobel Peace Prize), PROF. JAGMOHAN SINGH, MAJ. JASBEER SINGH, AMANPREET BAL, BALPREET SINGH BOPARAI, BIBI KIRANJOT KAUR (senior SGPC member), and COREY STEINBERG all provided valuable feedback.

I can trace my business acumen to my paternal grandfather, BABA JI KARTAR SINGH, who returned to India after a successful career in the U.K. in the 1930s and '40s. He taught me that hard work and perseverance pay off in life and business, and to always face challenges head-on.

My journey in Canada started with the help of my mother-in-law, DALIP KAUR DHALIWAL (bless her soul), and my brother-in-law LEHMBER SINGH DHALIWAL, and I will forever remain indebted to them for their support.

The city of Williams Lake was my home for four decades, a welcoming community from the beginning. Family friend AJIT SINGH HOTHI introduced me to its who's who, beginning my life in the public arena. May peace be with you, my friend.

HAZEL HUCKVALE, principal at my children's school, truly sympathized with our community; she worked late into the evenings to help me launch the Central Cariboo Punjabi Canadian Association and draft its constitution and bylaws. Her urging for me to put my education and administrative training to good use, instead of getting engrossed in menial sawmill lumber-piling jobs, gave me focus on a higher mission. I was privileged to be a pallbearer for her last journey on this Earth. Lawyer friend TOM SCOTT also helped me draft the World Sikh Organization's constitution and bylaws; I think of him every time I speak of the WSO's origins.

Thanks, JOHN BAS, for making me realize that the most effective method of convincing audiences is to practise what I preach. You brought me to the turning point of my life, and I became amritdhari and have worn my Sikh identity ever since. You are a true friend.

DR. JOHN SPELLMAN at the University of Windsor helped the WSO sail through media and government relations over its first decade. ANNE LOWTHIAN, WSO executive director for over 14 years, gave her all to articulate the Sikh perspective on Parliament Hill. Anne learnt more of our values, ethics, and history than most Sikhs ever do, and in recognition we gave her the Punjabi name Anninder. AMANPREET BAL and MAJ. (RET'D) JASBEER SINGH have been two of my closest, most reliable advisors.

DR. LORNE GREENAWAY, a veterinarian turned parliamentarian, became a friend who was always there to ease my access to government. He was also the first person to offer help when I was flat on my face with business losses.

My professional and academic education upgrades would not have been possible without the generous help and foresight of JAKE KERR, chairman of Lignum Limited. Two other role models and business mentors at Lignum, JOHN AILPORT and SIDNEY EGER, nurtured and honed my business skills — all who knew you miss you to this day.

At my company, Jackpine Group of Companies, RICK JONES (VP, Finance and Administration) and LINDA HILLEGEIST (my executive assistant), along with Lignum president and COO CONRAD PINETTE quietly nominated me for the Order of British Columbia. Receiving that award made me so proud and happy. I think of them every time I wear its insignia.

My successors at the head of the WSO (their names are listed in Note 1 on the next page) have carried on the legacy of our human rights work. I so appreciate your commitment and dedication to serving the community. It has been an honour to work with each of you, and I salute you.

My venture capital partners AVTAR SINGH SANDHU and PREM SINGH VINNING partnered with me at a time when I had hit rock bottom. I can still hear my critics telling you, "Don't support him!" I will never forget how both of you sold assets to sustain and support our dream. Thank you, my friends. I can also never forget the financial support of JOGINDER SINGH SIDHU, a relative and a true friend who mortgaged his house and loaned me $125,000 when it was really needed.

Last, to my granddaughters HARNEET, MANRAJ, MOHNAAM, and JASDEEP; my grandsons RAVDEEP, JUJAAR, AJEET, KURBAAN, EIMAAN, and TEJA; and a new member of my family, my grandson-in-law JASPAL — I hope that each of you finds this book inspiring as you continue your own life's journey.

GIAN SINGH SANDHU
Surrey, Canada, 2017

NOTES

Introduction: My Heart Is Open

1 The World Sikh Organization of Canada presidents, in chronological order: Gian Singh Sandhu, Williams Lake, B.C. (1984–89); Ram Raghbir Singh Chahal, Calgary, Alberta (1990–93); Inderjit Singh Bal, Toronto, Ontario (1994–97); Mohinder Singh Jawanda, Delta, B.C. (1998–2001); Ajit Singh Sahota, Ottawa, Ontario (2002–05); Gurpreet Singh Bal, Mississauga, Ontario (2006–09); Prem Singh Vinning, Surrey, B.C. (2010–13); Amritpal Singh Shergill, Surrey, B.C. (2014–15); and Mukhbir Singh, Ottawa, Ontario (2016–).

Chapter 1: The Stage Is Set

2 Nehru was speaking in Calcutta on July 6, 1946. The remarks were reported in the *Statesman* the following day.

3 Some reported even more casualties: one civil surgeon, identified only as "Dr. Smith," put the casualties at 1,526. This testimony is taken from *The Report of Commissioners* (Vol. 1, page 105), from the National Archives of India, New Delhi, published on September 20, 1920.

4 As with all great religions, to sum Sikhism up in a short paragraph will necessarily do it a disservice. Some main points: Sikhism is a monotheistic religion founded in India in 1469, by Guru Nanak. Sikhism holds as its basic tenets the equality of humankind, the equality of men and women, and the fundamental equality of all religions. It opposes idolatry and the caste system. After the inception of the religion by Guru Nanak, it went through a 200-year period of evolution, culminating in the creation of a distinctively separate group of followers who were outwardly identifiable (the Khalsa). Sikh women use Kaur (meaning "lioness" or "princess") and Sikh men use Singh (meaning "lion") as their middle or last name. For greater insights start with *World Religions: From Ancient History to the Present* and the section on Sikhism in *The Heritage of the Sikhs* by Harbans Singh.

5 In the Sikh faith, music is integral to meditation. Singing or listening to the kirtan, or spiritual music, is a large part of the meditative act.

6 Sikhs who are initiated into the Khalsa commit to follow the Sikh Rehat Maryada, or code of conduct. This includes a daily discipline of meditation and prayer, and also the wearing of the five Sikh articles of faith, or kakaars, at all times:

Kesh — unshorn hair symbolizing acceptance of God's will; the hair must be kept covered at all times with a keski or dastar (turban or head covering) representing spiritual wisdom

Kangha — a wooden comb representing self-discipline worn in the hair and used to keep it neat and tidy

Kara — an iron or steel bracelet worn on the wrist; the circle signifies the oneness and eternity of God and to use one's hands for the benefit of humanity

Kachhera — cotton undergarment representing high moral character and restraint

Kirpan — a stylized representation of a sword that must be worn sheathed, restrained in a cloth belt, next to the body; the kirpan signifies the duty of a Sikh to stand up against injustice. Most kirpans range in length from six to nine inches.

7   The Sant-Sipahi was bound to defend not only those who practised Sikhism, but all peoples, whether they be Hindu, Christian, Jain, Buddhist, or Muslim. Guru Tegh Bahadur, the ninth guru, died in service to this duty. He promised the Mughal ruler Aurangzeb that the Kashmiri Hindus would renounce their beliefs and embrace Islam — if he could be convinced to convert to Islam. But rather than convert, the guru chose death. Even today he is referred to as Hind dee Chader (protector of Hindustan, or what is now called India).

8   The parallel Ghadar movement, a political movement that aimed to liberate India from Britain, was active in the United States and Canada, foreshadowing political action later in the 20th century.

9   Congress passed this resolution at a meeting in Lahore in December 1929. For details, see *India's Struggle: Quarter of Century 1921–1946, Part 1* by Arun Chandra Guha, 1982. Also *Punjab through the Ages, Vol. 3*, by S.R. Bakshi and Rashmi Pathak, 2007.

10   In the 1870s, Sikhs in Punjab under the Singh Sabha movement strongly rejected being referred to as "Hindu," with Kahn Singh Nabha writing a seminal tract called "Ham Hindu Nahin" (We Are Not Hindus) in reaction to the Arya Samaj, trying hard to bring Sikhs back into the "Hindu fold," arguing publicly that Sikhs were, in fact, Hindus. So inserting the catch-all "Hindu" into the constitution was not accidental; the writers would have been well aware of a controversy and debate that had been going on for some time. For Sikhs, this was seen as a calculated decision to undermine all non-Hindu religious groups. The argument went that when you take away the land, the language, and the identity of a Sikh you strip them of their very essence. A parallel misuse would be if the Canadian Constitution stated that any reference to Anglophones would also be taken to include Francophones.

11 These states included Arunachal Pradesh, Assam, Jammu and Kashmir, Manipur, Mizoram, Nagaland, and Tripura.

Chapter 2: Operation Blue Star

12 On the return voyage, 19 of the *Komagata Maru* Sikhs were shot when they attempted to disembark at Budge-Budge, India. In May 2016, Canadian Prime Minister Justin Trudeau issued an official apology in the House of Commons for the tragedy.

13 Naseeb Kaur and her businessman husband Babu Singh Dhaliwal helped over two dozen relatives to successfully settle in Canada.

14 I will forever be grateful to Mohan Singh Dhaliwal and Gurmail Singh Samra for their early support.

Chapter 3: When a Great Tree Falls

15 Sikh resistance against the Mughals continued for the better part of the 18th century, and the Mughals for their part did their best to eradicate Sikhs entirely, capturing, torturing, and killing Sikhs in the most horrific ways possible to try to demoralize them, putting a price on their heads (literally: a reward was paid to anyone bringing the severed head of a Sikh). But the Raj of Banda Singh Bahadur, albeit brief, inspired Sikhs to believe they could control their own destiny in Punjab. Later, to fight against the Mughals, Sikhs broke into the independent misls, each fighting in and eventually taking control of different parts of Punjab. When a particular crisis or major decision needed to be made for the community, the misls would come together at the Golden Temple in Amritsar to discuss strategy and solutions. The Golden Temple by now was easily recognized as the centre of Sikh political life, and Mughals even destroyed it once in their attempts to eradicate Sikhs, a parallel that Sikhs in 1984 immediately drew to the Indian government's invasion.

16 Over the course of three decades after Partition, Pakistan and India had fought three wars. Generally, Pakistanis hated Indians, and Indians hated Pakistanis. But Punjab, which had been brutally divided into West Punjab (in Pakistan) and East Punjab (in India) at the time of Partition, still shared a common language and culture, despite the religious differences. In the wake of the attack on the Darbar Sahib, it seemed that the Pakistanis we were running into, including the average person on the street, were deeply empathetic of what the Sikhs had just gone through and their treatment by the Indian government.

17 The idea for an international Sikh convention came from an unlikely source. Not knowing what to do after the massacre of innocent Sikhs at Darbar Sahib, many Sikhs hoped that a peaceful protest outside the United Nations headquarters in NYC would

help bring international attention to the plight of Punjab's Sikhs. However, when a group comprising many different organizations arrived at the UN, they were met with officials who asked them who their representative was. The Sikhs had no answer. Up to this point, they had no international structure and were organized mostly at community levels with grassroots support. The Sikhs were advised that if they wanted to effect any real change in Punjab, they must present a unified voice to bring awareness to the wrongs perpetrated by the Indian government.

18   Although Delhi was the hardest hit, the violence wasn't confined to Delhi alone, and in the wake of Gandhi's death atrocities were committed throughout the country. But in Delhi, the retribution was fueled by the state-run media, the police, and certain politicians, making it uniquely dangerous.

Chapter 4: One Birth, Many Deaths

19   Not everyone embraced Bhullar. There were unsubstantiated rumours that he was an agent of RAW, India's CIA, but the evidence suggests otherwise. In a letter marked "Secret" from September 5, 1985, written by Richard Murphy, U.S. Assistant Secretary of State for Near Eastern and South Asian Affairs, to Robert Neptune, District Director Immigration and Naturalization, Murphy requested that "Bhullar's request to change his visa classification from H-1 to B-2" be denied because "Bhullar was one of the two key military advisors to Bhindranwale in the Golden Temple … outspokenly hostile to Government of India and would be a serious and continuing irritant to US–India relations." Recently, even more evidence has come to light. In January 2017, declassified CIA briefing notes from October 17, 1985, show that Murphy advised Deputy Secretary of State John C. Whitehead that during Whitehead's pending trip to India, "The Indians will welcome the news of INS's [Immigration and Naturalization Service] refusal, on foreign policy grounds, of Sikh activist Bhullar Singh's application for a visa adjustment, and the Service's initiation of deportation proceedings against him." In addition, before Bhullar's arrival in North America, my close friend Avtar Singh was advised by Bhindranwale that he would be coming. Taken together, this suggests that Bhullar was exactly who he said he was: an ally of Bhindranwale, not an RAW agent.

20   India's President Pranab Mukherjee, then a cabinet minister in the Gandhi government, recalls telling her that "it was the most dangerous decision" (*The Tribune*, Chandigarh, May 14, 2017). "As a student of history, I was afraid to do anything with the Golden Temple. I recalled [at a Cabinet committee meeting] how Ahmed Shah Abdali had to face serious consequences after the Third Battle of Panipat when he did something wrong with the Golden Temple," the president said.

21   Interestingly, I later found out that three young men among them were friends of the Indian consulate staff. They were never blacklisted, freely traveling to India and back.

22 Although there is no acknowledgment of the concept in Sikhism, it doesn't prevent some Sikhs from claiming to be avatars of the gurus.

23 The International Sikh Youth Federation (ISYF) was established in August 1984 in England by Jasbir Singh Rode, Jarnail Singh Bhindranwale's nephew, and Harpal Singh Ghuman. The former was deported to India from the U.K.; the latter (under the alias Harjinder Singh Nagra) eventually made his way to Canada, where he launched the Canadian branch of the ISYF, with Satinderpal Singh Gill as president and Labh Singh Rode, another nephew of Bhindranwale who also went by the name Lakhbir Singh, as convener. Labh/Lakhbir Singh was deported and apparently lives in Pakistan. Many of their efforts were directed at demonizing the WSO and attempting to control local gurdwaras rather than advancing the Sikh cause. In 1986, ISYF members were convicted for the attempted murder of a visiting Indian politician, Malkiat Singh Sidhu, near Gold River on Vancouver Island. In 2001 the ISYF was banned in the U.K.; in 2003 it was banned in Canada.

24 The WSO International founding constitution committee was made up of Dr. Gurcharan Singh (New York), Baldev Singh (New York), Gurcharan Singh (Ottawa), Bakhshish Singh (Ottawa), Dr. Sulakhan Singh (San Francisco), Gurcharan Singh Dhillon (Visalia, California), Baljit Singh (legal member), Dr. Sukhmandar Singh (San Francisco), and Prof. Manjit Singh (India). The WSO International founding governing council consisted of Didar Singh Bains (Yuba City, California), Karamjit Singh Rai (South Bend, Indiana), Jasbir Singh Sethi (Houston, Texas), Gian Singh Sandhu (Williams Lake, B.C.), Verinder Singh Lamba (Edmonton, Alberta), Raghbir Singh Samagh (Unionville, Ontario), Kesar Singh Mand (London, U.K.), Satwant Singh Soman (Southhall, U.K.), Maj.-Gen. (ret'd) Jaswant Singh Bhullar (Chandigarh, India), and Prof. Manjit Singh Sidhu (Chandigarh, India).

Chapter 5: "You Guys Did It"
25 Reconstructed from the film *Air India 182* (2008), directed by Sturla Gunnarsson and produced by David York.

26 One of the best outcomes of the meeting was to expedite the establishment of *World Sikh News*, a weekly English and Punjabi newspaper to counter Indian government false propaganda and cover Sikh news as it happened. Single-handedly Dr. Gurinder Singh Grewal, a cardiologist from Tracy, California, assumed the lead role and financially supported WSN for almost 12 years, until it went under close to the time that the WSO's U.S. branch closed its doors. It has been recently resurrected with Prof. Jagmohan Singh from India as its editor.

Chapter 6: The Long Arm of India

27   Even the act of having the same surname — Sandhu — could be a problem. Although they had valid travel visas, I know of two Canadian Sikhs, one from Ottawa and the other from Vancouver, who had to endure hours of interrogation by officials at the Delhi airport for the simple reason that their names were similar to mine.

28 In his 1994 book *Betrayal: The Spy Canada Abandoned*, David Kilgour, a long-serving and respected member of Parliament, recounts a story from a Russia-trained agent employed by CSIS who claimed that he was asked to participate in another Air India bombing attempt — this time in Europe — and that India, in collusion with rogue elements of the Canadian and Italian governments, may have been behind the plan. The possible reason cited was, again, to discredit the Canadian Sikh community.

29 "During interrogation of suspects, RCMP officers identified Mr. Gill as a spy for CSIS and a member of the inner circle in the Air-India conspiracy, according to court documents released this summer in response to media applications." ("Witness Told Police About Sikh Suspect," *Globe and Mail*, October 18, 2003). However, in response to a question by Air India Commission of Inquiry senior counsel Brian Gover, Bill Turner of CSIS responded, "No, he was not." Turner also confirmed that Gill resigned as a director of Babbar Khalsa "just before the bombing" and told the commission: "I think Surjan Singh Gill realized what was going to happen and didn't want to be a part of it." He was never called as a witness by either party and mysteriously all of his communication disappeared in the erased tapes.

Chapter 7: Et tu, Canada? Attacks From Within

30 In May 1986, Malkiat Singh Sidhu, a senior Akali Dal politician who was visiting Vancouver Island to attend his nephew's wedding, was attacked and shot near the town of Gold River by four men linked to the ISYF. (Sidhu took bullets to his arm and chest, but survived.) The four assailants were apprehended shortly after the incident, and all were convicted of attempted murder; each received a 20-year sentence. In 1987, however, lawyer Michael Code successfully argued that the wiretap evidence CSIS collected was fraudulently obtained; the convictions were subsequently overturned, and CSIS director Ted Finn resigned. Sidhu's four attackers would not remain free, however. In 1990, under appeal all four men had their convictions upheld. In 1991, Sidhu was murdered in India.

31 Notwithstanding our Indigenous peoples, the country known today as Canada was essentially founded by two nations, England and France. The French settled primarily in the province of Quebec, where, in the 1960s, a nationalist movement took root and grew, eventually spawning political parties that would have great success on the provincial (Parti Québécois) and national (Bloc Québécois) scenes. Like Akali Dal

in Punjab, these parties had a mandate to pursue the peaceful transition to an independent state; however, some militant splinter groups, most prominently the Front de Libération du Québec (FLQ), used violence in pursuit of the same ends, from bombing mailboxes to kidnappings and murder. (In 1970, during the so-called October Crisis, the FLQ kidnapped British Trade Commissioner James Cross and Quebec Liberal Party provincial cabinet minister Pierre Laporte, and murdered Laporte.) In Canada, while most non-Québécois disagree with the goals of the Quebec separatist parties, they are viewed as legitimate expressions of popular will. Conflating the aspirations of "Quebec nationalism" with the terror tactics employed by the FLQ would be seen in Canada as intellectually dishonest at the very least.

Chapter 8: Of Turbans and Turning Points

32 WSO members posted bonds amounting to over $750,000 to secure the release of all 174 refugees. This was a total community effort, but Daljit Singh Sandhu, Joginder Singh Sidhu, and Surinder Singh Jabal of Vancouver, and Harbhajan Singh Pandori, Inderjit Singh Bal, and Gurpreet Singh Bal of Toronto assumed leadership roles and deserve particular mention. We also appreciated the help of Narinderpal Singh, Gursharan Singh Toor, and Sardar Dhillon of the Halifax gurdwara. In addition, our legal team of David Gibbons and Mark Hillford (Vancouver), Mandel Green (Toronto), and Lee Cohen (Halifax) deserve mention for the work they did. David Gibbons deserves a special nod: he provided personal guarantees on behalf of the WSO for cash payments.

33 For the role he played in furthering Sikh rights, the WSO recognized Baltej Singh Dhillon in a special function held in Toronto in 1992.

Chapter 9: Advocacy Broadened

34 In 1994 B.C. premier Mike Harcourt, attempting to assuage the feelings of the Sikh veterans, invited them to have tea with Queen Elizabeth II, who was visiting British Columbia at the time.

35 They were accompanied and assisted by Senate liaison Bhupinder Liddar, who would go on to become a journalist and a Nairobi-stationed diplomat, and the WSO's Amanpreet Singh Bal, who helped organize meetings with human rights organizations and families of a few of the youth killed in false encounters. Justice Ajit Singh Bains, Darbara Singh Gill, Prof. Jagmohan Singh, and Mahavir Singh were of immense help in providing evidence for the delegation.

36 Formally passed in 1982, the Canadian Charter of Rights and Freedoms is part of the nation's Constitution Act. It is a broad, far-reaching document, covering everything from democratic and legal rights to language rights, among others.

Section 2 of the Charter deals with "fundamental freedoms," which include freedom of the press and of conscience, thought, belief, expression, association, and assembly — and, perhaps most importantly for the WSO, freedom of religion.

Chapter 10: The Sikh Community Today

37　According to recent WSO research, 101 Sikh youth have been killed in drive-by shootings since 2000. The comparable number for non-Sikhs is 111.

38　K.P.S. Gill's time in power coincided with the disappearance of thousands of young Sikh men whose remains Khalra had unearthed. By this time, among Sikhs Gill had already earned the nickname "the Butcher of Punjab" for his role in a state-sanctioned terror campaign. That Gill was commended by the government during the time of these disappearances, and was eulogized in glowing terms in much of India after his death in 2017, is a stark reminder of the vast interpretive chasm that exists between Punjabis and other Indians, even today.

SELECTED GLOSSARY OF PUNJABI TERMS

Akal Takht: The Sikh seat of authority in Amritsar (literally, Throne of the Timeless One)

amrit: the nectar used in the Sikh initiation ceremony

amritdhari: fully initiated Sikh

avatar: sage (literally, an incarnation)

azad: independent, free

babaji: paternal grandfather (literally, older/respected person)

bagh: garden

bhai: brother, also used to connote friendship and esteem

bhain: sister, also used to connote friendship and esteem

bhangra: traditional Punjab folk dance

brahmin: caste of scholars/priests

Darbar Sahib: Golden Temple

dastar: turban

dharam yudh: righteous war

diwan: court or association

goonda: hooligan

gurdwara: Sikh place of worship

guru: spiritual master, enlightener who dispels darkness

Guru Granth Sahib: the Sikh scripture, the final and eternal guru of the Sikhs

gyan: spiritual knowledge

hukamnamas: dictates

jatha: an assembled group, often for a particular purpose

jathedar: leader

ji: suffix connoting respect

kachhera: cotton undergarment, one of Five Ks

kangha: wooden comb, one of Five Ks

kara: iron or steel bracelet, one of Five Ks

karm: action

Kaur: princess (denoting initiated Sikh female)

kesh: uncut hair, one of Five Ks

Khalistan: Land of the Khalsa (literally, Land of the Pure)

Khalsa: fully initiated Sikhs, collectively

khuskhus: an aromatic Indian grass used for making mats

kirpan: stylized representation of sword, one of Five Ks

kirtan: the singing of Sikh hymns

kshatriyas: warrior caste

kutta: dog

langar: gurdwara free kitchen

lathi: long club

miri/piri: temporal and spiritual sovereignty

misl: small, independent region

Mool Mantar: first verse of Guru Granth Sahib

morcha: rally, movement

murdabad: a commonly used slogan of condemnation used during political rallies (literally, down with)

panth: Sikhs, collectively

purna swaraj: complete independence

sangat: congregation

sant: spiritual leader

sant-sipahi: saint-soldier

sarovar: pool found in many historical gurdwaras

seva: community service

shudra: worker caste

Sikh Rehat Maryada: Sikh code of conduct

Singh: lion (denoting initiated Sikh male)

tabla: a pair of small hand drums

taee: aunt

Vaisakhi: founding of the Order of the Khalsa, and the first of the month of Vaisakh; celebrated annually by Sikhs around the world as a harvest festival

vaishya: tradesperson caste

zindabad: long live

BIBLIOGRAPHY AND FURTHER READING

Part I: Annus Horribilis (June 1984–June 1985)

Barot, Rohit. "The Punjab Crisis and Bristol Indians." *International Journal of Punjab Studies* 2, no. 2 (1995): 195–215.

Bhullar, J.S., Gurtej Singh, and M.S. Sidhu. *The Betrayal of the Sikhs*. Chandigarh: Sikh Ex-Servicemen and Intellectuals Forum, 1984.

Bomball, K.R. "The Nation State and Ethno-Nationalism: A Note on the Akali Demand for a Self-Determined Political Status for Sikhs." *Punjab Journal of Politics* 9 (1983): 166–83.

Brar, K.S. *Operation Blue Star: The True Story*. New Delhi: UBS Publishers' Distributors, 1993.

Cunningham, Joseph Davey. *A History of the Sikhs: From the Origin of the Nation to the Battles of the Sutlej*. Delhi: S. Chand & Co, 1955. First published 1849 by J. Murray, London.

Gopal, S. *Politics of the Sikh Homeland, 1940–1990*. Delhi: Ajanta Publications, 1994.

Grewal, Gurdev. *The Searching Eye: An Insider Looks at the Punjab Crisis*. New Delhi: Rupa & Co., 2006.

Grewal, Jagtar S. *The Akalis: A Short History*. Chandigarh: Punjab Studies Publications, 1996.

Grewal, Jyoti. *Betrayed by the State: The Anti-Sikh Pogrom of 1984*. New Delhi: Penguin Books India, 2007.

Gunnarsson, Sturla. *Air India 182*, documentary film. Vancouver: Canadian Broadcasting Corporation, 2008.

Hajari, Nisid. *Midnight's Furies: The Deadly Legacy of India's Partition*. Boston: Houghton Mifflin Harcourt, 2015.

Hamdard, S.S. *Azad Punjab*. Amritsar: self-published, 1943.

Johnston, H. "The Development of Punjabi Community in Vancouver Since 1961." *Canadian Ethnic Studies* 20, no. 2 (1988): 1–19.

———. *The Voyage of the* Komagata Maru: *The Sikh Challenge to Canada's Colour Bar*. Delhi: Oxford University Press, 1979.

Joshi, Chand. *Bhindranwale: Myth and Reality*. New Delhi: Vikas, 1988.

Joss, Sohan Singh. *Hindustan Ghadar Party: A Short History.* 2 vols. New Delhi: People's Publishing House, 1977–78.

Kaur, Harminder. *Blue Star over Amritsar: The Real Story of June 1984.* Delhi: Ajanta Publications, 1990.

Kaur, Madanjit. *The Golden Temple: Past and Present.* Amritsar: Guru Nanak Dev University Press, 1983.

Kishwar, Madhu. "In the Name of Secularism and National Unity: How Congress Engineered the 1984 Pogroms." *Manushi* 5, no. 25 (1984).

Macauliffe, Max Arthur. *The Sikh Religion.* 6 vols. Oxford: Clarendon Press, 1909.

Mahmood, Cynthia. *Fighting for Faith and Nation: Dialogues with Sikh Militants.* Philadelphia: University of Pennsylvania Press, 1996.

McGregor, William Lewis. *The History of Sikhs.* 2 vols. London: James Madden, 1846.

Mitta, Manoj, and H.S. Phoolka. *When a Tree Shook Delhi: The 1984 Carnage and Its Aftermath.* New Delhi: Roli Books, 2007.

People's Union for Civil Liberties. "Who Are the Guilty? Report of a Joint Inquiry into the Causes and Impact of the Riots in Delhi from 31 October to 10 November 1984." 2003. http://www.pucl.org/Topics/Religion-communalism/2003/who-are-guilty.htm

Pettigrew, Joyce. "Betrayal and Nation-Building Among the Sikhs." *Journal of Commonwealth and Comparative Politics* 29, no. 1 (1991): 25–43.

Rao, Amiya et al. *Report to the Nation: Oppression in Punjab.* Chicago: Citizens for Human Rights and Civil Liberties, 1985.

Saini, R.S. "Custodial Torture in Law and Practice with Reference to India." *Journal of the Indian Law Institute* 36, no. 2 (1994): 166–92.

Sandhu, Ranbir Singh, ed. *Struggle for Justice: Speeches and Conversations of Sant Jarnail Singh Khalsa Bhindranwale.* Chelsea, MI: Sheridan Books, 1999.

Sarhadi, Ajit Singh. *Punjabi Suba: The Story of the Struggle.* Delhi: Uttar Chand Kapur, 1970.

Shiromani Akali Dal. *Anandpur Sahib Resolution.* Adopted at a meeting held at Sri Anandpur Sahib, Punjab, on October 16–17, 1973.

Sidhu, Jaspal Singh, and Anil Chamadia, eds. *Embedded Journalism: Punjab.* New Delhi: Media Studies Group, 2014.

Singh, Jarnail. *I Accuse: The Anti-Sikh Violence of 1984.* New Delhi: Penguin Books, 2009.

Singh, Khushwant. *A History of the Sikhs.* 2 vols. Oxford and New Delhi: Oxford University Press, 1999 and 2005.

Singh, Nikky-Guninder Kaur. *Sikhism: An Introduction.* I.B. Tauris: New York, 2011.

Singh, Patwant. *Of Dreams and Demons: A Memoir of Modern India*. London: Duckworth, 1994.

Singh, Patwant, and H. Malik. *Punjab: The Fatal Miscalculation*. Delhi: Patwant Singh, 1985.

Singh, Sirdar Kapur. *Betrayal of the Sikhs*. Delhi: Akali Dal, 1966.

Surjeet, Jalandhary. *Bhindranwale Sant*. Jalandhar: Punjab Pocket Books, 1984.

Swamy, Subramanian. "Three Days in the Darbar Sahib: An Incisive Report by a Member of Parliament." *Spokesman* (1984).

Tully, Mark, and Jacob Satish. *Amritsar: Mrs. Gandhi's Last Battle*. New Delhi: Rupa & Co., 1985.

Part II: A Community Under Siege (1985–1995)

Amnesty International. *Break the Cycle of Impunity and Torture in Punjab*. 2003.

———. *Determining the Fate of the "Disappeared" in Punjab*. 1995.

———. *Harjit Singh: A Case Study of "Disappearance" and Impunity*. 1995.

———. "India." *Amnesty International Report* (1986): 219–24.

———. *A Mockery of Justice: The Case Concerning the "Disappearance" of Human Rights Defender Jaswant Singh Khalra Severely Undermined*. 1998.

———. *Punjab Police: Beyond the Bounds of the Law*. 1995.

Bakshi, S.R., and Rashmi Pathak. *Punjab through the Ages*. Studies in Contemporary Indian History 3. New Delhi: Sarup & Sons, 2007.

Dhar, Maloy Krishna. *Open Secrets: India's Intelligence Unveiled*. New Delhi: Manas Publications. 2005.

Dharam, S.S. *Internal and External Threats to Sikhism*. Arlington Heights, IL: Gurmat Publishers, 1986.

Dhillon, G.S. *India Commits Suicide*. Chandigarh: Singh & Singh Publishers, 1992.

———. *Truth About Punjab: SGPC White Paper*. Amritsar: Shiromani Gurdwara Parbandhak Committee, 1996.

Fraser, T.G. "The Sikh Problem in Canada and Its Political Consequences, 1905–1921." *The Journal of Imperial and Commonwealth History* 7, no. 1 (1978): 35–55.

Jaijee, Inderjit Singh. *Politics of Genocide: 1984–1998*. New Delhi: Ajanta Publications, 1999.

Kashmeri, Zuhair, and Brian McAndrew. *Soft Target: How the Indian Intelligence Service Penetrated Canada*. Toronto: J. Lorimer, 1989.

Kilgour, David. *Betrayal: The Spy Canada Abandoned.* Scarborough, ON: Prentice-Hall Canada, 1994.

Kohli, A. *Democracy and Discontent: India's Growing Crisis of Governability.* Cambridge: Cambridge University Press, 1990.

Kumar, Ram Narayan. *The Sikh Unrest and the Indian State: Politics, Personalities, and Historical Retrospective.* New Delhi: Ajanta Publications, 1997.

Mulgrew, Ian. *Unholy Terror: The Sikhs and International Terrorism.* Toronto: Key Porter Books, 1988.

Mulgrew, Ian, and Tom Crighton. *Frontiers of Faith: World Sikhism Today,* documentary film. Vancouver: CMS Documentary Group, 1994.

Pettigrew, Joyce. "Martyrdom and Guerilla Organisation in Punjab." *Journal of Commonwealth and Comparative Politics* 30, no. 3 (1992): 387–406.

de Pierrebourg, Fabrice, and Michel Juneau-Katsuya. *Nest of Spies: The Startling Truth About Foreign Agents at Work within Canada's Borders.* Toronto: HarperCollins, 2009.

Privy Council. "Pre-Bombing." *Air India Flight 182 — A Canadian Tragedy: The Final Report of the Commission of Inquiry into the Investigation of the Bombing of Air India Flight 182,* vol. 2, part 1. Ottawa: Public Works and Government Services Canada, 2010.

Singh, Iqbal. *Punjab under Siege: A Critical Analysis.* New York: Allen, McMillan, and Enderson, 1986.

Vaughn, Bruce. "The Use and Abuse of Intelligence Services in India." *Intelligence and National Security* 8, no. 1 (2008): 1–22.

Part III: A Parallel Tack (1995–)

Grewal, Manraj. *Dreams after Darkness: The Search for a Life Ordinary under the Shadow of 1984.* New Delhi: Rupa & Co., 2004.

Mirza, Sarfaraz Hussain, Syed Farooq Hasnat, and Mahmood Sohail. *The Sikh Question: From Constitutional Demands to Armed Conflict.* Lahore: University of the Punjab, 1985.

Pettigrew, Joyce. *The Sikhs of the Punjab: Unheard Voices of State and Guerrilla Violence.* London and New Jersey: Zed Books, 1995.

Tatla, Darshan Singh. *The Sikh Diaspora: The Search for Statehood.* London: UCL Press, 1999.

Wallace, Paul, and Surendra Chopra, eds. *Political Dynamics of Punjab.* Amritsar: Guru Nanak Dev University Press, 1981.

THIS BOOK WAS DESIGNED AND PRODUCED BY:

ECHO STORYTELLING AGENCY
1616 West 3rd Avenue
Vancouver, BC, Canada
V6J 1K2

www.echostories.com
1.877.777.ECHO

CREATING INSPIRING BOOKS, VIDEO AND DIGITAL CONTENT SINCE 1999.
Design © ECHO